STYLE IN THE
FRENCH NOVEL

To
MY WIFE

STYLE IN THE FRENCH NOVEL

BY

STEPHEN ULLMANN, Ph.D., D.Litt.

*Professor of Romance Philology in the
University of Leeds*

CAMBRIDGE

AT THE UNIVERSITY PRESS

1957

PUBLISHED BY
THE SYNDICS OF THE CAMBRIDGE UNIVERSITY PRESS
Bentley House, 200 Euston Road, London, N.W.1
American Branch: 32 East 57th Street, New York 22, N.Y.

Printed in Great Britain by
Western Printing Services Ltd., Bristol

CONTENTS

PREFACE

ONE of the most striking developments in contemporary linguistics has been the emergence of a new science of style. This science, which lies astride the border-line between linguistic and literary studies, has already aroused wide interest; a recent bibliography of stylistic work in the Romance languages lists well over 1500 titles. At the same time, there is as yet no coherent doctrine, agreed terminology or established method in this field. It is hoped that the present book will help to direct attention to these problems by surveying what has been achieved so far and by suggesting a new approach to style, based on a closer integration of linguistic and literary viewpoints.

Most of the material contained in these essays appears here for the first time. The chapter on Proust is drawn mainly from an article published in *French Studies*, 1954, and the section on Vigny in chapter I from an article which appeared in 1950 in the same journal. In the chapter on word-order, I have utilized the data of three articles which were printed in *The Modern Language Review*, 1952, and in *Le Français Moderne*, 1952 and 1955. The introduction has a number of points in common with an article in *Journal de Psychologie*, 1953. I am very grateful to the Editors of these journals for authorizing me to use this material.

The book has greatly benefited by the help and encouragement of Professor L. C. Harmer of Trinity College, Cambridge, to whom my sincere thanks are due. It also gives me much pleasure to express my thanks to the following scholars for advice and assistance on various points: Professor G. T. Clapton and Dr G. Hainsworth, of the University of Leeds; Professor H. Hatzfeld, of the Catholic University of America, Washington; Mr T. E. Hope, of the University of Durham (King's College, Newcastle-upon-Tyne); Dr Stanley Jones and Mr Francis H. Scarfe, of the University of Glasgow.

STEPHEN ULLMANN

Leeds
September 1956

INTRODUCTION:
LANGUAGE AND STYLE

1

'WHAT is time?', Saint Augustine once exclaimed, having searched in vain for a definition. 'If no one asks me, I know. If I am asked and try to explain it, I do not know.' The student of style is faced with a similar problem. How are we to define style and to delimit its field? How can we grasp the essence of this term, familiar and yet elusive and ambiguous; how can we find the connecting link between its various meanings?

The history of the word, as plotted by the dictionaries, will provide no answer to these questions. It will, however, give some idea of the ramifications of the term: the Oxford Dictionary records it in twenty-seven different meanings. It is also significant that all these meanings have a common root. Style is primarily a quality of writing; it comes from the Latin *stilus*, the name of the writing-rod, and it is only by metaphor that it came to be applied to other activities. As Sir Walter Raleigh once remarked,

... the fact that we use the word *style* in speaking of architecture and sculpture, painting and music, dancing, play-acting, and cricket, that we can apply it to the careful achievements of the housebreaker and the poisoner and to the spontaneous animal movements of the limbs of man or beast, is the noblest of unconscious tributes to the faculty of letters.[1]

A glance at some of the classic definitions of style seems at first sight to make confusion worse confounded. But if we look more closely at these conflicting and overlapping definitions, a certain pattern begins to emerge. Like other high-order abstractions, the concept of style has many facets and can be approached from a variety of angles. Some of the definitions have little to offer to the twentieth-century reader; when, for example, Swift declares: 'Proper words in proper places, make the true definition of a style', he is merely echoing the ideas of

---

[1] W. Raleigh, *Style*, 2nd ed. (1897), pp. 1–2.

traditional rhetoric. But there are also more original conceptions which seem to foreshadow the main trends of contemporary thinking on the problem. These more modern ideas fall broadly into two groups. According to one school of thought, each writer has his own peculiar form of style which bears the stamp of his personality. Buffon had something slightly different in mind when he coined his famous formula: 'Le style, c'est l'homme même'; but he had the merit of crystallizing a view of style which, within certain limits, has proved correct and helpful. Schopenhauer went further when he defined style as 'the physiognomy of the mind'. Flaubert was even more categorical: 'Le style', he proclaimed, 'est à lui tout seul une manière absolue de voir les choses.' These ideas were developed by Proust into an ingenious theory. In his view, whatever a great artist writes has his own unmistakable hallmark because he will extract from each object those elements which are congenial to him and have an affinity to his own mind. In this sense, style is inimitable. Explaining why the manner of the writer Bergotte remained completely distinct from that of his imitators, the narrator of Proust's novel remarks:

Cette différence dans le style venait de ce que 'le Bergotte' était avant tout quelque élément précieux et vrai, caché au coeur de chaque chose, puis extrait d'elle par ce grand écrivain grâce à son génie . . . en ce sens chaque nouvelle beauté de son oeuvre était la petite quantité de Bergotte enfouie dans une chose et qu'il en avait tirée.[1]

And a few pages further on, the same idea is expressed through another image: '. . .le génie consistant dans le pouvoir réfléchissant et non dans la qualité intrinsèque du spectacle reflété'.[2]

The second school of thought is interested in the expressive qualities of style and regards it as the means of formulating our thoughts with the maximum of effectiveness. This view was stated most succinctly, though somewhat cumbrously, by Stendhal when he claimed that the essence of style is 'ajouter à une pensée donnée toutes les circonstances propres à produire tout l'effet que doit produire cette pensée'.[3] Flaubert has ex-

---

[1] *A l'ombre des jeunes filles en fleurs*, vol. I, p. 114.

[2] *Ibid.*, p. 117.

[3] This definition was adopted and developed by J. Middleton Murry in his book, *The Problem of Style* (1922), ch. I.

pressed the same conception in an image which brings back the word *style* to its etymological origins. 'Je conçois un style', he wrote in his correspondence, 'qui nous entrerait dans l'idée comme un coup de stylet.' In our own time, Paul Valéry has outlined the programme of a science based on this principle:

> En somme, l'étude dont nous parlions aurait pour objet de préciser et de développer la recherche des effets proprement littéraires du langage, l'examen des inventions expressives et suggestives qui ont été faites pour accroître le pouvoir et la pénétration de la parole.[1]

These two fundamental ways of looking at style underlie the two main branches of a new discipline which has come to be known by the somewhat ungainly name of *stylistics*.[2] The two branches began to take shape almost simultaneously, in the opening years of our century. Prior to that date, there was no proper science of style: traditional rhetoric had outlived its usefulness and lost contact with modern thought, and nothing had yet come to take its place. Occasionally a plea was heard in favour of a systematic attack on the problem of style. In 1852 Herbert Spencer published an essay on *The Philosophy of Style*,[3] but he oversimplified the whole issue by reducing it to a single factor, economy of effort. A few years later, Steinthal spoke of the need for a 'rational stylistics' which would study 'the conditions governing the peculiarities and effects of any form of style'.[4] But these views had little influence on the main body of philological research. Studies of style were by no means lacking, but they were inarticulate and unorganized, without any guiding principle and established method.[5] Much valuable material was accumulated in monographs on the language of classical authors. Some students of style were still dominated by rhetorical categories. Others turned to more practical pur-

---

[1] *Introduction à la poétique*, pp. 12f., quoted by R. A. Sayce, *Style in French Prose*, Oxford (1953), p. 7.

[2] The term *stilistik* has been in current use in German since the early nineteenth century; the first example recorded by Grimm's dictionary is from Novalis. In English, the noun *stylistic* is found as early as 1846; *stylistics* is first attested in 1882–3 (*OED*). In French, the first example of *stylistique* is from 1872 when Littré included the word in his dictionary.

[3] Reprinted in *Essays, Scientific, Political, and Speculative* (1858), pp. 228–61.

[4] H. Steinthal, 'Zur Stilistik', *Zeitschrift für Völkerpsychologie und Sprachwissenschaft*, vol. IV (1866), pp. 465–80.

[5] See on this early phase E. P. Morris, 'A Science of Style', *Transactions and Proceedings of the American Philological Association*, vol. XLVI (1915), pp. 103–18.

poses and tried to inculcate an 'art of good writing' by example and precept.[1] Certain critics revolted against these pedantic methods and published astute and perceptive essays on style,[2] but these did not pretend in any way to lay the foundations of a systematic discipline.

The new stylistics of the early twentieth century did not derive directly from these antecedents; it owed its existence to new attitudes to language which began to gain ground at that time. Nineteenth-century linguistics had treated language as an object of purely historical study pursued by rigorously positivistic methods. These had been erected into a doctrine by the 'Neo-grammarian' school. Around the turn of the century, there was a sharp reaction against the Neo-grammarian orthodoxy. Among the various forms which this reaction took, two were to prove particularly fruitful for the study of style. A group of linguists headed by de Saussure evolved a new concept of language: they regarded it as a social institution and also as an articulate totality whose elements were interdependent and derived their significance from the system as a whole. It was on this 'structural' conception of language that de Saussure's pupil Bally modelled his idea of style. The branch of stylistics which he started has the ambitious programme of surveying the entire system of expressive resources available in a particular language.

The other main branch of stylistics had very different origins. Under the influence of Benedetto Croce's aesthetic philosophy, some linguists began to look upon language as an artistic activity, a process of creative self-expression. In contrast to the other school, their emphasis was mainly literary and individualistic; and in the hands of the most forceful exponent of the doctrine, Leo Spitzer, it acquired, and still retains, a strong psychological bias.

It might be argued that the two stylistics are not irreconcilable: they are simply complementary to one another. Each writer has, as Valéry once put it, his own language within the the language, and the unique features of his style can only be

---

[1] Conspicuous among these were the arid treatises of Albalat which earned him this wicked paraphrase of a famous line from Hugo: 'Albalat, Albalat, Albalat, morne plaine.'

[2] Esp. Remy de Gourmont, *Le Problème du style*, first publ. in 1902.

INTRODUCTION

determined against the background of the expressive resources at his disposal. We cannot hope to detect deviations from the norm unless we are familiar with the norm itself. This is perfectly true in theory; in practice, however, the two approaches imply two entirely different temperaments, casts of mind and habits of thought. In the history of this young science, the tension between two opposing points of view has not been altogether unfruitful. Meanwhile, it is possible to bridge the gap between the two. The present book occupies such an intermediate position: it takes the expressive resources of language as its starting-point, but only to show how these are fitted into the structure of a work of art and, if necessary, adapted to its requirements. Nevertheless, each of the two approaches has its distinctive procedures which may be combined but must not be confused.[1]

2

Stylistics as a study of *expressiveness* in language has seen its field considerably broadened since its aims were first defined by Bally.[2] In the early stages, Bally had envisaged it as the study of the emotive resources of language.[3] Subsequently, the

---

[1] The entire field of stylistics is covered by H. Hatzfeld's valuable *Critical Bibliography of the New Stylistics Applied to the Romance Languages, 1900–1952*, The University of North Carolina Studies in Comparative Literature, Chapel Hill (1953). A brief introduction to the various branches of stylistics will be found in P. Guiraud, *La Stylistique*, Paris, 1954 (Collection 'Que sais-je?'). See also W. Kayser, *Das sprachliche Kunstwerk*, Berne (1948), pp. 271–330; R. Wellek and A. Warren, *Theory of Literature*, London ed. (repr. 1954), ch. IX; several articles in the volume *Literature and Science*, Oxford (1955); Ch. Bruneau, 'La stylistique', *Romance Philology*, vol. v (1951), pp. 1–14; and my article, 'Psychologie et stylistique', *Journal de Psychologie*, vol. XLVI (1953), pp. 133–56. Some students also distinguish a third main branch of stylistics: the study of the characteristic structure of a given language. At one time it was customary to class such studies under stylistics, but they are now scarcely referred to as such; cf., however, A. Malblanc, *Pour une stylistique comparée du français et de l'allemand* (1944). A survey of the relevant literature is given, under the heading 'Idiomatology', in ch. x of Hatzfeld's bibliography.

[2] See esp. his *Traité de stylistique française*, 2 vols., 2nd ed., Heidelberg (1919–21) and *Le Langage et la vie*, 3rd ed. revised, Genève—Lille (1953). The following books have fundamentally the same approach as Bally, though they differ from him on many essential points: J. Marouzeau, *Traité de stylistique latine*, 2nd ed., Paris (1946); *Précis de stylistique française*, 3rd ed., Paris (1950); M. Cressot, *Le Style et ses techniques*, Paris (1947); G. Devoto, *Studi di stilistica*, Firenze (1950); H. Seidler, *Allgemeine Stilistik*, Göttingen (1953); Sayce, *op. cit.*

[3] See *Traité* I, p. 16; cf. also Seidler's definition: 'Stil ist die durch die Sprache erwirkte, bestimmt geartete Gemüthaftigkeit eines Sprachwerks', *op. cit.*, p. 62.

criterion of emotiveness proved too narrow and was replaced by the wider notion of expressiveness. In another respect, too, there has been a significant shift of emphasis and widening of scope. Bally had originally confined stylistics to ordinary speech and debarred it from the study of literary style which, so he felt, was something *sui generis* and had its own special forms of expressiveness.[1] It was, however, somewhat paradoxical to place the purest and most distilled form of style outside the boundaries of stylistics, nor was there any justification for completely divorcing literary language from everyday speech. The ban was therefore relaxed and at present all types and levels of style, from the most literary to the most vulgar, are included within the purview of stylistics.

The pivot of the whole theory of expressiveness is the concept of *choice*. There can be no question of style unless the speaker or writer has the possibility of choosing between alternative forms of expression. Synonymy, in the widest sense of the term, lies at the root of the whole problem of style.

The choice between two or more alternatives may be dictated by a variety of motives. If there are several words, several constructions, several grammatical forms, or even several ways of pronunciation, conveying the same meaning, we shall choose the one which is best suited to the emotions we wish to express or to arouse, to the tone at which we aim, to the kind of language—formal, colloquial, familiar etc.—which is appropriate to the occasion. We shall also choose the one which is most pleasing and euphonious, the one which gives the right degree of emphasis to the utterance, and which carries the right associations and overtones. At the risk of oversimplification, one might say that everything which, in language, transcends pure communication belongs to the province of style. Whether the choice, and the effects which it produces, are conscious or not is fundamentally irrelevant to a purely stylistic inquiry, and it is also most difficult to determine.[2]

The mechanism of choice and effect can best be illustrated by

---

[1] Cf. *Traité* I, pp. 17–20, and *Le Langage et la vie*, pp. 68ff. For a spirited critique of this and other aspects of Bally's doctrine, see Dámaso Alonso, *Poesía española; ensayo de métodos y límites estilísticos*, Madrid (1950), pp. 621–34.

[2] It is therefore hardly practicable to distinguish between 'expressive' (unconscious) and 'impressive' (conscious) effects of style, as recommended by Professor Guiraud, *op. cit.*, p. 47.

a concrete example. It is common knowledge that most adjectives have no fixed place in French; they can either precede or follow the noun: *un intéressant livre—un livre intéressant.* Some adjectives are not mobile: one can only say *société parisienne, garde républicaine, robe noire, belle maison, petit garçon.* In a few cases, different shades of meaning attach to the two positions: *sa main propre—sa propre main, un ami vieux—un vieil ami, sacré menteur—amour sacré de la patrie.* But even these rules are not absolute, and in most cases the two orders are interchangeable as far as meaning is concerned. The French language, with its customary fondness for discreet nuances, can exploit this possibility of choice to achieve a number of stylistic effects.

1. The basic function of the two orders is to differentiate between subjective and objective attitudes. Placed before the noun, the adjective will imply emotional participation, whereas the opposite order is purely factual or rational. *Une découverte importante* is a statement of fact, *une importante découverte* an emotive utterance. Differences in rhythm and accent between the two arrangements help to underline the contrast.

2. As there is a certain emotive tinge in figurative language, an adjective preceding the noun will sometimes have a metaphorical sense: *une robe noire—un noir forfait, une feuille verte—une verte semonce.*

3. Considerations of euphony may make one order preferable to the other. We shall say *un homme riche,* but *un riche propriétaire. Un coup sec* is more pleasing than *un sec coup* because it avoids an awkward sequence of sounds.

4. An adjective may receive special emphasis by being placed before the noun: 'Il ne s'agissait pas de la *banale* résignation ni de la *difficile* humilité' (A. Camus, *La Peste,* p. 248). This effect becomes even more insistent when the same adjective is repeated:

> Le ciel faisait sans bruit avec la neige épaisse
> Pour cette *immense* armée un *immense* linceul
> (Victor Hugo, *L'Expiation*).

5. An adjective placed before the noun is apt to denote an inherent quality. This impression of inherence is particularly strong when adjectives which would normally follow the noun are made to precede it: 'une *parisienne* journée'; 'ce Luna Park

aux *américaines* délices';[1] 'le passage a comme une *baudelairienne* beauté'.[2]

6. The sequence adjective+noun may have a poetic and slightly archaic flavour as it was once current in a number of combinations where it is rare to-day:

> Et l'ombre de la voile errante sur sa joue,
> Elle écoutait le chant du *nocturne* pêcheur
> (Lamartine, *Le premier regret*).

7. If an adjective is displaced from its normal position, the effect may be ironical: 'Les *rituelles* consultations de M. Vincent Auriol' (*Le Monde*, 21 July 1948); 'ils abdiqueront peut-être jusqu'à leur *républicaine* prétention à la souveraineté' (Roger Martin du Gard, *Les Thibault* VIII, p. 195).

8. Occasionally a writer will depart from ordinary syntax without any particular reason: 'les *jumelles* tours de Notre-Dame';[3] '*Aboli* bibelot d'inanité sonore' (Mallarmé, *Ses purs ongles*). The device is even more artificial when a whole adjectival phrase is placed in front of the noun, as for example when Laforgue writes: 'C'est un *très au vent d'octobre* paysage.'[4]

9. When the same adjective occupies two opposite positions in the sentence, the result is the figure known in rhetoric as *chiasmus*, from its resemblance to the Greek letter *khi* which has the shape of an X. Chiasmus is sometimes cultivated for its own sake, as an ornament: 'la *nouvelle* nature et les moeurs *nouvelles* que j'ai peintes';[5] 'cette musique *sans analogue* due à ce *sans analogue* génie'.[6] Elsewhere it will imply a contrast between inherent and contingent qualities, as in Musset's line: 'Une robe *blanche* et de *blanches* mains.' The writer may even hint that between the two uses of the adjective there is a subtle difference in meaning which it would be difficult to put into words: 'On annonce quelques *nouveaux* journaux, mais aucun

---

[1] Cf. Spitzer, *Zeitschrift für französische Sprache und Literatur*, vol. XLI, pp. 105ff.

[2] Quoted from Maurois in L. C. Harmer, *The French Language Today*, London (1954), p. 307.

[3] Quoted from Gautier in Ch. Bally, *Linguistique générale et linguistique française*, 3rd ed., Berne (1950), p. 232.

[4] Cf. Cressot, *op. cit.*, p. 194.

[5] Quoted from Chateaubriand in F. Brunot, *La Pensée et la langue*, 2nd ed., Paris (1926), p. 643.

[6] Cf. Harmer, *op. cit.*, p. 311.

journal *nouveau*'; 'Non, pas un *admirable* ambassadeur, mais un ambassadeur *admirable*.'[1]

From this brief and incomplete survey it will have become clear how the principle of choice works in practice. All the examples quoted—except figurative expressions like *une verte semonce*—could have been phrased in the reverse order; in some of them, the alternative sequence would actually have sounded more normal. In each case, the choice was motivated by some specific reason, or possibly several reasons some of which could only be established in the light of the context.

Three further principles of stylistic explanation emerge quite clearly from our collection of examples:

(*a*) The same device of style may give rise to a variety of effects. One might term this the *principle of polyvalency* in stylistics. As we shall see later, this principle has a counterpart: the same effect may be obtained from a number of different devices.

(*b*) The expressive force of a device depends in no small measure on whether it deviates from ordinary usage. Some of the above examples owed their effect solely to this factor. This second basic feature may be termed the *principle of deviation from the norm*.

(*c*) There are two kinds of expressive devices: direct and indirect. The former are expressive in themselves, the latter derive their force from their associations. Any linguistic element—accent, suffix, word, idiom, grammatical form or turn of phrase—which is peculiar to a certain social milieu or level of style will become associated with its environment and will be able to call it up in any context. The atmosphere of its habitat will cling to it whenever it is used: a vulgarism, an archaic term, a foreign word will each carry its own connotations which must be carefully handled and judiciously blended by the writer. These connotations have been known since Bally as *evocative values*.[2] They underlie the entire technique of

---

[1] Cf. F. Boillot, *Psychologie de la construction dans la phrase française moderne*, Paris (1930), pp. 76ff.

[2] Professor Devoto (*op. cit.*, pp. 23ff.; cf. also *Mélanges Marouzeau*, pp. 125f.) has argued that there is no essential difference between direct and indirect devices: in the case of expressiveness proper, the choice made by the writer is purely psychological, whereas in the case of evocative values it is dictated by social considerations.

portrayal through style, and also a number of oblique effects such as irony and parody.

These four principles—choice, polyvalency, deviation and evocation—are fundamental to any form of stylistic analysis. They will frequently recur on the pages of this book.

3

Stylistics is not a branch of linguistics; it is a parallel science which examines the same problems from a different point of view. It will therefore have the same subdivisions as linguistics.

One scheme which has proved useful in the study of language[1] and can easily be extended to that of style distinguishes between three basic units: the sound, the word and the phrase. We shall thus have three divisions of stylistics, each dealing with one of these three units. This is not the place to survey in detail the field of stylistics; on the following pages, I shall confine myself to outlining a few characteristic problems which will arise at each of these levels.

Stylistics of the *sound*, or 'phonostylistics', as it has been called,[2] investigates the expressive qualities of speech-sounds and other phonetic features such as accent, intonation and rhythm. Its primary task will be to study those phonetic devices which, in a given language, are at the speaker's disposal to express emotion or to emphasize a particular word. In French, for example, there is a choice between three different modes of accentuation. Pronounced without any particular feeling or emphasis, every word will be stressed on the last syllable, though this accent is so weak that, in connected speech, it can only be heard at the end of a breath-group. When a word is spoken with strong feeling, it receives a special kind of accent, a heavy expiratory beat which will fall on the first syllable if the word begins with a consonant, and on the second if it starts with a vowel: 'c'est un *mi*sérable!—c'est a*bo*minable!'. The effect will be reinforced by other phonetic devices: the preceding consonant will be lengthened, and a glottal stop will be prefixed to an initial vowel. Finally, there is a third type of accent, mainly musical in nature, which always falls on the first syllable

---

[1] Cf. my book, *The Principles of Semantics*, Glasgow (1951), ch. i.
[2] See N. S. Troubetzkoy, *Principes de phonologie*, Paris (1949), pp. 16–29.

of the word and helps to emphasize it and to contrast it with some other term: 'Ce n'est pas *subjectif*, c'est *objectif*.'[1]

An important but delicate subject of stylistic inquiry is the problem of *onomatopoeia* and its role in style. Since the Symbolist movement, harmony between sound and sense has been raised to an aesthetic principle, but Pope was already alive to its importance and gave some happy illustrations of how it works:

> 'Tis not enough no harshness gives offence,
> The sound must be an echo to the sense.
> Soft is the strain when zephyr gently blows,
> And the smooth stream in smoother number flows;
> But when loud surges lash the sounding shore,
> The hoarse, rough verse should like the torrent roar:
> When Ajax strives some rock's vast weight to throw,
> The line too labours, and the words move slow
>
> *Essay on Criticism*, ll. 364–71.[2]

Unfortunately, the study of these effects has been brought into disrepute by unrestrained and dilettantish speculation on the problem. Yet some modern investigations have shown that it can be examined by strictly scientific methods, though there will always remain a subjective element which ultimately defies analysis.[3]

Stylistics will also explore the evocative values of speech-sounds: the accent and pronunciation peculiar to a certain social class, a foreigner, etc. The 'hypercorrect' pronunciation of an *h* by people afraid to 'drop their aitches' has been ridiculed in many English plays and novels; the same tendency was already rampant in Latin and was stigmatized by Catullus in the portrait of the social climber Arrius who would say *hinsidias* for *insidias*. The pronunciation of a foreign language has similar pitfalls: one of Proust's characters says *laift* for *lift* to parade his knowledge of English. Occasionally, such features may play a vital part in the unfolding of the plot; Bernard Shaw's *Pygmalion* is the supreme example.

---

[1] Cf. esp. J. Marouzeau, *Le Français Moderne*, vol. XVI (1948), pp. 1–10, and vol. XXIV (1956), pp. 241–8.

[2] Cf. J. Orr, 'On Some Sound Values in English', in *Words and Sounds in English and French*, Oxford (1953), ch. II.

[3] See esp. M. Grammont, *Traité de phonétique*, 3rd ed., Paris (1946), Pt. II; cf. recently G. V. Smithers, 'Some English Ideophones', *Archivum Linguisticum*, vol. VI (1954), pp. 73–111.

Stylistics of the *word* will concern itself both with word-forms and with word-meanings. One formal feature which has points of stylistic interest is 'emotive derivation': suffixes which add a special overtone to the basic idea. Some languages have a profusion of emotional derivatives: terms of endearment, pejorative formations and the like. Modern Italian is particularly rich in diminutives; there is nothing in English or French to match a series like *donna, donnetta, donnina, donnettina, donnuccia, donnicciuola*.[1]

Apart from coining an occasional neologism, writers have little freedom in the matter of word-forms. Yet in the hands of some of them—Rabelais, Laforgue, Lewis Carroll, James Joyce—words have become plastic, and comical effects have been obtained from playful 'portmanteau' forms like Carroll's *chortle* (*chuckle* + *snort*) and Rostand's *ridicoculiser*. There may be deeper implications. In *The Psycho-Pathology of Everyday Life*, Freud has suggested that some slips of the tongue may be manifestations of the subconscious; before him, Laforgue had risked formations like *volupté, sangsuelle, sexciproque*. Joyce had a special theory about what he called the 'polyphonic' word which would emit two meanings just as a chord emits several notes in one sound. Hybrid words like *bespectable, funnominal, beehiviour, mincethrill* abound in *Finnegans Wake*; sometimes the whole sentence will convey two meanings running concurrently through it: 'the wedding will take bloss as oranged'.

Word-meanings are less precise than word-forms, and lend themselves more easily to stylistic effects. The very vagueness of a word—its 'blurred edges', as a philosopher has called them —may increase its powers of suggestion. Some schools of poetry have deliberately cultivated this kind of vagueness. The Symbolist position is summed up in Mallarmé's warning: 'Le sens trop précis rature Ta vague littérature' (*Toute l'âme résumée*) and, more explicitly, in Verlaine's *Art poétique*:

> Il faut aussi que tu n'ailles point
> Choisir tes mots sans quelque méprise.
> Rien de plus cher que la chanson grise
> Où l'Indécis au Précis se joint.

[1] Cf. W. v. Wartburg, *La Posizione della lingua italiana*, Firenze (1940), pp. 89f.

Gide relates that, under the influence of Symbolism, he used to be fond of words

. . . qui laissent à l'imagination pleine licence tels que *incertain*, *infini*, *indicible*. Les mots de ce genre, qui abondent dans la langue allemande, lui donnaient à mes yeux un caractère particulièrement poétique. Je ne compris que beaucoup plus tard que le caractère propre de la langue française était de tendre à la précision.[1]

Yet even in a mature work like *Les Faux-Monnayeurs*, he felt impelled to revive a negative word of this type, the verb *illimiter*: 'L'amour et le beau temps *illimitent* ainsi nos contours' (p. 455).

Semantics, the study of word-meanings, has made great strides forward in the last half-century, and it has become apparent that most aspects of meaning have stylistic implications. Four sets of semantic problems will claim special attention. The first of these, *synonymy*, is in a sense the prototype of all stylistic devices, the purest and simplest example of a choice between alternative expressions.[2] The main task here will be to determine the motives behind the choice: the overtones and associations which distinguish synonyms from each other. In *As You Like It*, Act v, sc. 1, Shakespeare has given, through the mouthpiece of Touchstone, an object-lesson in the analysis of synonymic nuances:

Therefore, you clown, abandon—which is in the vulgar leave—the society—which in the boorish is company—of this female—which in the common is woman—which together is: abandon the society of this female; or clown, thou perishest; or, to thy better understanding, diest; or, to wit, I kill thee, make thee away, translate thy life into death.

Stylistics will also study combinations and accumulations of synonyms and the purposes which they may serve: variety, symmetry, precision etc. There are also more special functions. An accumulation of synonyms may provide an emotional outlet to an over-excited speaker.[3] It may even help to reproduce the process of a thought taking shape and groping for the right word. Most writers would carefully delete any traces of this

[1] *Si le grain ne meurt*, 37th ed., Paris (1928), p. 246.
[2] Cf. my *Précis de sémantique française*, Berne (1952), pp. 192ff.
[3] See e.g. Harpagon's monologue in *L'Avare*, Act IV, sc. 7.

process, but some take a special pride in recording them. They abound in Péguy's prose:

Je sens déjà l'*incurvation*, l'*incurvaison* générale, latérale, trans-versale, horizontale aux épaules, verticale aux reins. Il faut aussi dire que c'est le *courbement*, la *courbure*, la *courbature*, l'*inclinaison* de l'écri-vain sur sa table de travail (*Cahiers de la Quinzaine*, 23 October 1910).

Synonymy is an invaluable linguistic resource, but it has its dangers. It may distort the meaning of a sentence by suggesting that there is a slight difference between two terms when there is none. It may produce artificial variety, what H. W. Fowler has called 'elegant variation'. It may lead to padding, the great vice of Renaissance poetry:

> Des arbres et des murs, lesquels tour dessus tour,
> Plis dessus plis il *serre*, *embrasse* et *environne*
>
> (Ronsard, *Sonnets pour Hélène*, II, 29).

Synonymy may even degenerate into cumbersome over-emphasis such as is often encountered in legal jargon.

Here we have, then, a valuable linguistic resource which may become a defect of style. Another semantic feature, *ambiguity*, is in the opposite position: it is obviously a deficiency in lan-guage, but can be turned into an effective stylistic device. Much work has been done in recent years on the use of ambi-guity in literature.[1] Linguistically, we shall have to distinguish between two main types of ambiguity, according to whether the equivoque lies in the words used or in the structure of the sentence. Either of these may be deliberately contrived as a figure of style. In single words, there are two sources of ambiguity. Two different meanings of the same word may arise simultaneously in a given context; when, for example, Pyrrhus says in Racine's *Andromaque*, Act I, sc. 4: 'Brûlé de plus de *feux* que je n'en allumai', he plays on two meanings of *feu*, and the reader has to follow him from one plane of experience to another, from the material flames which he kindled in Troy to the flames of love which now consume his heart. But ambiguity

---

[1] See esp. two books by W. Empson, *Seven Types of Ambiguity* (1930), and *The Structure of Complex Words* (1951). Cf. also W. B. Stanford, *Ambiguity in Greek Literature*, Oxford (1939). On stylistic aspects of ambiguity, cf. my *Précis de sémantique française*, pp. 215ff. and 233ff.

may also result from chance homonymy, as for instance in Mercutio's sinister pun: 'Ask for me to-morrow, and you shall find me a *grave* man' (*Romeo and Juliet*, Act III, sc. 1). In either case, the equivoque can be more forcibly driven home by repetition. The same word may appear twice, each time in a different meaning, as in this bitter remark by an old trade unionist in Jules Romains's *Hommes de bonne volonté*: 'La civilisation ne peut pas *se passer* de nous, mais elle *se passe* au-dessus de nous' (*Le 6 octobre*, p. 291). Similarly, there may be a clash of homonyms within the sentence:

> Not on thy *sole*, but on thy *soul*, harsh Jew,
> Thou mak'st thy knife keen
> > (*The Merchant of Venice*, Act IV, sc. 1).

In all these cases, there is a strong tension between the two terms of the pun as they belong to widely different spheres of experience. There is a fundamental similarity here between the structure of ambiguity and that of imagery.

Imagery, the third semantic feature with stylistic implications, takes us to the very heart of an author's style. It is the field where his creative power has full scope, untrammelled by linguistic conventions. In the last two chapters, I shall study this process of image-making and shall also explore a special form of imagery which is prominent in the style of Proust. One question which the student of imagery has to ask himself is how far a particular image is still felt as such. There is much wear and tear in figurative language; metaphors and other images are exposed to a process of weakening in which Bally has, somewhat schematically, distinguished three successive phases: 'Images concrètes, saisies par l'imagination; images affectives, saisies par le sentiment; images mortes, saisies par une opération intellectuelle.'[1] But such is the freedom in this field of language that the process can be reversed: a faded image can be revitalized, brought back to its etymological origins. This can be done by bringing a word into contact with another term which will remind us of its derivation. The French verb *avaler* 'to swallow' originally meant 'to descend' and was a derivative of *val*, but the ordinary speaker is quite unaware of this connection. Rabelais, however, succeeds in restoring the

---

[1] *Traité de stylistique*, vol. I, p. 195.

link by contrasting *avaler* with *monter*: 'Si je *montasse* aussi bien comme je *avalle*, je feusse désjà au dessus la sphere de la lune.'[1] T. S. Eliot proceeds in the same way when he tries to give back to the word *revision* its full etymological force:

> And time yet for a hundred indecisions,
> And for a hundred *visions* and *revisions*,
> Before the taking of a toast and tea
> (*The Love Song of J. Alfred Prufrock*).

Elsewhere the author himself or one of his characters will speculate on the changed meanings of words. Thucydides had already noted how words had depreciated in meaning during the Peloponnesian War. In one of A. Camus's plays, a modern dictator juggles cynically with meanings and etymologies:

> L'essentiel n'est pas qu'ils comprennent, mais qu'ils *s'exécutent*. Tiens! C'est une expression qui a du sens, ne trouvez-vous pas? . . . Magnifique! On y trouve tout! L'image de l'exécution d'abord qui est une image attendrissante et puis l'idée que l'exécuté collabore lui-même à son exécution, ce qui est le but et la consolidation de tout bon gouvernement. . . . Je les ai *concentrés*. Jusqu'ici, ils vivaient dans la dispersion et la frivolité, un peu délayés pour ainsi dire! Maintenant ils sont plus fermes, ils se concentrent! . . . *Ils s'exécutent, ils s'occupent, ils se concentrent.* La grammaire est une bonne chose et qui peut servir à tout! (*L'Etat de siège*, pp. 117–18 and 121).

Strong stylistic effects can also be obtained from words with a marked evocative value. There is a wide gamut of such terms, stretching from the highly literary to the most vulgar, and including such diverse elements as archaisms, neologisms, foreign words, dialect features, slang, and technical terms. Since the Romantic movement, these resources have been systematically exploited to produce local colour and to achieve verisimilitude in dialogue. The beginnings of this technique will be discussed in the first chapter of this book.

In *syntax*, there is an extremely wide range of stylistic possibilities. These will arise at three distinct levels: the level of grammatical elements, of the sentence as a whole, and of higher units.

---

[1] Cf. Wartburg, *Evolution et structure de la langue française*, 4th ed., Berne (1950), p. 171.

Although grammar is far more closely organized than the vocabulary, it leaves a considerable margin for choice and personal preference. When relating a past event, for example, French can choose between four or five different verbal forms. In Old French, these were used quite indiscriminately; since then, they have each acquired their distinctive meanings and overtones. To give but one example, the student of style will seek to determine why, and in search of what effects—variety, dramatic tension, deviation from current usage—La Fontaine should have employed a narrative Infinitive in some cases where one would normally expect a finite form:

> Et Grenouilles de se *plaindre*, Et Jupin de leur *dire* . . .
> (*Les grenouilles qui demandent un roi*);
> Grenouilles aussitôt de *sauter* dans les ondes;
> Grenouilles de *rentrer* en leurs grottes profondes
> (*Le lièvre et les grenouilles*).

There is also a certain amount of freedom in the use of the minor parts of speech: pronouns, conjunctions, prepositions and articles. The article in particular lends itself to many stylistic effects. There was no article in Latin; in French there are three: definite, indefinite and partitive—or even four, if we count the absence of the article, 'l'article zéro', as a separate possibility.[1] This system leaves a wide field for choice, and in the hands of a great writer, this seemingly small and trivial element of speech may be fraught with significance. It is not by accident that Racine uses the indefinite article rather than the possessive adjective when Andromaque recalls the wishes of her dead husband:

> Voilà ce qu'*un* époux m'a commandé lui-même
> (*Andromaque*, Act IV, sc. 1),[2]

or that Rilke prefers the definite article to the indefinite when speaking of experiences of which we have some kind of mysterious foreknowledge:

---

[1] Cf. G. Guillaume, 'Logique constructive interne du système des articles français', *Le Français Moderne*, vol. XIII (1945), pp. 207–29.

[2] Cf. Spitzer, *Romanische Stil- und Literaturstudien*, vol. I, pp. 136ff.

Nur wer die Leier schon hob
Auch unter Schatten,
Darf *das* unendliche Lob
Ahnend erstatten
(*Orpheus Sonnets*).[1]

The system of word-classes also leaves some room for effects of style. In English, words can be moved freely from one category to another: *to house—to savage—to down tools—to be in the know*. Some writers will go considerably further and startle the reader by constructions like Shakespeare's 'it *out-herods* Herod' (*Hamlet*, Act III, sc. 2), or Gerard Manley Hopkins's '*feel-of-primrose* hands' (*The Habit of Perfection*). On a major scale, there is the famous 'nominal syntax' of the Goncourt brothers: their preference for a noun where an adjective or verb would be more normal. This technique, which was closely bound up with their Impressionist aesthetic, will be the subject of the third chapter of this book.

At the level of the sentence, the most significant stylistic problem is that of word-order. French, like other uninflected languages, has a rigidly regulated pattern of sentence-structure; yet it has retained two valuable resources: the virtually unrestricted mobility of the adjective and the limited but effective mobility of the subject. The first of these has already been mentioned; the second will be studied in chapter IV.

Stylistic effects may even transcend the limits of a single sentence and influence the syntax of larger units. The most intriguing problem here is that of reproduced speech: the way an author will report the words and thoughts of his characters. For a long time it was believed that only two possibilities were open to him: direct and indirect discourse. Now we know that there is also a third alternative, a compromise solution, free indirect style; and quite recently it has been suggested that there may exist yet a fourth method of speech-reporting.[2] Flaubert was a pioneer in this field, and a direct precursor of the modern 'stream of consciousness' technique. His experiments will be discussed in the second chapter.

[1] Quoted by W. Kayser, *op. cit.*, p. 106.

[2] Professor Harmer (*op. cit.*, pp. 300f.) describes as 'style direct libre' cases like the following, where the author passes from narrative to direct speech, without explicitly indicating the change: 'Il se détourna brusquement: quelqu'un a cogné à la vitre.'

18

Syntax is also rich in evocative effects. People are particularly sensitive to the exact tone of grammatical forms and constructions; if the latter are used out of place, there is immediately a strong impression of clumsiness, affectation or pedantry, as the case may be. It is interesting to observe, for example, how a modern dramatist will handle a correct but pretentious form like the Imperfect Subjunctive.[1] He will hardly ever risk it in ordinary dialogue, but will fully exploit it as a source of stylistic effects. It is a powerful weapon of parody and satire and will appear almost inevitably in the linguistic portrait of a pedant:

Il serait excellent pour ma tranquillité à venir que je ne m'en *allasse* pas sans un petit résultat (J. Romains, *M. Le Trouhadec*, Act I, sc. 1—the speaker is a Professor in the Collège de France);

in the speech of an affected aristocrat:

Il *eût été* bien malséant que je vous *oubliasse* (Abel Hermant, *Le Faubourg*, Act I, sc. 3);

or in the hypercorrect language of a foreigner:

Il *eût préféré* que nous lui en *fissions* part nous-mêmes (J. Romains, *Démétrios*).

The Imperfect Subjunctive may become the vehicle of irony:

Oh! par exemple! . . . on te pince avec mon concurrent . . . et il faudrait que je te *remerciasse* (V. de Cottens-P. Veber, *L' Elu des femmes*, Act IV, sc. 10).

It may also have a genuinely comic effect, especially where there is a discrepancy between the pompous form and the familiar or popular quality of the verb:

> Oui, Mode, pour que d'eux tu *t'emberlucoquasses*,
> Coquine! ils n'ont voulu, ces coqs, qu'être cocasses
> (E. Rostand, *Chantecler*, Act III, sc. 4).

Sometimes there is explicit comment on these points, as in this conversation in one of Sacha Guitry's plays:

HÉLÈNE: Je n'ose pas t'en dire davantage . . . et *j'eusse préféré* sans doute . . .

[1] Cf. my article, 'Le passé défini et l'imparfait du subjonctif dans le théâtre contemporain', *Le Français Moderne*, vol. VI (1938), pp. 347–58.

LEVAILLÉ: Pourquoi dis-tu '*J'eusse préféré*' ? Parle donc simplement. Qu'est-ce que tu aurais préféré ? (*Un sujet de roman*, Act I).

Elsewhere, the careless grammar of one speaker will be corrected by another. In Rostand's *Chantecler*, the woodpecker is the custodian of grammatical orthodoxy:

FAISANE: Plus qu'elle je voudaris que tu m'*adores*.
LE PIVERT (doctoral): *rasses* (Act IV, sc. 2).

In a modern play, an ex-teacher who has become a prosperous businessman still retains his professional reflexes:

SUZY: Vous méritiez qu'on vous le *cache*.
TOPAZE: *Cachât*!
SUZY: Comment, *cachât* ?
TOPAZE: Qu'on vous le *cachât*
（M. Pagnol, *Topaze*, Act III, sc. 2).

It would almost seem that the obsolescent form has received a new lease of life as a source of stylistic effects.

4

Stylistic elements, it will be remembered, are 'polyvalent'; the same device may produce several effects, and conversely, the same effect may be obtained from several devices. There are therefore two possible methods in stylistics. So far I have taken devices of style as my starting-point, and I shall continue to do so throughout this book. But the opposite route is also possible: one may start from a particular effect and study the means available for achieving it. A Swiss thesis has examined, for example, the resources which a French speaker has at his disposal for emphasizing an idea.[1] But it is hard to see how the stylistic system as a whole could be surveyed in this way; divorced from their linguistic expression, effects of style are too vague and fluid to provide a framework for synthesis.

Whichever of the two methods is followed, stylistics as a study of expressiveness is primarily a *descriptive* discipline. It is concerned with linguistic values, not with historical development. Naturally, any stage in the evolution of a language can

[1] M. L. Müller-Hauser, *La Mise en relief d'une idée en français moderne* (1945); cf. M. Mangold, *Etudes sur la mise en relief dans le français de l'époque classique* (1950).

become the subject of stylistic inquiry, but the approach will always be descriptive: we shall try to reconstruct stylistic values as they existed at the time, and shall disregard any changes that may since have occurred. The great temptation one has to guard against is the tendency to project modern reactions into the interpretation of earlier material. An amusing example of this fallacy is given in Wellek and Warren's *Theory of Literature* (p. 181). In Andrew Marvell's poem *To His Coy Mistress*, there occurs the couplet:

> My *vegetable* love would grow
> Vaster than empires and more slow.

These lines sound irresistibly comical to the modern reader who will call up the grotesque image of 'an erotic cabbage outlasting the pyramids and overshadowing them'. But there was naturally no such intention in the poet's mind; in the seventeenth century, *vegetable* meant 'vegetative, life-giving'. Commenting on this example, Wellek and Warren wonder whether it is 'desirable to get rid of the modern connotation', whether the retention of the modern association cannot be defended as an enrichment of meaning. The answer surely is that, from a strictly scientific point of view, it is desirable and even imperative to eliminate modern connotations; whether it is always possible to do so is a different matter.

In the case just discussed, it was easy to establish the contemporary value of the word. But it may sometimes be extremely difficult to reconstruct the precise overtones and implications of a linguistic form. How, for instance, are we to interpret the following couplet in the famous sonnet scene of *Le Misanthrope*:

> Je voudrois bien, pour voir, que, de votre manière,
> Vous en *composassiez* sur la même matière
> > (Act i, sc. 2).

The speaker is the affected and pompous Oronte who is incensed over Alceste's lack of admiration for his sonnet. The conclusion seems almost inescapable that the pretentious verbal form is used here to portray and ridicule the speaker, in much the same way as Jules Romains had done in his caricature of a pedantic professor. But can we be sure that it had the same effect on a seventeenth-century audience? Only close scrutiny of other texts would show whether the Imperfect Subjunctive already had the same overtones as at present, or whether, in fact, it had any overtones at all.[1]

There is thus a very real danger that one may be reading too much into a passage, looking for effects of style where there are none. But it may also happen that the modern student will miss a genuine stylistic value because he is not sufficiently familiar with the background. The position of the Past Definite in French classical drama provides a good example of this pitfall.[2] By the middle of the seventeenth century, the rivalry between the Past Definite and the Past Indefinite had reached a critical stage. In spoken French, the Past Definite was rapidly losing ground. In literature, there was an uneasy truce between the two tenses, regulated by the so-called 'rule of twenty-four hours'. According to this rule, events which happened prior to the previous night had to be related in the Past Definite, whereas those which happened since would be put in the Past Indefinite: '*je vis* hier—*j'ai vu* ce matin.' This had important consequences for classical drama where the whole action was restricted to twenty-four hours. The Academy had blamed Corneille for infringing the rule, and in the vast majority of cases, writers found it wiser to conform to it. They did, however, deviate from it for special reasons. An interesting example occurs in Act IV, sc. 4 of Racine's *Mithridate*. A few scenes earlier (Act III, sc. 5) Mithridate had tricked Monime into believing that he no longer wanted to marry her himself, but wished her to marry his younger son, Xipharès. Now he curtly informs her that he has changed his mind:

[1] Cf. Professor Dauzat's comments: 'Et dans la fameuse scène du sonnet, quand le prétentieux Oronte prend avec véhémence la défense de ses vers, il ne manque pas, pour impressionner son critique, de lui asséner un imparfait du subjonctif, du type le plus lourd et le plus pédant, en lui lançant son défi' (*Etudes de linguistique française*, 2nd ed., Paris (1946), p. 73). Professor Marouzeau is more cautious: he merely remarks: 'Il (viz. the Imperfect Subjunctive) nous paraît convenir excellemment à l'Oronte de Molière' (*Précis de stylistique française*, p. 98).

[2] See my article, 'The Vitality of the Past Definite in Racine', *French Studies*, vol. II (1948), pp. 35–53, and, more recently, H. Saunders, 'The Obsolescence of the Past Definite and the Time-Perspective of French Classical Drama', *Archivum Linguisticum*, vol. VII (1955). On eighteenth-century usage cf. G. Gougenheim, 'La valeur psychologique des temps dans le monologue de Figaro', *Journal de Psychologie*, vol. XLIV (1951), pp. 472–7.

MITHRIDATE: . . .Venez, et qu'à l'autel ma promesse accomplie
  Par des noeuds éternels l'un à l'autre nous lie.
MONIME: Nous, seigneur?
MITHRIDATE: Quoi, madame! osez-vous balancer?
MONIME: Et ne *m'avez-vous pas défendu* d'y penser?
MITHRIDATE: *J'eus* mes raisons alors: oublions-les, madame.
  Ne songez maintenant qu'à répondre à ma flamme.

In a modern work, there would be nothing remarkable in this
use of the Past Definite. In a seventeenth-century context, it is
a direct contravention, by the most careful of writers, of a rule
which he knew his critics might invoke against him. The
reasons for his departing from the norm are not far to seek.
Although the meeting referred to had taken place only a short
while before, Mithridate dismisses it as irrevocably past and
therefore irrelevant; he brushes it aside with the arbitrariness
of an oriental despot: '*J'eus* mes raisons alors: oublions-les,
madame.' By using the Past Definite, he relegates it to the
remote past: it is done with once and for all, and ought to be
forgotten. This contrasts sharply with the attitude of Monime
for whom the arrangement so recently made is still valid, and
who quite naturally speaks of it in the Past Indefinite, the tense
which establishes a link between present and past. In Mithridate's brutal retort we have what might be called a 'pregnant'
use of the Past Definite, which could only be recognized as
such in the light of contemporary grammatical theory and
practice.

5

The tasks of stylistics are, as we have seen, primarily descriptive. It will not, however, necessarily stop at the descriptive stage. Once one has described the expressive resources of a
language at different periods, one can start comparing these
cross-sections and plot the changes which may have occurred.
Stylistic changes[1] may happen in three different ways. A
linguistic element may lose its expressive force; it may acquire
new expressive values; finally, there may be a change in the

---

[1] Cf. Marouzeau, *Actes du IVe Congrès International de Linguistes* (1938), pp.
105f.; *Traité de stylistique latine*, pp. 337f. The scheme here suggested is closely
parallel to the classification of phonological changes put forward by R. Jakobson
in the Appendix to Troubetzkoy, *op. cit.*

expressive values themselves. Each of these possibilities will be illustrated by examples from the field of onomatopoeia.

1. *Loss of expressive values.* The French word *pigeon* is stylistically neutral, but it derives from a Vulgar Latin formation which was clearly onomatopoeic: *pipio, pipionem.* The phonetic development of the word has deprived it of its expressive force. It might be objected that *pipio* is a poor imitation of the cooing of a pigeon; but this objection lapses when it is realized that the word originally meant 'young pigeon'; Italian *pippione* still retains that meaning.[1]

2. *Acquisition of expressive values.* The name *Cicero* has given the common noun *cicerone* in Italian. The modern meaning of 'guide' was at least partly suggested by the form of the word which almost sounds like a parody of the cicerone's babble. In this way the word has become onomatopoeic in Italian.[2]

3. *Change in expressive value.* Changes in the pronunciation of a word may alter its expressive quality without depriving it of all expressiveness. Latin *murmur*, French *murmure* and English *murmur* are all three onomatopoeic, but they suggest different noises. The Latin back vowel *u* has been fronted to *y* in French, which gives the word an entirely different tonality. English *murmur*, with the central vowel ə, stands somewhere between the two, though rather nearer to Latin. One typical example from each of the three languages will show these nuances more tellingly than any analysis:

> Strepit omnis *murmure* campus
> > (*Aeneid*, VI, 709).

> Comme un enfant bercé par un chant monotone,
> Mon âme s'assoupit au *murmure* des eaux
> > (Lamartine, *Le Vallon*).

> Now entertain conjecture of a time
> When creeping *murmur* and the poring dark
> Fills the wide vessel of the universe
> > (*King Henry V*, Act IV, Prologue).

---

[1] Cf. Bloch-Wartburg. The other Italian form, *piccione*, is a borrowing from Southern French (Meyer-Lübke, *Romanisches Etymologisches Wörterbuch*, 3rd ed., no. 6522a). It may also happen that a word resists a phonetic change which would cancel out its expressive qualities; thus, the first *i* in French *charivari* would normally have disappeared, but it has been retained to preserve the onomatopoeic effect of the word (Bloch-Wartburg). Cf. Orr, *loc. cit.*, pp. 17f.

[2] See B. Migliorini, *Dal nome proprio al nome comune*, Geneva (1937), pp. 141, 276, 282.

The scheme outlined above gives an ideally simple picture of stylistic change. When we pass from single words to major devices of style, the historical process becomes infinitely complicated. Many stylistic values are so delicate and evanescent that it will be impossible to recapture them. Nevertheless, the broad lines of evolution can sometimes be reconstructed from a close study of contexts. The fourth chapter of this book, though confined to the literary language, may be regarded as a contribution to the history of word-order as a stylistic device.

Historical stylistics may set itself even more ambitious tasks. The evolution of the expressive system as a whole will probably elude its grasp, but it might be possible to trace the development of some major sectors of the system. Here again, the procedure will be essentially comparative: successive stages in the history of the language will be first described separately, then set against one another. In this way, it will become apparent, for example, how radically certain stylistic resources of French have been impoverished since the end of the Old French period. Seemingly diverse processes like the reduction of onomatopoeic effects, the loss of figurative locutions and idioms, the curtailment of derivation, the pruning of synonyms, the regularization of word-order, and others, will have to be viewed as part of a general tendency, of a fundamental change in the physiognomy of the language. Historical stylistics will seek to relate these processes to changes in the language itself, in the mentality of the speakers and in the structure of the speech-community; it will also examine their bearing on literary style. But such syntheses can only be profitably attempted when we possess many more descriptive monographs than are at present available; and reconstruction is bound to prove increasingly difficult as one probes deeper into the past.

6

The second main branch of contemporary stylistics starts from an entirely different point of view. It limits its attention to the literary language and is mainly concerned with *individual style*. At the root of this approach there are two basic assumptions: (1) that there is such a thing as 'individual style', a set of linguistic habits peculiar to a given writer; and (2) that this individual style is closely bound up with the writer's mind and experience and bears the stamp of his personality.

That there is an element of truth in both of these assumptions is self-evident; and they have received experimental confirmation from psychologists interested in the problem of style. Some of these experiments were based on direct observation, others were conducted on statistical lines. In one set of experiments, a number of essays by a group of schoolchildren were tested for idiosyncrasies of style, and it has been found possible to single out, on stylistic grounds alone, those written by the same pupil. Having carried out some non-verbal tests on the pupils, the investigator also succeeded in identifying the authors of the various essays.[1] Statistical analysis has ventured even further: by applying 'stylometrical' criteria, a correlation has been established between the ratio of verbs and adjectives and the emotional stability of the subjects examined.[2]

Literary stylistics deals with rather different problems and has begun to devise its own methods for attacking them. Here, too, there are two main possibilities: we may proceed either by direct observation or on a numerical basis. In addition to these two methods, several ancillary techniques have also been evolved in recent years. So far, the most spectacular results have been achieved by the method of direct observation, of which Professor Leo Spitzer is the most influential advocate.[3]

Spitzer's method is sometimes described as 'psychological stylistics', because of its strong emphasis on connections between an author's mental make-up and his language. Spitzer's conception of style has been moulded by two major influences. Like Croce and Vossler, he regards language as creative and artistic self-expression which finds its purest form in literary style. At the same time, he is inclined to interpret this process

[1] See F. H. Stanford, 'Speech and Personality', *Psychological Bulletin*, vol. XXXIX (1942), pp. 811–45.

[2] Cf. W. Johnson (ed.), 'Studies in Language Behaviour', in *Psychological Monographs*, vol. LVI, 2 (1944), and F. Rostand, *Grammaire et affectivité*, Paris (1951), pp. 15ff. and *passim*. Some of M. Rostand's conclusions must, however, be treated with extreme caution.

[3] The following are Spitzer's most important contributions to the subject: *Aufsätze zur romanischen Syntax und Stilistik* (1918); *Stilstudien. I, Sprachstile; II, Stilsprachen* (1928); *Romanische Stil- und Literaturstudien*, 2 vols. (1931); *Linguistics and Literary History. Essays in Stylistics* (1948); *A Method of Interpreting Literature* (1949).

of self-expression on Freudian lines. In his early writings, the psycho-analytical element was very prominent, and he was mainly interested in abnormal idiosyncrasies of style. More recently, he has been concerned with more discreet deviations from ordinary usage, but his fundamental position has remained unchanged. He still starts from the axiom that every stylistic peculiarity has its roots in the author's mind and temperament. In order to identify these peculiarities of style, and to trace them to their psychological 'radix', he has elaborated an interesting procedure which he terms the 'philological circle'.

The philological circle is an operation with three distinct phases. In the first phase, the student will merely read and re-read the text and allow it to act on him until he is struck by some persistently recurrent peculiarity: a type of imagery, a syntactical construction, a rhythmic pattern or any other feature. Next, he will try to relate this stylistic trait to some element in the author's psyche. In the third phase, he will make the return journey from the centre to the periphery and will look for further manifestations, linguistic or otherwise, of the same mental feature.

Spitzer has given an impressive demonstration of his technique in his analysis of the style of Diderot.[1] On reading various works by that author—his narrative prose, his Encyclopaedia articles, his correspondence—Spitzer was struck by a characteristic and persistent rhythmic pattern in which, as he puts it, 'I seemed to hear the echo of Diderot's speaking voice: a self-accentuating rhythm, suggesting that the "speaker" is swept away by a wave of passion which tends to flood all limits.' A short passage from *Le Neveu de Rameau* will give an idea of this rhythm which will be immediately recognized by all readers of Diderot:

. . . avec des joues renflées et bouffies, et un son rauque et sombre, il rendait les cors et les bassons; il prenait un son éclatant et nasillard pour les hautbois; précipitant sa voix avec une rapidité incroyable pour les instruments à corde dont il cherchait les sons les plus approchés; il sifflait les petites flûtes, il roucoulait les traversières; criant, chantant, se démenant comme un forcené, faisant lui seul les danseurs, les danseuses, les chanteurs, les chanteuses, tout un orchestre, tout un théâtre lyrique, et se divisant en vingt rôles divers; courant,

---

[1] *Linguistics and Literary History*, ch. iv.

s'arrêtant avec l'air d'un énergumène, étincelant des yeux, écumant de la bouche.

Once this stylistic peculiarity had been recognized, the next step was clearly indicated: the rhythmic pattern had to be related to Diderot's nervous temperament of which he himself had given a caricature in the figure of Rameau's nephew. Nor was it difficult to discover other expressions of the same nervous temperament, such as Diderot's philosophy of mobility, his 'perpetual desire to transcend the rationally graspable'. The circle had thus been closed; a correspondence had been established between three facets of the writer's personality: his nervous system, his philosophy and his style.

It was inevitable that the doctrine of the philological circle, and the assumptions on which it rests, should give rise to a number of objections.[1] The method has been criticized because of its essentially subjective and intuitive nature. Indeed, Spitzer himself has emphasized that the first step in the circle, the discovery of a stylistic idiosyncrasy, must come as a sudden illumination, a kind of 'click', and that there can be no recipe for it and no guarantee that it will take place. It has also been suggested that the linguistic facts are sometimes too slender for the far-reaching conclusions which Spitzer draws from them. The very basis of the doctrine has been called into doubt; some critics have pointed out that a stylistic trait is not necessarily symptomatic of the author's mental processes: it may be a mannerism or a mere tic. Finally, the sequence of the various phases in the philological circle has been contested; it has been argued that the mental feature identified by stylistic analysis was in most cases already known beforehand and may have influenced the choice of linguistic criteria. Professor Spitzer has strongly repudiated this allegation;[2] but even if it is true, it does not really affect the value of the method. As long as the demonstration is conclusive, it surely does not matter in what

[1] Spitzer has given a full account of his method in *Linguistics and Literary History*, ch. I. For criticisms, see esp. R. Levy, 'A New Credo of Stylistics', *Symposium*, vol. III (1949), pp. 321–34; J. Hytier, 'La méthode de M. L. Spitzer', *Romanic Review*, vol. XLI (1950), pp. 42–59; Wellek and Warren, *op. cit.*, pp. 187f.; Bruneau, *loc cit.*, pp. 11ff. A useful evaluation of Spitzer's doctrine will be found in H. Hatzfeld, 'Stylistic Criticism as Art-minded Philology', *Yale French Studies*, vol. II (1949), pp. 1–9.

[2] *Archivum Linguisticum*, vol. III (1951), pp. 1f.

order the various steps were taken; the main point is that a link
has been established between a stylistic peculiarity, its root in
the author's psyche, and other manifestations of the same mental
factor. The great merit of Spitzer's procedure is indeed that it
has lifted stylistic facts out of their isolation and has related
them to other aspects of the writer's experience and activity.

Spitzer has disclaimed any intention of founding a school,
but his influence has been widely felt, and there are now vigorous
centres of stylistic studies in a number of universities.[1] One
of the most active branches is the Spanish school headed by
Professor Dámaso Alonso.[2] The main purpose of this school
is to give a 'semantic' interpretation of literary style by estab-
lishing a relation between form and meaning at every level,
from single sounds to the significance of an entire work of art.
Unlike Spitzer, whose analyses always start from a linguistic
detail, Dámaso Alonso practises two alternative methods: he
will either work his way from outer form to inner meaning, or
follow the reverse route. Meaning itself is defined as a combination of three factors: reason, feeling and imagination. The
dosage of the three elements is variable; Dámaso Alonso
actually outlines a rudimentary typology of style by distinguishing six cardinal types, according to the relative importance of
the three components. Apart from these and a few other
principles, he recognizes no general method or canon for stylistic
analysis. More even than Spitzer, he emphasizes the intuitive
nature of the process: the method to be followed must emerge
from the text itself and must be grasped in a sudden flash of
illumination. Summarized in this way, his doctrine may appear
rather abstruse and schematic, but he has applied it with great
skill and sensitivity to the study of Góngora and other Spanish
classics.

7

The method of direct observation is not interested in numbers
as such. It is content to note the significant recurrence of some
linguistic feature, without inquiring into precise numerical

[1] There is in particular the group around Professor Hatzfeld in Washington,
and the Swiss school headed by Th. Spoerri.
[2] See Dámaso Alonso, *op. cit.*, pp. 9–13, 19–29, 421–45, 513–27. Cf. also
Amado Alonso, 'The Stylistic Interpretation of Literary Texts', *Modern Language
Notes*, vol. LVII (1942), pp. 489–96.

details. The *statistical* method[1] goes considerably further; it deliberately disregards quality and subjects the raw material of style to mathematical analysis. Most students of style lack the necessary equipment for such an approach and are also temperamentally averse to it. It is obvious that such a method will be too crude to catch the finer nuances of style. Statistics can never be more than a strictly ancillary technique in stylistic studies. As such, however, it can render useful services in dealing with certain specific problems and in placing stylistic elements in a proper perspective.

Numerical criteria can be profitably applied in inquiries where style is examined not for its own sake but for some ulterior purpose. They may help, for example, to establish the chronology of an author's works, as has been done with some measure of success in the case of Plato's dialogues. Problems of authorship may also be approached in this way; thus, the attribution of the *Imitation of Christ* to Thomas à Kempis has recently been re-examined in the light of statistical evidence.[2] Another problem which may yield to this kind of treatment is the unity of a work of art; the *Chanson de Roland* is an obvious example.[3]

Numerical data may also have some importance in dealing with the central problems of style. While there is no need for mathematical analysis proper, some rough idea of frequency may be of considerable value. When assessing the role of a particular device of style, it is not a matter of indifference whether it occurs on every page or only once or twice in a book. Some works on the subject are very unhelpful on this point; they list a number of devices and cite one or two examples for each, without explaining whether they are common or exceptional. In the essays which follow, I shall always try to give some indication of the density of each device, and of the relative frequency of its various types. This is the only way of avoiding serious errors of perspective. But such data must never be regarded as an end in themselves; they are merely the first step

[1] Cf. Guiraud, *op. cit.*, pp. 104f., and the same author's *Les Caractères statistiques du vocabulaire*, Paris (1954). See also G. Herdan, *Language as Choice and Chance*, Groningen (1956).

[2] G. U. Yule, *The Statistical Interpretation of Literary Vocabulary*, London (1944).

[3] Cf. L. Priestley, 'Reprise Constructions in the *Song of Roland*', *Archivum Linguisticum*, vol. II (1950), pp. 114–57.

towards what remains the principal task of stylistics: a qualitative interpretation of the facts of style.

8

Among the ancillary methods of literary stylistics, there is one which deserves special attention as it holds out the promise of quick and interesting results. It is based on the assumption that a writer reveals himself through his *choice of images*, that he draws them mainly from personal experience, and in particular from those experiences which have held his attention, fired his imagination or made a strong impression on him.

There is a striking example of this principle in Hugo's poem *Booz endormi*. After a hard' day's work on the land, Ruth is gazing up at the night sky, but her mind is still full of the objects and experiences of the day: the starry sky reminds her of a field, and the new moon of a sickle:

> Le croissant fin et clair parmi ces fleurs de l'ombre
> Brillait à l'occident, et Ruth se demandait,
> Immobile, ouvrant l'oeil à moitié sous ses voiles,
> Quel dieu, quel *moissonneur* de l'éternel été,
> Avait, en s'en allant, négligemment jeté
> Cette *faucille* d'or dans le *champ* des étoiles.

No important conclusions can be drawn from an isolated image, but if there is a persistent pattern or motif, it might possibly provide a clue to the author's mind and experiences. The best-known application of this technique is C. F. E. Spurgeon's book, *Shakespaere's Imagery and what it tells us*, which aims at nothing less than an inner biography of Shakespeare, a reconstruction of his personal background, his interests, his likes and dislikes, in the light of his imagery. Shakespeare is of course an ideal subject for such a reconstruction: his imagery is rich and powerful, and very little is known about his life and personality. Some of Miss Spurgeon's theories may appear fanciful and even naive; others have been disproved by closer study of Elizabethan usage.[1] But she was probably right on certain points, as for example when she interpreted Shakespeare's

[1] A detailed discussion of Miss Spurgeon's method will be found in L. H. Hornstein, 'Analysis of Imagery: A Critique of Literary Method', *Publications of the Modern Language Association of America*, vol. LVII (1942), pp. 638–53.

flood-images as boyhood memories of floods of the river Avon. It is known that the Avon was frequently in flood in Shakespeare's day, as it still is in our time.[1] This would be the psychological motivation of images like the following, which are fairly common in Shakespeare:

> my particular grief
> Is of so flood-gate and o'erbearing nature
> That it engluts and swallows other sorrows,
> And it is still itself
> (*Othello*, Act i, sc. 3).

There are indeed cases where the choice of images seems to have been dictated by some vivid experience or strong emotion in the writer's mind. Alfred de Vigny's railway images are an example in point. We know that that writer was profoundly shocked by the railway accident at Versailles in 1842 and developed a strong emotional hostility towards railways. In *La Maison du berger*, he warned against the dangers of the new invention:

> Sur ce taureau de fer qui fume, souffle et beugle,
> L'homme a monté trop tôt. Nul ne connaît encor
> Quels orages en lui porte ce rude aveugle.

Now it is interesting to find Vigny using the words *rail* and *dérailler* in a figurative sense.[2] He speaks of someone losing his head in a discussion and getting constantly off 'les *rails* de la conversation', and of writers who '*déraillent* terriblement de leurs lignes accoutumées'. He seems to have been the first writer to use the verb *dérailler* in this sense. One may safely assume that he was so much exercised by the problem of trains and derailments that they came to his mind even when he was talking of other matters. In any case, railways were still a novelty at the time, and images drawn from that sphere were uncommon and must have had a strong stylistic effect.

Images can even be deliberately used as a means of portrayal. A conscientious writer will try to adapt the speech of his char-

[1] Spurgeon, *op. cit.*, pp. 93ff.
[2] Cf. *French Studies*, vol. iv (1950), p. 9. On early railway images in Balzac and other writers, see P. J. Wexler, *La Formation du vocabulaire des chemins de fer en France, 1778–1842*, Genève-Lille (1955), pp. 130f; cf. also G. Charlier in *Literature and Science*, pp. 250ff.

acters to their milieu, interests and experience. It is an old adage that people are fond of talking about what concerns them directly:

> Navita de ventis, de tauris narrat arator,
> Et numerat miles vulnera, pastor oves
> (Propertius, *Elegies*, II, i).

This is also reflected in their choice of similes and metaphors. The peasants of George Sand, for example, draw such images as they use from their own activities and experiences. Their speech is perfectly attuned to the idyllic setting of the story:

> Toute chose a son terme, mère Maurice: quand le cheval est trop chargé, il tombe; et quand le boeuf n'a rien à manger, il meurt (*La Mare au Diable*, p. 143).

A writer may go even further and conform his imagery as a whole to the theme and atmosphere of the work. As we shall see in the last chapter, the images in Giono's novel *Regain* form a closed circle. The various aspects of country life in his native Provence are described with a wealth of imagery drawn almost exclusively from the same sphere: animals, plants, natural phenomena, farming activities peculiar to the region. An image from an outside source, for example from urban life or technological civilization, would be almost inconceivable in such a stylistic milieu; it would disturb the inner harmony of the work.

At the same time, the assumption that a writer's imagery is necessarily related to his interests and experiences can lead to absurd results. Many images and image-patterns are too conscious and deliberate to reveal anything of the author's psyche; others, though spontaneous, may result from the caprice of association; others again may have a literary source or model. A concrete example will show where an uncritical application of the method may lead. In Sartre's novel, *La Mort dans l'âme*, there is, as we shall see, an almost obsessive recurrence of insect images. The heat is likened to a gigantic octopus; the people and vehicles on the roads of France during the great exodus of 1940 are pictured as hosts of painfully crawling insects, and as the novel progresses, the insect image develops into a major symbol. Are we to interpret this as a sign of Sartre's interest in entomology, or are we perhaps to assume that as a child he had some traumatic experience connected with insects? And are we to extend the same psychological explanation to other writers in whom the insect motif is equally prominent, such as for example Malraux?[1] There may no doubt be cases where such a connexion could be plausibly argued, but on the whole it will be sufficient to suppose that all these writers were struck by an analogy with strong expressive possibilities, and developed it into a symbol, each in his own way.

Nor is it permissible to draw any inferences from the absence of a sphere as a source of imagery. It has been found, for example, that in Izaac Walton's *Life of Donne*, there is not a single image drawn from fishing. If we knew no other work by Walton, it would be impossible for us to guess from the imagery the absorbing interest which inspired the *Compleat Angler*.[2]

It is clear, then, that this method can be usefully applied in certain cases, but that it is on the whole too narrow and facile, and has serious pitfalls. A more broadly based study of imagery may, however, grant valuable insights into the workings of a writer's mind. It is hardly surprising that some of these problems should have been attacked on psycho-analytical lines, Freudian as well as Jungian.[3] But there is one great danger here: one may be tempted to construct ingenious and perfectly plausible hypotheses while there is a much simpler explanation which will remain for ever inaccessible to us. The case of Rimbaud's sonnet *Voyelles* may serve as a salutary warning. In this well-known poem, Rimbaud endows each vowel with a specific colour embodied in a series of visual images:

A noir, E blanc, I rouge, U vert, O bleu, voyelles,
Je dirai quelque jour vos naissances latentes.
A, noir corset velu des mouches éclatantes
Qui bombillent autour des puanteurs cruelles. . . .

The conclusion seems indicated that Rimbaud had the rare, but by no means unique gift known as coloured hearing. It would seem, however—though one cannot be quite sure—that the poet derived his images from quite a different source: the colours which he attributes to the various vowels, and the

[1] G. O. Rees, 'Animal Imagery in the Novels of André Malraux', *French Studies*, vol. IX (1955), pp. 129–42.
[2] Hornstein, *loc. cit.*, p. 651.
[3] Cf. Wellek and Warren, *op. cit.*, ch. IV, and the works of G. Bachelard.

objects to which he likens them, can be traced back to a spelling-book used in his childhood.[1]

9

Various other methods have been experimented with in literary stylistics. Some students have tried to grasp the essence of an author's outlook and philosophy of life by carefully examining some of his key-words, terms which occupy a special place in his vocabulary and epitomize his ideals. Corneille, for example, has been studied in the light of his use of half a dozen key-words: *mérite, estime, devoir, vertu, générosité, gloire.*[2] Another formula has become very popular in research theses at the Sorbonne: a number of monographs have been published on 'the language and style' of a particular author, giving a detailed inventory and analysis of his stylistic resources. This method has one great disadvantage: it tends to become more and more mechanical as the same problems arise and the same categories reappear in one author after another.[3] But Professor Bruneau, who was mainly responsible for the vogue of such monographs, was too modest when he described them as 'travaux d'approche . . . et de ramassage' designed to provide raw material for a future synthesis;[4] some of the theses based on this principle are important and original contributions in their own right.[5]

Literary stylistics can also transcend the study of a single work or author. It can examine the stylistic features characteristic of a group of writers, of an epoch[6] or of a *genre*. The essays

[1] H. Héraut, 'Du nouveau sur Rimbaud', *Nouvelle Revue Française*, vol. XLIII (1934), pp. 602–8. Cf. also R. Etiemble, 'Le sonnet des Voyelles', *Revue de Littérature Comparée*, vol. XIX (1939), pp. 235–61, and J.-F. Barrère, 'Rimbaud, l'apprenti sorcier', *Revue d'Histoire Littéraire de la France*, vol. LVI (1956), pp. 50–64.

[2] O. Nadal, *De quelques mots de la langue cornélienne*, Paris (1948). On the concept of 'key-words', see G. Matoré, *La Méthode en lexicologie*, Paris (1953), pp. 67 ff.

[3] Cf. Marouzeau, *Précis de stylistique française*, p. 16.

[4] *Loc cit.*, pp. 8ff. A number of relevant works are briefly discussed by Bruneau in *Où en sont les études de français*, 2nd ed., Paris (1949), Supplement, ch. VII.

[5] M. Cressot, *La Phrase et le vocabulaire de J.-K. Huysmans*, Paris (1938); J. Schérer, *L'Expression littéraire dans l'oeuvre de Mallarmé*, Paris (1947); P. Nardin, *La Langue et le style de Jules Renard*, Paris (1942). Professor Bruneau himself has embarked on a synthesis along these lines, in the volumes he has added to F. Brunot's *Histoire de la langue française*: vol. XII, *L'Epoque romantique* (1948); vol. XIII, pt. 1, *L'Epoque réaliste: Fin du romantisme et Parnasse* (1953).

[6] See ch. IX of Hatzfeld's *Bibliography*.

contained in this book might perhaps be regarded as a contribution to the stylistics of a *genre*; although they are based on the study of particular novels, attention will also be paid to what might be called the constants of the language of fiction: those stylistic problems and potentialities which are inherent in the *genre* itself.

Literary stylistics is primarily a descriptive discipline, but it can also deal with certain historical questions. One can investigate, for example, how the same stylistic problem was faced and solved by successive authors and epochs. In this way, E. Auerbach has examined, in his book *Mimesis* (1946), the history of a stylistic technique, the representation of reality in literature, by analysing nineteen representative passages which range from the *Odyssey* to Virginia Woolf. One can also trace the history of specific devices of literary style. In his monumental work on European literature and the Latin Middle Ages, E. R. Curtius has studied the survival and development of a number of stock images, allegories and similar figures. Some important themes and motifs of Western literature can be synoptically surveyed by this method: the picture of the world as a stage, fully developed in Jaques' speech in *As You Like It*, but which recurs elsewhere in Shakespeare:

> Life's but a walking shadow, a poor player,
> That struts and frets his hour upon the stage,
> And then is heard no more
> > (*Macbeth*, Act v, sc. 5);

the book as a symbol of the universe:

> In nature's infinite book of secrecy
> A little I can read
> (*Antony and Cleopatra*, Act i, sc. 2);

the temple of nature:[1]

> La Nature est un temple où de vivants piliers
> Laissent parfois sortir de confuses paroles
> > (Baudelaire, *Correspondances*).

On a more modest scale, the development of a device of style

[1] Cf. H. Flasche, '*Similitudo Templi*. Die Geschichte einer Metapher', *Deutsche Vierteljahrsschrift für Literaturwissenschaft und Geistesgeschichte*, vol. XXIII (1949), pp. 81–125.

may be followed in the works of a single author or over a longer period. Two of the essays in this book are partly historical: chapter II examines the evolution of Flaubert's technique of speech-reporting, and chapter IV outlines the changing values of word-order in the style of the nineteenth- and twentieth-century novel.

10

After this survey of the field of contemporary stylistics, it is now time to explain my own approach to these problems. The method here applied has affinities with both of the main branches of stylistics. Like the first school, it is concerned with expressive values and with the effects produced by certain stylistic devices. Like the second, it is confined to the study of literary style and tries to relate linguistic peculiarities to other aspects of a work of art.

The distinctive feature of these essays is the perspective which has been adopted. In any form of scientific research, the delimitation of the field of inquiry is of crucial importance; in stylistics, it assumes special significance. We have to find the type of context within which stylistic analysis can most profitably operate. Here the student of style is faced with a curious antinomy. He can do one of two things, but not both at the same time. He can limit himself to short texts, study each element in its natural setting, and observe their interaction. This is what Dr Sayce did in his recent book, *Style in French Prose*, where the expressive resources of French are actually seen at work in ten brief passages from prose writers of the last four centuries. This procedure has great advantages, but it also has obvious limitations. We can never recognize this way the significant recurrence of a stylistic feature, nor can we determine the relative importance of the various elements of style and their role in the structure of a major work. Alternatively, the student of style may range over a wider field where significant trends will clearly stand out; but he will do so at the risk of losing in intension what he has gained in extension, and of tearing linguistic elements out of their immediate context. Both methods are legitimate; neither is complete in itself.

In the essays which follow, the second method has been

37

adopted, though attention has also been paid to the actual setting and situation in which particular instances occur. The question arose, however, as to how wide a context one should choose for an inquiry of this type. It seemed to me, on the whole, that the optimum context would be the one set by the author himself: *the whole work of art.* This would be obviously insufficient in a short poem, and might even be so in a play, but it would be ideal in the case of a novel.

Once this point had been settled, the whole problem of stylistic method was placed in a new perspective. Linguistic elements acquired a fresh significance; they became part of a wider system and had to be related to other aspects of the novel and to its structure as a whole. A work of art is an independent and self-contained world organized in a unique way, and it will be the task of stylistic analysis to determine the role of each device in this organization, to show how far it promotes the total effect of the novel and contributes to its impact. This perspective will be consistently adhered to in these essays, whether a device of style is studied in one novel only or in a series of novels, each of them examined in its entirety. The only exception will be the chapter on Proust where, for practical reasons, the inquiry has been limited to a substantial section of the *Temps perdu.*

There can be no question of giving in half a dozen essays an account, however sketchy, of the stylistic evolution of the French novel. But the material has been so selected as to throw light on the main phases of that evolution. At the risk of oversimplifying, it would seem that there have been three distinct phases since the early nineteenth century. The first was summed up by Hugo himself when he wrote: 'Guerre à la rhétorique et paix à la syntaxe!' (*Réponse à un acte d'accusation*). In the sphere of style, the main effort of the Romantics was directed towards freeing the vocabulary from the shackles of the rhetorical tradition, and adapting it to the requirements of the new aesthetic. It was essentially a lexical revolution which left syntax practically undisturbed. In the latter half of the nineteenth century, the 'peace to syntax' turned out to have been no more than a truce: Flaubert first, then the Goncourt brothers started a revolution in syntax which received a further impetus from the Symbolists and reached its high watermark in the prose of Proust. The effects of this revolution are still very much felt in our time, but since the Symbolist movement there has been a further shift of emphasis: imagery has come to be recognized as the supreme creative principle in style. The inner structure of this book is designed to reflect this historical movement which is at the same time a progress in depth: from the surface layer of the vocabulary we shall penetrate to the deeper stratum of syntax and eventually to that subsoil of stylistic creation where images are generated and where a new vision of the world is evolved.

CHAPTER I

SOME ROMANTIC EXPERIMENTS
IN LOCAL COLOUR

I n the programme of the Romantic movement, the quest for local colour occupied a prominent position. It soon became a fashionable slogan, and some of the leading Romantics felt it necessary to protest against its excesses.[1] In the *Préface de Cromwell*, Hugo sounded a note of caution against the new manner:

> Non qu'il convienne de *faire*, comme on dit aujourd'hui, de la *couleur locale*, c'est-à-dire d'ajouter après coup quelques touches criardes çà et là sur un ensemble du reste parfaitement faux et conventionnel. Ce n'est pas à la surface du drame que doit être la couleur locale, mais au fond, dans le coeur même de l'oeuvre.

In a more jocular vein, Musset echoed the same misgivings in *Namouna*:

> Si d'un coup de pinceau je vous avais bâti
> Quelque ville aux toits bleus, quelque blanche mosquée,
> Quelque tirade en vers, d'or et d'argent plaquée,
> Quelque description de minarets flanquée,
> Avec l'horizon rouge et le ciel assorti,
> M'auriez-vous répondu: 'Vous en avez menti!'

Looking back in 1840 to the early days of the Romantic movement, Mérimée remarked ironically:

> Point de salut sans la couleur locale. Nous entendions par *couleur locale* ce qu'au XVIIIe siècle on appelait les *mœurs*; mais nous étions très fiers de notre mot et nous pensions avoir imaginé le mot et la chose.[2]

---

[1] Cf. also this denunciation of local colour by a writer in the *Journal de la langue française* (1829): 'Une bande de brouillons littéraires, exhumant des mots barbares de tous les dialectes, parlent un jargon qu'ils ne comprennent pas eux-mêmes.' Quoted by G. Matoré, *Le Vocabulaire et la société sous Louis-Philippe*, Genève-Lille (1951), p. 159.

[2] In the preface to the second edition of *La Guzla*, quoted by J. W. Hovenkamp, *Mérimée et la couleur locale. Contribution à l'étude de la couleur locale*, Nijmegen (1928), p. 1. The first chapter of Hovenkamp's book contains a detailed account of the history of the term and of the concept.

Mérimée was quite right in pointing out that neither the word nor the idea was a Romantic invention. The expression *couleur locale* was originally a technical term used in painting ; it occurs in French as early as 1699[1] and in English only a few years later, and is defined as 'the colour natural to each object or part of a picture'.[2] For a long time it was thought that Chateaubriand had been the first to use it in its modern sense when he spoke in 1811, in the *Itinéraire de Paris à Jérusalem*, of his anxiety to give 'à la peinture de ces lieux célèbres les couleurs locales'. Recently, however, some earlier uses of the term have come to light. Speaking of Racine's *Bajazet*, the critic La Harpe wrote in 1772:

C'est là sans doute posséder la science des *couleurs locales* et l'art de marquer tous les sujets d'une teinte particulière, qui avertit toujours le spectateur du lieu où le transporte l'illusion dramatique.[3]

Several other examples of this usage are found in the same author. One cannot of course be sure that he was the originator of the new meaning, but it cannot have been much older, as painting terms only began around that time to penetrate into literature. It is also symptomatic that the modern sense of *couleur locale* is not found in the 1802 edition of the Academy dictionary; it was first recorded in the 1835 edition. In the interval, the expression had not only passed into common use but had developed into one of the key-terms of the language of criticism.[4]

More important than the history of the word is that of the aesthetic principle itself. The local colour of the Romantics had a long and distinguished ancestry. Its beginnings can be traced back to the early days of mediaeval literature. As far back as the twelfth century, English words were sporadically used by writers like Wace and Marie de France when dealing with happenings in England. Not much later, argot made its first

[1] F. Brunot, *Histoire de la langue française*, vol. VI, p. 738.

[2] *OED*, s.v. local 4 e. The earliest example quoted is from 1721, but the *Shorter OED* (3rd ed., 1952 impr.) gives one from 1706. The subsequent history of the term is not quite clear, and it is impossible to say whether the modern sense of *couleur locale* is an Anglicism, as has been suggested (F. Mackenzie, *Les Relations de l'Angleterre et de la France d'après le vocabulaire*, vol. I, Paris, 1939, pp. 44 and 277).

[3] E. Malakis, 'The First Use of *Couleur Locale* in French Literary Criticism (?)', *Modern Language Notes*, vol. LX (1945), pp. 98–9. Cf. also W. v. Wartburg, *Französisches Etymologisches Wörterbuch*, s.v. *localis*.

[4] Cf. Matoré, *La Méthode en lexicologie*, p. 107.

appearance in literature: in Jean Bodel's *Jeu de Saint Nicolas*, the three thieves converse in a kind of cant. In subsequent centuries, such effects became bolder and more persistent. The fifteenth-century mystery plays are rich in local colour; learned Latinisms, foreign words, dialect and argot help to characterize the various speakers and to determine their social status. Anticipating Rabelais's linguistic parodies, Villon composed a ballad in 'vieil françois'; his poems written in the jargon of the Coquillard bands to which he belonged had no doubt a practical rather than a stylistic purpose. People from the countryside are made to speak in their local dialect in the works of Bonaventure Despériers and other Renaissance writers.[1] All these trends found their most concentrated expression in Rabelais where archaisms, technical terms, provincialisms, foreign elements and argot are employed lavishly and with great gusto.

The advent of the classical era marked a recession of local colour as of all other forms of colour in literature.[2] Comedy could still freely use evocative effects of all types: Molière's physicians discourse in a pseudo-Latin jargon, while peasant speakers in *Don Juan* and *Monsieur de Pourceaugnac* talk in their native patois. There was some local colour in narrative prose, but the higher reaches of literature were inhospitable to all elements alien to the 'bel usage'. Even foreign names had to be avoided if they sounded harsh to French ears:

> D'un seul nom quelquefois le son dur ou bizarre
> Rend un poëme entier ou burlesque ou barbare
> (Boileau, *L'Art poétique*, Chant III).

Yet a touch of linguistic colour appears occasionally even in classical tragedy. When Don Rodrigue recounts his victory over the Moors, he uses an 'exotic' word in describing their particular kind of sabre:

> Contre nous de pied ferme ils tirent leurs *alfanges*
> (*Le Cid*, Act IV, sc. 3).

It is not without interest that the original version had *épées*; in the 1644 edition, Corneille replaced it by the Hispano-Arabic *alfange* which he was the first to use in French.[3]

---

[1] See Nyrop, *Grammaire historique de la langue française*, vol. I, p. 41.

[2] On local colour in the seventeenth and eighteenth centuries, see Hovenkamp, *op. cit.*, ch. II.

[3] *Ibid.*, p. 16; cf. Dauzat, *Dictionnaire étymologique*, s.v.alfange.

The eighteenth century brought a widening of horizons and a relaxation of classical restraints. There were some timid attempts at linguistic portrayal on the stage,[1] and a certain amount of local colour in Montesquieu's *Lettres persanes*[2] and in novelists like Lesage. Towards the end of the century, the exotic trend in literature received a powerful impetus from Bernardin de Saint-Pierre's *Paul et Virginie*, while the classical trend was crystallized in André Chénier's poetic evocation of the ancient world. Both trends were vigorously developed by Chateaubriand in whose historical and exotic novels, travel books and other writings the Romantic technique of local colour appeared for the first time on a grand scale. Recent investigations have shown that his use of exotic terms was both well-informed and discreet, taking good care that they should be readily intelligible and embedded in suitable contexts.[3] The many strange names of animals, plants, objects and institutions, and especially the strings of sonorous and exotic proper names, enhanced the picturesque effect of his prose and stirred the imagination of his readers.

It was almost inevitable for the young Romantics to give local colour an important place in their aesthetic. It satisfied at once two of their fundamental aspirations: the cult of the picturesque, and the interest in characteristic, distinctive qualities. It was also a tempting outlet for Romantic escapism in the face of a society where they felt neglected and out of place. As Gautier told the Goncourts many years later:

Ce qui nous distingue, c'est l'exotisme. Il y a deux sens de l'exotisme: le premier vous donne le goût de l'*exotisme dans l'espace*; le goût de l'Amérique; le goût des femmes jaunes, vertes, etc. Le goût le plus raffiné, une corruption plus suprême, c'est le goût de l'*exotisme à travers le temps*.[4]

At the same time, the growing preoccupation of writers with

[1] Cf. my article, 'Couleur locale anglaise et théâtre français', *Mélanges Dauzat*, Paris (1951), pp. 339–50.

[2] Cf. P. Nardin, *Le Français Moderne*, vol. xx (1952), p. 281.

[3] See esp. J.-M. Gautier, *L'Exotisme américain dans l'oeuvre de Chateaubriand. Etude de vocabulaire*, Manchester (1951); Id., 'Le vocabulaire de Chateaubriand. La couleur locale dans *Les Martyrs* et *L'Itinéraire*', *Le Français Moderne*, vol. xviii (1950), pp. 33–43.

[4] Quoted by Matoré, *Le Vocabulaire et la société*, pp. 157f.

the lower strata of society, urban as well as rural, opened up further possibilities for linguistic portrayal.

Local colour in the widest sense of the term comprises a variety of types and aspects. Some authors distinguish between *internal* and *external* colour;[1] the former is psychological, bringing out the characteristic temperament and moral attitudes of a nation or period, whereas external colour is picturesque, based on physical detail. Another distinction, which overlaps with the preceding one, is that between *linguistic* and *non-linguistic* colour. Linguistic colour has three main varieties: foreign, archaic and social. The latter includes a number of different elements: dialect, slang, the language of the various trades and professions, the speech of women and children, etc.

The present chapter will be confined to the study of four stylistic techniques: portrayal of a foreign milieu (Italian, Spanish and English), of a historical period, of country life, and of the Parisian underworld. Each of these techniques will be seen at work in one Romantic novel. The texts chosen are free from the excesses and eccentricities indulged in, for example, by a Petrus Borel; yet they contain a sufficiently concentrated and diverse element of local colour to give some idea of the stylistic value of the device.

1. PORTRAYAL OF A FOREIGN MILIEU

ITALY: Stendhal, *La Chartreuse de Parme*

No French writer was more passionately attached to Italy than Stendhal. His epitaph: 'Arrigo Beyle Milanese . . .'[2] was more than a mere pose; it epitomized one of the deepest aspirations of his life. His single-minded devotion to Italy is a typical example of Romantic escapism. In the spiritual climate of the Italy of Carbonarism and of the Risorgimento, he discovered certain qualities which he particularly valued and which he had sought in vain in contemporary France: the intensity and spontaneity of feelings, the quest for happiness, and the para-

---

[1] On these and other classifications see Hovenkamp, *op. cit.*, pp. 6ff.; Bruneau, *Histoire de la langue française*, vol. XII, pp. 132ff.; Matoré, *Le Vocabulaire et la société*, pp. 157ff.

[2] See on this epitaph H. Martineau, *Le Coeur de Stendhal*, vol. II, Paris (1953), pp. 414ff.

mount importance of love as a motive force in private life and in society. This sense of affinity with, and of nostalgia for, Italy became a decisive factor both in his career and in his work as a writer. It has been calculated that he spent altogether some sixteen years in Italy, nearly half his adult life, and that more than two thirds of his printed works were directly inspired by that country.[1] It was in the course of these contacts that he accumulated the vast fund of information and experience from which his great Italian novel grew with astonishing speed at the very end of his creative period.

This attitude towards Italy was also reflected in his interest in the language. He began learning Italian at the time of his first visit to the country, nearly forty years before he wrote the *Chartreuse*. Several passages in his correspondence show that he was a keen student of foreign languages.[2] Very occasionally, there are traces of Italian influence in his choice of words and turns of phrase. In *La Vie de Henri Brulard*, for example, he had written: 'Séraphie, assez jolie, faisait l'amour avec mon père'; later on he made a note on the margin: 'italianisme à ôter.' This did not prevent him from using the same phrase in the *Chartreuse* (p. 103), but this time it fits naturally into the situation as it occurs in the speech of an Italian. Elsewhere in the same novel, he hazards a somewhat unorthodox image to illustrate the difference between the two national temperaments: 'Ce ministre, malgré son air léger et ses façons brillantes, n'avait pas une âme *à la française*; ne savait pas oublier les chagrins. Quand son chevet avait une épine, il était obligé de la briser et de l'user à force d'y piquer ses membres palpitants'—adding, with a touch of irony: 'Je demande pardon pour cette phrase, traduite de l'italien' (pp. 110f.).[3] But such cases are rare; on the whole, his language was immune from Italian influences, and the simplicity and sobriety of his style was far removed from the Italian tradition. He did, however, make a consistent and the deliberate attempt in the *Chartreuse* to evoke the Italian

---

[1] P. Martino, *Stendhal*, Paris (1934), p. 88.

[2] See J. C. Alciatore, 'Stendhal et l'étude des langues', *French Review*, vol. XXIII (1949–50), pp. 278–88.

[3] See H. Martineau's critical edition of the *Chartreuse*, Garnier, Paris (1949), p. 585, n. 429, and p. 593, n. 476; cf. also J. Prévost, *La Création chez Stendhal*, Paris (1951), p. 361, and M. Wandruszka, 'Zum Stil Stendhals', *Zeitschrift für französische Sprache und Literatur*, vol. LII (1939), pp. 429–36.

background and to give an air of authenticity to the narrative by a skilful admixture of linguistic colour.

There are in the novel some sixty Italian words and phrases, which fall into several distinct groups. Some Italianisms—names of human types, objects and institutions peculiar to that country—have a purely *documentary* function. One or two are genuinely untranslatable; others could have been expressed in French, but in the process they would have lost their evocative power and their Italian flavour. Some of the titles used are inevitably conventional (*podestate, Monsignore*); others bear witness to close familiarity with conditions in Italy. When introducing Fabrice del Dongo, Stendhal describes him as a *marchesino* and adds in a footnote: 'On prononce *markésine*. Dans les usages du pays, empruntés à l'Allemagne, ce titre se donne à tous les fils de marquis, *contine* à tous les fils de comte, *contessina* à toutes les filles de comte, etc.' (p. 29). The upstart Rassi is described as a *contino*, no doubt with a slightly ironical overtone: 'les yeux offensés par la figure ridicule du *contino* Rassi' (p. 473). Other Italianisms show that Stendhal was sensitive to the social connotations of words and knew in what contexts to use them. Thus, it was not by oversight that he spoke of the marriage of *signora*, not *signorina* Giulia Crescenzi (p. 376): although young girls are usually referred to as *signorina*, it was customary at the time to use *signora* when speaking of an unmarried young woman of noble birth.[1] Similarly, the insolent and high-handed manner in which the gaoler treats his aristocratic prisoner is conveyed, among other things, by the pronoun of address he uses, *voi* instead of the more courteous *lei*: 'Il lui adressait la parole en l'appelant *voi*, ce qui est en Italie la façon de parler aux domestiques' (p. 262).

Still in the human field, the *Chartreuse* contains a gallery of characteristic Italian types with their local labels. Some of these, such as *sbire* and *faquin*, had been known in France for a long time and had become so thoroughly acclimatized that there was no need to put them in italics;[2] but most of them still had a foreign air and were therefore italicized. Curiously enough, all these types belong to the lower strata of Italian society. At the

---

[1] Cf. Garnier ed., p. 651, n. 934.

[2] The history of *faquin* is not clear: some dictionaries (Dauzat, Battisti-Alessio) regard it as an Italianism in French, others (Prati, Bloch-Wartburg) as a Gallicism in Italian.

bottom end of the scale we find *bravo*, which was comparatively new in the sense of 'assassin',[1] and *bulo*, defined in the novel as 'une sorte de fier-à-bras subalterne' (p. 213). At a higher social level we have *cameriere* (p. 236), *vetturino* (p. 290), and *mammacia*, the old woman who looks after the actress Marietta (p. 160). Somewhat higher still is the *impresario*, a recent Italianism introduced by Stendhal himself:[2]

Les troupes d'opéra sont formées par un *impresario* qui engage de côté et d'autre les sujets qu'il peut payer ou qu'il trouve libres, et la troupe amassée au hasard reste ensemble une saison ou deux tout au plus (p. 157).

Another theatrical term is 'comédie *dell'arte*':

Chaque personnage invente le dialogue à mesure qu'il le dit, le plan seul de la comédie est affiché dans la coulisse (p. 414).

In the realm of material civilization, there are some conventional Italianisms: names of money, streets (*via, vicolo, corso*) and buildings (*trattoria, casa, palazzetto*). Stendhal also mentions *sediola* 'sorte de tilbury champêtre et rapide' (p. 161) and *mortaretto*, a special kind of small mortar (p. 173), as well as a famous poison, the *aquetta* of Perugia (p. 303). How well-informed he was on all these matters can be seen from his reference to a Piedmontese wine, the *nébieu* of Asti (p. 308); it has been pointed out that *nébieu* is the local pronunciation of *Nebiolo*, name of a village near Asti where this brand of wine is grown.[3]

Rather different from these 'documentary' Italianisms are a second group which have a purely *decorative* function. There is nothing specifically Italian about the ideas they denote; the only reason why they are given in Italian is to heighten the effect of local colour. This device is comparatively rare; there are only half a dozen examples, most of them in direct speech. There is perhaps some justification for it where the Italian word is more expressive than the French equivalent:

Voici la dénonciation de cet infâme *col-torto* (hypocrite) (p. 102);
Puis aller habiter le château de Grianta avec un abominable *secatore*, ce marquis del Dongo! (p. 103)

[1] P. 233; cf. Dauzat, *Dictionnaire étymologique, s.v. brave*, and Matoré, *Le Vocabulaire et la société*, p. 247.
[2] See Wartburg, *Französisches Etymologisches Wörterbuch, s.v. imprehendere*.
[3] Garnier ed., p. 642, n. 857.

Elsewhere, the use of idle Italianisms may appear somewhat artificial:

Eh quoi! le *porco* s'est donc défendu? (p. 201);
Eh bien! votre belle générosité nous ruine, nous perdons l'*avviamento* (l'achalandage) (p. 219).

This impression of artificiality is even stronger when such words are found, not in the speech of Italians but in the narrative itself:

Mais c'était en vain que son oeil *aggrottato* cherchait parmi tant de figures . . .(p. 469);
Ce jeune homme était fort riche, se croyait tout permis, et comme ses *prepotenze* lui avaient attiré des menaces, il ne se montrait guère qu'environné de huit ou dix *buli* (sorte de coupe-jarrets) (p. 223).

Far more significant than documentary and decorative Italianisms is a third group which takes us to the very heart of Stendhal's attitude towards Italy. The primary function of these elements is *psychological*: they epitomize certain fundamental traits, qualities and tendencies of the Italian mind. Some of them are real key-words, in the sense given to that term in the preceding chapter: they denote those features of the Italian temperament and way of life which had a special attraction for Stendhal. The fact that they are left untranslated emphasizes their uniqueness; the implication is that these qualities and attitudes are peculiar to Italy and are not found elsewhere in the same form.

One of the most striking characteristics of the Italian mind is a particular kind of gaiety, 'une gaieté pleine de *brio* et d'imprévu' (p. 43). Stendhal himself had introduced *brio* into French some years earlier,[1] and, as we shall see, he was still fascinated by that quality when he came to revise the text of the *Chartreuse*. Another trait which aroused his curiosity was the free and easy manner, the lack of constraint of most Italians: 'La franchise, la *disinvoltura* avec laquelle parlait ce ministre d'un prince si redouté' (p. 108). *Disinvoltura* had already been used by Rousseau, and the Gallicized form *désinvolture* by Madame de Staël.

[1] Cf. the dictionaries of Dauzat and Bloch-Wartburg. In *La Cousine Bette*, Balzac describes *brio* as 'mot italien intraduisible, que nous commençons à employer' (Bruneau, *Histoire de la langue française*, vol. XII, p. 382). Cf. also M. Wandruszka, *Romanische Forschungen*, vol. LXVII (1955), pp. 20f.

For obvious reasons, Stendhal preferred the Italian form; in *Le Rouge et le Noir* he had already spoken of the '*disinvoltura* de tous les mouvements' of Mathilde de la Mole.[1]

A third distinctive feature of Italian psychology is the *puntiglio* or point of honour, which must not be mistaken for vanity. This is a theme which Stendhal had developed on several occasions, arguing that vanity, a vice very common in France, was very rare in Italy except in the form of wounded pride. He returned to the problem in the preface to the *Chartreuse*:

> Les Italiens sont sincères, bonnes gens, et, non effarouchés, disent ce qu'ils pensent; ce n'est que par accès qu'ils ont de la vanité; alors elle devient passion, et prend le nom de *puntiglio* (pp. 19f.).[2]

Stendhal also quotes two interesting expressions from the language of love in Italy. In his book *De l'Amour* he had already noted some of the typical euphemisms used by lovers in that country: 'Les savants d'Académie voient les moeurs d'un peuple dans sa langue: l'Italie est le pays du monde où l'on prononce le moins le mot *d'amour*, toujours *amicizia* et *avvicinar* (*amicizia* pour amour et *avvicinar* pour faire la cour avec succès)'.[3] *Amicizia* reappears in the concluding section of the *Chartreuse*, in the account of the secret love-affair of Fabrice and Clélia Conti: 'Jamais cette *amicizia*, comme on dit en Lombardie, ne fut même soupçonnée' (p. 485). From the same sphere Stendhal also borrows the phrase *terzo incomodo* which he finds admirably expressive: 'Ici même que suis-je autre chose que le *terzo incomodo* (cette belle langue italienne est toute faite pour l'amour)! *Terzo incomodo* (un tiers présent qui incommode)!' (p. 153). There may be a childhood memory behind our author's interest in this locution: in *La Vie de Henri Brulard* he relates how, as a child, he used to play the part of a 'tiers incommode' during the walks of his father with his aunt.[4] Yet another expression from the same field is *casto Giuseppe*: 'Quel rôle jouerai-je à ses yeux? exactement le *casto Giuseppe* (proverbe italien, allusion au rôle ridicule de Joseph avec la femme de l'eunuque Putiphar)' (p. 154).

[1] Pléiade ed., p. 332; Bloch-Wartburg and Wartburg, *Französisches Etymologisches Wörterbuch* (*s.v. involvere*), give wrongly '*désinvolture* de tous ses mouvements'. Cf. Dauzat, *Dictionnaire étymologique*, Supplément chronologique to the 1954 ed., and Matoré, *Le Vocabulaire et la société*, p. 248.
[2] Cf. Garnier ed., pp. 532f., n. 7.   [3] *Ibid.*, pp. 675f., n. 1148.
[4] *Ibid.*, p. 616, n. 660.

Other locutions also serve to evoke certain aspects of Italian life and mentality. One of them contains an allusion to political events: 'Alors commença cette époque de réaction et de retour aux idées anciennes que les Milanais appellent *i tredici mesi* (*les treize mois*)' (p. 28). Several idiomatic phrases are given in Italian because of their expressive and picturesque quality: 'un jour qu'elle avait la *luna*, comme on dit dans le pays' (p. 358); 'une fête à coups de couteau (*un trattamento di cortellate*)', (p. 396); 'Tout est fini, *siamo a cavallo*. (Proverbe italien: nous sommes sauvés)' (p. 209).

The *Chartreuse de Parme* also contains several short quotations in Italian. Some of these derive from literary sources: the epigraph of the novel is taken from Ariosto; a line from Monti: '*Come face al mancar dell'alimento* (comme la petite lampe quand l'huile vient à manquer)' (p. 167), is quoted by the abbé Blanès; Cimarosa's aria, '*Quelle pupille tenere!*' (p. 456), is sung in church. The remaining quotations all occur in direct speech. Their sole function is to contribute to local colour; otherwise they could have been translated like all other conversations in the novel. They include Gina's code message to Fabrice: *Gina pensa a te* (p. 337); a form of salute : *Eccellenza, la riverisco* (p. 199); and the traditional cheers: *E viva del Dongo!* (*ibid.*).

There is, however, one episode in the novel where the use of Italian phrases is psychologically justified. Young Fabrice, it will be remembered, becomes involved in the battle of Waterloo without really understanding what is going on. In this part of the story, all the characters converse in French, but such is Fabrice's confusion and excitement that he sometimes forgets himself and lapses into Italian. When, in the thick of the battle, a French general asks him where he got his horse,

Fabrice était tellement troublé qu'il répondit en italien: '*L'ho comprato poco fa*. (Je viens de l'acheter à l'instant)' (p. 59).

A little later, his horse is taken from him:

. . . il se mit à courir après eux en criant: '*Ladri! ladri!* (voleurs! voleurs!)' (p. 65);

then he realizes his position and goes on protesting in French. After the battle, when he is recovering in a Flemish inn,

. . . par un effet singulier de la perte du sang et de la faiblesse qui en était la suite, Fabrice avait presque tout à fait oublié le français; il s'adressait en italien à ses hôtesses, qui parlaient un patois flamand, de façon qu'on s'entendait presque uniquement par signes (p. 87).

Unfortunately, Stendhal has refrained from giving a closer analysis of this partial amnesia and of the way Fabrice communicated with the Flemish girls nursing him.

When estimating the intensity of Italian colour in the *Chartreuse de Parme*, it must be remembered that some Italianisms are used several times, and that one or two—admittedly the least interesting ones, such as titles—are frequently repeated. We must also take proper names into account. They too possess some measure of evocative power, and there are certain ways in which their expressive force can be heightened. They can be provided with Italian suffixes. Several proper names can be combined to form an impressive and sonorous sequence; thus, the duchess signs a letter as *Angelina-Cornelia-Isota Valsera del Dongo, duchesse Sanseverina* (p. 254). A proper name can even be 'rejuvenated' by being brought back to its etymological origins: '*Belgirate*, village charmant et qui tient tout ce que son nom promet (voir un beau tournant du lac)' (p. 398).

By these varied effects, Stendhal has contrived to produce a vivid impression of local colour, and has shown himself a connoisseur of the finer nuances of Italian. Yet, on the whole, his technique of linguistic portrayal is rather restrained and discreet in this novel. Here a comparison suggests itself with an episode in *Le Rouge et le Noir*, chapter XXIII, where the appearance of the Italian singer Geronimo is accompanied by a spate of Italianisms: *maestro, caro, lascia fare a me, credete a me, carta canta*, and others. Nowhere in the *Chartreuse* can one find such a concentration of linguistic colour. It would indeed have been impossible to maintain this dosage throughout a story which takes place almost entirely in Italy; but it is also conceivable that, during the interval of nine years between the two novels, Stendhal's method had matured and had become more discriminating.

There are signs that Stendhal meant to intensify the local colour in the second edition of the *Chartreuse*. Encouraged by Balzac's searching but laudatory review of the novel in the *Revue de Paris*, Stendhal set to work to revise the style and texture of his book. He never completed the task, but his notes, written on the margin of a copy of the *Chartreuse*, have been published in H. Martineau's critical edition. It is clear from these notes that Stendhal had decided to introduce a number of further Italianisms. Thus, 'le majordome de la maison' was to be changed into 'le majordome de la *casa* del Dongo' (p. 542, n. 47); the sentence: 'Entre ici, ami de mon coeur' was to be followed by the Italian version: '*Di quà, amico del cuore*' (p. 675, n. 1145); the statement on 'la gaieté italienne, pleine de *brio*' was to be made more explicit: 'cette gaieté italienne, peu connue parmi nous, pleine de *brio*' (p. 555, n. 164). Italianisms also appear in the new passages which were to be incorporated into the text: 'Le marquis son père, d'après une idée du Prévôt de Saint-Jean *alle case rotte*' (p. 548, n. 98); '*Eh! viva il signor contino!* s'écria Barlass' (p. 579, n. 371). Elsewhere, two lines by Foscolo were to be quoted in Italian (pp. 635f., n. 804). One may wonder whether these and other alterations would, on balance, have been beneficial to the novel. Contradictory opinions have been expressed in recent years about the style of the *Chartreuse*. Some critics praise its limpidity: 'il s'applique à la pensée comme un vernis translucide qui semble n'avoir d'autre rôle que d'aviver la couleur primitive'.[1] Others detect in it a certain dryness, monotony and lack of warmth.[2] But even its detractors would agree that it has one supreme virtue: spontaneity. This spontaneity in style is in harmony with the composition of the book, the free and unconstrained way, somewhat reminiscent of the picaresque novel, in which one episode follows another.[3] It is also in harmony with the central theme of the work: the *brio* and *disinvoltura*, the strong emotions and impetuous actions, which Stendhal admired in the Italian temperament. There is a subtle correspondence between the three planes of artistic creation, and an over-careful revision of the text, however useful on points of detail, might have disturbed the inner balance of the book.

[1] H. Martineau, on p. xvii of his introduction to the Garnier edition.
[2] Cf. A. Lytton Sells, '*La Chartreuse de Parme*: The Problem of Style', *Modern Language Quarterly*, vol. XI (1950), pp. 486–91, and Wandruszka, *loc. cit.*
[3] Cf. A. Lytton Sells, '*La Chartreuse de Parme*: The Problem of Composition', *Modern Language Quarterly*, vol. XII (1951), pp. 204–15. See also M. Bardèche, *Stendhal romancier*, Paris (1947), pp. 393 ff.

Spain: Mérimée, *Carmen*

The term *couleur locale* recurs in Mérimée's writings with the persistence of a *leit-motiv*. It appears at every stage of his career and in the most diverse works: letters, travel books, fiction, critical prefaces.[1] A comparison of these passages reveals a somewhat ambiguous attitude to the whole problem. At times, he seems to be firmly attached to local colour; at others, he treats it ironically and almost condescendingly. As late as 1859, fourteen years after the publication of *Carmen*, he speaks in a letter of 'nous autres amateurs de couleur locale'. His eagerness to learn about local conditions at first hand is expressed almost naively in some of his earlier letters: he hopes to experience 'quelque aventure pleine de couleur locale telle que nous l'aimons tous les deux', and to cultivate the friendship of Turkish bandits in order to get some touches of local colour. In fiction and criticism, however, he shows himself more sophisticated and adopts a tone of ironical detachment, as in the following passage from a story about Turkey:

> . . . Il avait à la main une espèce de vilain coutelas . . .
> —Un yataghan? dit Châteaufort qui aimait la couleur locale.

Elsewhere he appears to dismiss local colour as one of the slogans which were fashionable in his youth. In the preface to the second edition of *La Guzla*, which has already been mentioned (see above, p. 40), he states in no uncertain terms: 'Le procédé était si simple, si facile, que j'en vins à douter du mérite de la couleur locale elle-même.' Some years earlier he had told a friend that one of his reasons for writing *La Guzla* was precisely 'de me moquer de la couleur locale dans laquelle nous nous jetions à plein collier vers l'an de grâce 1827'. And in *Colomba*, he goes so far as to declare: 'couleur locale . . . caractère. Explique qui pourra le sens de ces mots, que je comprenais fort bien il y a quelques années, et que je n'entends plus aujourd'hui.'[2]

It is difficult to reconcile these contradictory utterances. Some critics discount them as a mere pose of scepticism and self-mockery, others interpret them as symptoms of a gradual change

---

[1] For details see Hovenkamp, *op. cit.*, pp. 11, 142ff., 174ff.
[2] Cf. L. Cazamian, *A History of French Literature*, Oxford (1955), p. 332.

in Mérimée's outlook.[1]   It may also be that he felt alternately attracted by local colour and repelled by its excesses. Yet, as far as his own practice is concerned, there seems to be little difference in the density of linguistic colour between his earlier and later works. In *Le Théâtre de Clara Gazul*, published in 1825, one critic has counted 150 Spanish words on as many pages, and the dosage is much the same in *Carmen*, written twenty years later, though the technique is of course more mature.

Local colour in *Carmen* is technically interesting because of its extraordinary complexity. It has three distinct layers: Spanish, Basque and Romany. The three are intermingled in the story, and each of them is applied with gusto and with a lavish display of colourful detail. To elucidate all these diverse linguistic elements, the author had to give a number of explanations which he accommodated in the text itself, in the notes, and in a special appendix on the Romany language. In a narrative told in the first person singular, it is of course fairly easy to introduce extraneous matter of this type; nevertheless it was a *tour de force* to have all this intricate linguistic documentation without in any way slowing down the story.

Of the three layers of local colour, the *Spanish* one is the most elaborate. Spain held a unique place in the art and experience of Mérimée. It is perhaps an exaggeration to suggest that it had the same magnetism for him as Italy had for Stendhal;[2] but he did visit the country on several occasions, had many Spanish contacts, and frequently treated Spanish themes in his writings. In *Carmen* he goes out of his way to show his knowledge of, and affection for, the language. When the narrator first meets Carmen, he thinks—wrongly, as it turns out—that she must be Andalusian:

Vous êtes du moins Andalouse. Il me semble le reconnaître à votre doux parler. . . . Je crois que vous êtes du pays de Jésus, à deux pas du paradis (p. 23).

And he goes on to explain that he had heard this metaphorical description of Andalusia from a well-known picador. He also refers to a characteristic feature of Andalusian pronunciation, the

[1] Hovenkamp, *op. cit.*, *passim*, esp. pp. 176f.; cf. A. Dupouy, '*Carmen*' *de Mérimée*, Paris (1930), pp. 99ff.

[2] Dupouy, *op. cit.*, p. 24.

so-called *ceceo*, which makes the *s* sound like a voiceless *th*: 'Sur le seul mot *Señor* on peut reconnaître un Andalous' (p. 7). Andalusia had a particular fascination for Mérimée, and he extended his affection even to the dialect.[1]

Mérimée delights in picturesque proverbs and idiomatic locutions typical of Spanish mentality. Some of the most striking ones occur in the speech of Carmen herself, which not only abounds in local colour but is carefully contrived to reflect her temperament and the workings of her mind:

Demain il fera jour! (*Mañana será otro dia!*) (p. 47);
Eh bien, moi, je te ferai des abreuvoirs à mouches sur la joue, et je veux y peindre un damier (p. 38).

As explained in a footnote, this is a free translation of the locution *pintar un javeque* 'peindre un chebec', as the side of these barges is usually painted in red and white squares in Spain.

The expression in Carmen's eyes reminds the narrator of the Spanish proverb: 'Oeil de bohémien, oeil de loup' (p. 25). He also notes several phrases about ethnical peculiarities: *Navarro fino* (p. 72), to dress *a la francesa* (p. 22), and the description of British soldiers as 'crabs' (*écrevisses*) because of their red uniform.

Mérimée was also struck by another trait of the Spanish language: its richness in diminutives, which contrasts rather sharply with the relative paucity of such resources in French. In a letter to Madame de Montijo, the mother of the future Empress Eugénie, he spoke early in 1845 of a Madrid girl who was so small that a double diminutive was required to describe her; her friends called her *Mariquita*.[2] In *Carmen*, a number of diminutives are used, formed mainly from Christian names: *Carmencita, Joseito, Juanito, Inglesito, candilejo, gitanilla*.

The same meticulous accuracy in the observation of details is evident in the use of Spanish words for local types, objects and institutions. Prominent among these are the names of various succulent dishes: *yemas* 'jaunes d'oeufs sucrés' (p. 48), *turon* (*turrón*) 'espèce de nougat' (*ibid.*), *gaspacho* 'espèce de salade de piments' (p. 12). Still in the gastronomical sphere,

---

[1] On Mérimée's interest in Andalusia, see M. Bataillon, 'L'Espagne de Mérimée d'après sa correspondance', *Revue de Littérature Comparée*, vol. XXII (1948), pp. 35–66, esp. p. 65.
[2] *Ibid.*, p. 42.

Mérimée mentions *manzanilla* (p. 48) and *chufas* 'racine bulbeuse dont on fait une boisson assez agréable' (p. 57). *Neveria* 'café pourvu d'une glacière' (p. 22) and *papelito* (*ibid.*), a contemporary term for cigarette,[1] belong to the same field. Other names of specifically Spanish objects—not counting assimilated ones like *mantille* and *castagnette*—include *patio* and *zaguán* 'entrance' (p. 46) as well as *divisa* 'cocarde du taureau' (p. 79). The strong local colour produced by these and other words is reinforced by Spanish names of human types and occupations: *gitana, hidalgo, picador, corregidor*, and by several geographical and administrative terms: *sierra, fuero, presidio, partido*, etc.

Compared to the rich Spanish colour in *Carmen*, the *Basque* material may appear rather slight. It is mainly introduced as a linguistic and ethnographical curiosity, and also to emphasize the special background of Don José, so that the Basque bandit and his Gipsy girl form an alien element sharply detached from the Spanish environment. Don José is proud of his Basque origin:

> Je m'appelle Don José Lizzarrabengoa, et vous connaissez assez l'Espagne, monsieur, pour que mon nom vous dise aussitôt que je suis Basque et vieux chrétien. Si je prends le *don*, c'est que j'en ai le droit (p. 32).

He is also proud of his language:

> Notre langue, monsieur, est si belle, que, lorsque nous l'entendons en pays étranger, cela nous fait tressaillir (p. 40).

The Spaniards' inability to learn Basque is dismissed with contempt: 'il n'y en a pas un qui puisse seulement apprendre à dire *baï, jaona* (oui, monsieur)' (p. 39). This is confirmed by a Spanish Dominican who admits that he is unable to pronounce José's Basque name (p. 30). Carmen, on the other hand, has mastered this difficult idiom; most of the few Basque words and phrases which occur in the novel are actually found in her speech, adding yet another touch to her complex linguistic portrait: *barratcea* 'enclos, jardin' (p. 40); *Laguna ene bihotsarena* 'camarade de mon coeur' (p. 40); *Agur laguna* 'Bonjour, camarade' (p. 46).

The *Romany* element in *Carmen* is the most exotic of the three

[1] Cf. Matoré, *Le Vocabulaire et la société*, p. 98, and Bruneau, *Histoire de la langue française*, vol. XIII, 1, p. 135.

layers. Though less substantial than the Spanish one, it is more striking because of its strangeness. Once again, it shows the scholarly thoroughness with which Mérimée approached the problem of local colour.[1] His friend Estebanez Calderon had initiated him into the mysteries of the Gipsy tongue; when presenting him with a copy of *Carmen*, Mérimée called him in the autograph 'mon maître en *chipecalli*', the Romany of Spain. Other friends were also consulted: the French consular agent at Janina was asked, for example, about the speech of the Bohemians of Albania. But the main sources were literary, foremost among them two works by George Borrow, *The Zincali* and *The Bible in Spain*, to which the author acknowledges his debt in the appendix. Most of the Romany words in *Carmen* also occur in one or the other of these books, and it has even been suggested that the appearance, a few months before the composition of *Carmen*, of a French translation of *The Bible in Spain* may have been a factor of some importance in the genesis of the story.[2]

Most of the general information—historical, linguistic, ethnographical—about the Bohemians of Spain is relegated in *Carmen* to the appendix, but in the text itself there are references to their language, 'la *rommani* ou *chipe calli*' (p. 26), and to its international diffusion (pp. 39f.). Occasionally, a small detail will add to the authenticity of the narrative: the Gipsies call Portugal *Laloro*, 'la terre rouge' (p. 52); Gipsy women are known in Spanish slang as *Flamenco de Roma* (p. 56), etc. The Bohemian element itself shows the same taste for humorous and picturesque expressions as the Spanish layer. Many of these are found in Carmen's speech and contribute to its vivid and graphic quality. Figurative locutions and proverbs are quoted in great profusion, with the Romany wording given in the notes: 'Chien qui chemine ne meurt pas de famine' (p. 48); 'Je suis habillée de laine, mais je ne suis pas mouton' (p. 52); 'Gale avec plaisir ne démange pas' (p. 60); 'Rivière qui fait du bruit a de l'eau ou des cailloux' (p. 77). A second group of Romany words denote certain features of their life and organization: fortune-telling (*la baji*, p. 23), charms (*bar lachi* 'pierre d'aimant', p. 39), Gipsy dances (*la romalis*, p. 46), the queen of the

---

[1] On the Bohemian background of *Carmen* see Dupouy, *op. cit.*, ch. v.
[2] *Ibid.*, pp. 78ff.

Bohemians (*Bari Crallisa*, p. 82). Finally, some general terms are thrown in to add to local colour and also because of their expressive quality: *payllo* 'foreigner' (p. 24); *calo*, literally 'black', the name by which the Bohemians call themselves (p. 50); *minchorro* 'mon amant, ou plutôt mon caprice' (p. 69). In Carmen's speech, two Romany words are sometimes combined to heighten the effect: 'Tu es mon *rom*, je suis ta *romi*' (p. 50), where *rom* means 'husband' and *romi* 'wife'; 'Ah! les *lillipendi* qui me prennent pour une *erani*' 'Les imbéciles qui me prennent pour une femme comme il faut' (p. 64).

Carmen probably represents the extreme limit in local colour to which a writer may go without overloading the narrative. In what purports to be a travel story told in the first person singular, the reader will be prepared to accept an unusually heavy concentration of local colour; yet one may wonder whether the experiment was altogether successful, whether the colour was not out of proportion with the rest of the story and whether its elements were harmoniously blended. Such doubts may have been partly responsible for the cold reception of the novelette: Tolstoy dismissed it as 'feeble' and Sainte-Beuve found it 'sec, dur, sans développement'.[1] In the long run, however, the verve and virtuosity of local colour played a decisive part in the success of the book and the opera.[2] Historically, Mérimée's technique is interesting because it faces both backwards and forwards, towards Romanticism and towards Realism. He is essentially Romantic in his fondness for the picturesque, the strange and the exotic. Yet he anticipates Realism by his scrupulously careful documentation and by the psychological verisimilitude of his portrayal through speech.[3] This is his significance in the history of local colour.

England: Vigny, *Stello*

Vigny was perhaps the most thoroughly Anglicized of all the major Romantics.[4] He was married to an Englishwoman, had

---

[1] Cf. Hovenkamp, *op. cit.*, p. 204.
[2] See P. Trahard, *Prosper Mérimée de 1834 à 1855*, Paris (1928), p. 224.
[3] On the fortunes of *Carmen*, see Dupouy, *op. cit.*, ch. VIII.
[4] An account of Vigny's English contacts will be found in my article, 'The Stylistic Role of Anglicisms in Vigny', *French Studies*, vol. IV (1950), pp. 1–15.

many English friends, and visited England on two occasions, in 1836 and again in 1838–9. At one stage he even had hopes of being appointed ambassador in London. Though he was strongly critical of the excesses of dandyism, he developed certain Anglicized habits: he wrote an English hand, dressed with what a contemporary described as 'English elegance', and, on his own admission, emulated the taciturnity of the British. His debt to English literature was considerable: he translated *Othello* and *The Merchant of Venice* into French and played a leading part in the vogue of Byron and Walter Scott. Yet he had some difficulty in mastering the English language. When he met Scott in Paris in 1826, he was unable to converse with him in English. A study of his manuscripts has revealed some elementary mistakes in the use and spelling of English words, and his command of the language was so uncertain that when he wanted to employ an Anglicism he usually left a blank space for it in the draft version.[1] Eventually, however, he acquired a reasonable fluency in the language; an Englishman who met him in 1844 wrote:

> Il parlait anglais correctement, mais avec un fort accent et il était évident qu'il avait fait des études d'anglais longues et laborieuses. Quand je lui demandai où il l'avait appris, il répondit: 'De ma femme et de Shakespeare'.

Like other Romantics, Vigny was interested in local colour, though he was too detached and reserved by temperament to indulge in any excesses. How alive he was to the importance of this principle can be seen from his comment on Iago's words: 'By Janus, I think, no', which struck him while he was translating *Othello*:

> Sans affirmer que Shakespeare ait pensé à faire jurer Yago par le dieu *au double visage*, comme l'assure Letourneur, je vois du moins là dedans une grande fidélité de couleur locale que j'ai précieusement conservée: les Italiens jurent encore aujourd'hui par les dieux du paganisme: *Per Bacco*, etc. (*Théâtre*, vol. I, p. 13).

There is a certain amount of linguistic colour in Vigny's

For a fuller treatment, see M. Citoleux, *Alfred de Vigny. Persistances classiques et affinités étrangères*, Paris (1924), Part II, ch. III, and E. Lebbin, *Alfred de Vignys Beziehungen zu England und zur englischen Literatur*, Halle (1936).

[1] Cf. Baldensperger's critical ed. of *Stello* in the Conard ed. of Vigny's works, p. 432.

novels: in *Cinq-Mars*, in the *Canne de Jonc* episode of *Servitude et Grandeur Militaires*, which centres on the figure of Admiral Collingwood, and in the history of Chatterton and Kitty Bell, which forms the second part of the novel *Stello*.

It is perhaps somewhat surprising that Vigny should have thought it necessary to introduce local colour into a book like *Stello*. His aim was to write, not so much a work of fiction as a study of the poet's predicament in the midst of an unsympathetic society, exemplified by three incidents: the fate of Gilbert under the *Ancien Régime*, that of Chatterton in the England of the Industrial Revolution, and that of André Chénier under Robespierre's Reign of Terror. At times Vigny actually appeared to scorn the ordinary methods of story-telling: he once told Villemain that

. . . on devait diminuer à l'avenir l'action matérielle et ses puérilités pour tout donner à l'action spiritualiste et au développement métaphysique d'une vérité morale ou d'une idée philosophique (*Théâtre*, vol. II, p. 60).

In his handling of the Chatterton theme, he disclaimed any attempt at historical accuracy; in the preface to the dramatized version he declared:

Chatterton n'était qu'un nom d'homme, et je viens d'écarter, à dessein, des faits exacts de sa vie pour ne prendre de sa destinée que ce qui le rend un exemple à jamais déplorable d'une noble misère (*ibid.*, p. 242).

But if he was uninterested in authenticity, he was not entirely indifferent to artistic verisimilitude, and local colour was one of the means he used for achieving it.

The form of the story lent itself easily to such treatment. Once again we have a narrator, the Docteur Noir, relating his experiences abroad in the first person singular, and it is quite natural for him to use some English words when talking about things English. There is even further justification for the use of Anglicisms. The Docteur Noir obviously takes a snobbish delight in displaying his knowledge of English, even though he has 'un accent anglais d'une pesanteur insupportable' (p. 57) and, after listening to him for half an hour, Kitty Bell has to confess that she does not know any German (pp. 50f.).

Linguistic colour in the Chatterton episode is formed of two elements. The author's main effort goes into the picture of England in the late eighteenth century. This picture is entirely conventional, and it is mainly achieved by conventional means. Names of persons and of London landmarks are freely used; occasionally, several names are combined to strengthen their evocative power: 'le moine Rowley paraissait aussi grand qu'Homère à lord Chatham, à lord North, à sir William Draper, au juge Blackstone' (p. 61). Trite Anglicisms like *gentleman*, *lord*, *bill* contribute to this conventional setting; here again, they are sometimes combined and thus become a little more effective: 'les gros *Lords* et les longues *Ladies*' (p. 52); 'un *Quaker* noir et un *Lord* rouge' (p. 80). Other Anglicisms are more specific. The description of Kitty Bell's sweet-shop includes a number of English terms which had become fashionable in France during the Restoration period:[1] 'les membres des deux Chambres . . . venaient manger des *buns* et des *mince-pies* en continuant la discussion sur le Bill' (p. 49); 'elle me faisait verser du *soda-water*' (p. 51); 'prendre sur le comptoir des macarons, des *cracknels* et des *plumbuns*' (p. 79). English words are also used in direct speech. In the portrait of the Lord Mayor, the chief target of Vigny's satire, they produce a grotesque effect: 'Les *young Ladies* aiment cela' (p. 79); '*Well, very well!* cria le gros Beckford, c'est bien, mon enfant! c'est noblement représenter notre bienheureuse patrie! *Rule Britannia!* chanta-t-il en fredonnant l'air national' (p. 82). In the melodramatic death-scene, John Bell's repeated summons to his wife: '*Come, mistress Bell!*', may derive additional poignancy from the use of a foreign language (p. 89). Elsewhere, the presence of English words and tags might seem incongruous, but the Docteur Noir's habit of parading his English provides a plausible excuse: 'Monsieur . . . *you* . . . médecin . . . achetez-moi mon corps, et payez ma dette' (Chatterton's last words, p. 88); '*The Lord-Mayor! Lord-Mayor!* s'écria tout à coup Kitty' (p. 75). This mannerism of the narrator is noticed by Stello himself who occasionally interrupts the story to chaff him about it. The novel thus becomes, in a sense, a mild satire on contemporary Anglomania by

[1] Cf. J. Bertaut, 'L'Anglicisme en France sous la Restauration', *Revue de Paris*, vol. xxv (1918), pp. 153–83, esp. pp. 171ff. and 177ff, and Mackenzie, *op. cit.*, p. 212, *s.v.crackers*.

someone who was himself by no means immune from that malady.[1]

The Docteur Noir is also fond of allusions to English literature and of actual quotations: '*Othello's occupation's gone*' (p. 92); '*He was violent and impetuous to a strange degree*' (p. 80), etc. These literary reminiscences form a connecting link between the two layers of English colour in the story: the evocation of modern Britain and that of the mediaeval scene.

Chatterton's famous piece of literary forgery, the poems he wrote in archaic[2] English and attributed to the fifteenth-century priest Thomas Rowley, could not fail to arouse Vigny's antiquarian interest. He had been intrigued by certain aspects of English philology long before he set pen to *Stello*. While translating Shakespeare he had been struck by the fundamental affinity of the English and French vocabularies:

En les cherchant avec soin, on trouve d'étonnantes et fraternelles analogies entre la langue anglaise et la nôtre, qui fut entée par Guillaume le Conquérant sur le vieux saxon. Le vieil anglais conserve l'*e* muet du français dans une foule de mots, et la première édition de Shakespeare . . . est remplie d'expressions de notre ancien langage: en les remettant en usage, on pourrait, *en prose*, traduire l'ancien anglais mot à mot (*Théâtre*, vol. I, p. 23).

This line of thought is pursued in chapter xvi of *Stello*, 'où le drame est interrompu par l'érudition d'une manière déplorable aux yeux de quelques dignes lecteurs'. In this philological digression, which includes quotations in Greek, Latin, Old French, Middle English and Spanish, some comments are made on the phonetics and prosody of Middle English and also on 'la perte irréparable des vieux mots si naïfs et si expressifs de *emburled* au lieu de *armed*, de *deslavatie* pour *unfaithfulness*, de *acrool* pour *faintly*; et des mots harmonieux de *myndbruche* pour

---

[1] See pp. 57, 65f., 77. For protests against the fashion of Anglomania, cf. my article, 'Anglicisms in French', *Publications of the Modern Language Association of America*, vol. LXII (1947), pp. 1153–77, esp. pp. 1166f.

[2] Archaic in a very superficial sense. 'The Rowley poems', writes George Sampson, 'are not an imitation of fifteenth-century English verse; they are really new poetry of the eighteenth century. . . . All that is old about them is the spelling, freely imitated from the worst fifteenth-century practice, and the vocabulary, taken from available dictionaries. Chatterton does not seem to have cared for Chaucer, except as a source of words. He studied the glossary, not the text' (*The Concise Cambridge History of English Literature*, Cambridge University Press (1942), p. 537).

firmness of mind, *mysterh* pour *mystic*, *ystorven* pour *dead'* (p. 68). Vigny also tries to give some idea of the archaic flavour of the Rowley poems by quoting a few lines from them (pp. 62, 70); at one point he prints seven consecutive lines in pseudo-Middle-English (p. 73). The Docteur Noir's pedantry gives the author a convenient excuse for indulging his antiquarian hobby.

Three years after the publication of *Stello*, Vigny produced a dramatized version of the Chatterton story, which was performed at the Comédie-Française, with Marie Dorval in the part of Kitty Bell. A comparison between the novel and the play is instructive as it shows the influence of *genre* on this aspect of style. When rehandling the story, Vigny was compelled to reduce local colour for a number of reasons: stage realism, dramatic condensation, and the replacement of the Docteur Noir by the Quaker who now provides a very chastened *raisonneur*. The second layer of Anglicisms, the antiquarian and philological element, disappeared in the process, except for a few colourless references. The use of English words and phrases in direct speech was also abandoned as it would have been out of place on the stage. Names of English foods and drinks were relegated to the stage directions: 'John Bell, gonflé *d'ale*, de *porter* et de *roastbeef'* (*Théâtre*, vol. ii, p. 244). The more conventional vehicles of English local colour: proper names, titles, money, proverbs and literary allusions are retained and even expanded by quoting sayings like: 'Gardons bien les sous, les shellings se gardent eux-mêmes' (p. 252). To compensate for the loss of English words unusable in a play, some Anglicisms which were then fashionable in France are introduced: *confortable* and *groom* occur in the stage directions, *bas bleu*, *toast* and *gentleman* in the text itself. English dandies are made to use English words current in the speech of French dandies: 'Moi, je n'ai rien appris à Oxford si ce n'est à *boxer'* (p. 281); 'J'ai le *spleen*, mais ce n'est que pour une heure ou deux. . . . Ah! mistress Bell, vous êtes une *puritaine'* (p. 282). The author was obviously trying to retain as much local colour as his medium would allow, but he did not succeed in making the play even remotely English. 'Trop tournée au rêve et trop décolorée pour être applaudie des Français, mais trop étrangement peu anglaise pour être ratifiée par moi' was the verdict of one of Vigny's English friends.

Beside the vivid and exuberant colour of *Carmen*, *Stello* is bound to appear rather pale. It also lacks the finesse and self-assurance with which Stendhal evokes the Italian atmosphere in the *Chartreuse*. The contrast is hardly surprising. As a novelist, Vigny did not possess the skill of a Stendhal or a Mérimée, and he was also less interested in the story itself than in its symbolic significance. The narrative form he adopted was unsuited to the more imaginative uses of local colour. But there was also a more personal reason. When Stendhal wrote the *Chartreuse*, he had spent many years in Italy; when Mérimée wrote *Carmen*, he had already been twice to Spain; *Stello*, on the other hand, was published in 1832, some years before Vigny's first visit to Britain. Local colour in the novel is entirely second hand: it is made up of information gleaned from English friends and mainly from literature. The England of *Stello* is half-conventional, half-bookish: it lacks the hall-mark of personal observation and experience.

2. PORTRAYAL OF A HISTORICAL PERIOD

Hugo, *Notre-Dame de Paris*

In a letter to his publisher, written while he was working on *Notre-Dame de Paris*, Hugo summed up in these terms the aims of his new novel:

C'est une peinture de Paris au quinzième siècle, et du quinzième siècle à propos de Paris. . . . Le livre n'a aucune prétention historique, si ce n'est de peindre peut-être avec quelque science et quelque conscience, mais uniquement par aperçus et par échappées, l'état des moeurs, des croyances, des lois, des arts, de la civilisation enfin, au quinzième siècle.

This statement, though modestly worded, shows the magnitude of the task which Hugo had set himself. In the broader canvas of a historical novel, he was trying to put into practice what he had written about drama in the *Préface de Cromwell*:

Le drame doit être radicalement imprégné de cette couleur des temps; elle doit en quelque sorte y être dans l'air, de façon qu'on ne s'aperçoive qu'en y entrant et qu'en en sortant qu'on a changé de siècle et d'atmosphère. Il faut quelque étude, quelque labeur pour en venir là; tant mieux.

This insistence on historical colour had its roots in a funda-mental tendency of the Romantic movement.[1] Throughout Europe, the interests of writers were turning towards the past and in particular towards the Middle Ages. This was another symptom of that mood of escapism and nostalgia which we have seen at work in a different medium. In France, there had been various signs of that trend since the Pre-Romantic period. The late eighteenth century saw the birth of the so-called trouba-dour manner which endeavoured to re-create the atmosphere of the Middle Ages by evoking the objects peculiar to mediaeval civilization. This movement received a strong impetus from Chateaubriand's *Génie du Christianisme* and especially from Mar-changy's *Gaule poétique*, published in 1813–17. Half a century later, Gautier coined the adjective *moyenâgeux* to describe the temper of that generation. With the advent of Romanticism, the troubadour manner gave way to the bolder and more strident archaisms of the *machicoulis* style where obsolete words were resurrected from mediaeval texts and glossaries. The progress of philological studies was another contributory factor in the rise of mediaevalism. Various attempts were made to revive old expressions which had fallen into disuse. Nodier, the linguist of the movement, wrote:

L'archaïsme consiste à reprendre dans les écrivains originaux de la langue des locutions ingénieuses et expressives que l'usage a laissé perdre ou qu'un sot purisme a rebutées. Ceci est, entre nous, la meilleure manière de rajeunir, de revivifier les langues.[2]

Soon mediaevalism invaded other spheres of public taste: fashion, architecture, furnishing, interior decoration. Victor Hugo himself furnished his rooms in what was then known as 'Gothic' style. In historical fiction, Walter Scott's influence reigned supreme and gave rise to a manner which its opponents contemptuously called 'la Walterscotterie'. The disciples even outdid the master in their cult of archaism; as Balzac pointed

---

[1] For the vogue of archaism in the Romantic period, see esp. Matoré, *Le Voca-bulaire et la société*, pp. 162–9. Cf. also Bruneau, *Histoire de la langue française*, vol. XII, *passim*, esp. pp. 214, 285ff., 303ff., and vol. XIII, 1, pp. 88f. On archaism as a device of style, see J. Damourette, 'Archaïsmes et pastiches', *Le Français Moderne*, vol. IX (1941), pp. 181–206.

[2] *Notions élémentaires de linguistique* (1834), quoted after Bruneau, *op. cit.*, vol. XII, p. 214.

out in an attack on 'le bibliophile Jacob', 'Walter Scott a écrit pour les lecteurs du XIXᵉ siècle, M. Jacob a écrit pour ceux du XVIᵉ.'[1] Yet such was the power of fashion that, a little later, Balzac himself published the *Contes drôlatiques*, his famous pastiche of the language of the sixteenth century. To give some idea of these affectations, it will be sufficient to quote a short passage from one of the worst offenders, Aloysius Bertrand:

—Qui vous baillera, à vous, si grosse chevance?
—La guerre.
—Où?
—Es Espagne. Mécréants y remuent l'or à la pelle, y ferrent d'or leurs haquenées. Le voyage vous duit-il?[2]

Set against such eccentricities, Hugo's use of archaisms in *Notre-Dame* gives an impression of moderation and self-restraint which one would not normally associate with this writer. He employs them freely and with characteristic zest, and accumulates them on occasion to enhance their evocative power, but he never allows them to imperil intelligibility or to disturb the flow of the narrative.

Hugo took his role of chronicler of the past very seriously and made a thorough study of a number of reference works, some of which are actually mentioned in the novel.[3] He drew heavily on the three volumes of Sauval's *Histoire et recherches des antiquités de la ville de Paris* (1724) and went carefully through the accounts of the Prévôté, published in that work, to find authentic fifteenth-century names for his characters. He also consulted Du Breul's *Théâtre des antiquités de Paris*, various chronicles, and, for the passages on occult practices, Collin de Plancy's *Dictionnaire infernal*. Many of the obsolete

---

[1] Quoted after Matoré, *Le Vocabulaire et la société*, p. 166.

[2] Quoted after Bruneau, *op. cit.*, vol. xii, p. 286. Bertrand, like many other writers, did not realize that *ès* was a plural form, a contraction of *en les*. Similarly, Baudelaire dedicated *Les Fleurs du mal* to Théophile Gautier, 'parfait magicien *ès langue française*'; subsequently he changed it to *ès lettres françaises*. The same mistake is sometimes made by contemporary writers; cf. A. Dauzat in *Mélanges Bruneau*, Genève (1954), p. 3, n. 2.

[3] These sources are fully examined in E. Huguet's monograph, 'Quelques sources de *Notre-Dame de Paris*', *Revue d'Histoire Littéraire de la France*, vol. viii (1901), pp. 48–79, 425–55, 622–49. See also O. H. Moore, 'How Victor Hugo Created the Characters of *Notre-Dame*', *Publications of the Modern Language Association of America*, vol. lviii (1942), pp. 181–206, and G. Huard, *Revue d'Histoire Littéraire de la France*, liii (1953), pp. 319–44.

terms scattered all over the book can be traced back to one or the other of these sources. To give but one or two examples, among the shady characters who throng the Cour des Miracles, there is an *hubin* and a *sabouleux*: 'Ailleurs un jeune *hubin* prenait leçon d'épilepsie d'un vieux *sabouleux* qui lui enseignait l'art d'écumer en mâchant un morceau de savon.' These are two terms of fifteenth-century argot transcribed from Sauval: 'Les *Hubins* disoient et montroient avec un certificat, qu'un chien ou loup enragé les avait mordus, et qu'ils alloient faire le voyage de St Hubert . . . les *sabouleux* contrefaisoient les malades de Saint (les épileptiques) avec un morceau de savon en la bouche qui jettoit bien de l'écume . . .'[1] Elsewhere, Hugo follows even more closely the wording of his source: 'un méchant page qui s'amusait à *escailbotter* les écoliers en faisant courir son cheval dans les boues' (vol. ii, p. 37) is an exact replica of a passage in Du Breul: 'un de leurs pages, qui avoit *escailbotté* quelques Escholiers en faisant courir son cheval dans les boues.'

Archaic colour in *Notre-Dame* is intense and persistent: there are hundreds of obsolete terms and phrases, very diverse in nature and in tone. On the fringes of archaism proper are the many quotations in mediaeval Latin. Some of them are reasonably correct; others are couched in Low Latin or in barely Latinized French with a distinctly comic flavour. The style of official documents is often ridiculed: 'ce que le beau latin des chartes appelle *tota via, cheminum et viaria*' (vol. i, p. 122); '*tunicam dechiraverunt*, dit la plainte' (vol. ii, p. 37). But the device is most effective when it occurs in direct speech and reflects the general attitude of the speaker: the self-mockery of the poet Gringoire: 'J'ai vendu la semaine passée ma dernière chemise; c'est-à-dire, puisque vous ne comprenez que la langue de Cicero: *Vendidi hebdomade nuper transita meam ultimam chemisam*' (vol. i, p. 126); or the flippancy and mock erudition of the young student Jehan Frollo: 'avec mon laquais, *cum meo laquasio*' (vol. ii, p. 40); 'la petite boucherie, *parva boucheria*' (vol. ii, p. 61); 'à je ne sais quels garçons et marmousets, *quibusdam marmosetis*—vous voyez, bon frère Claude, qu'on sait son latin' (vol. ii, p. 39).

A number of archaisms occur in quotations from a wide variety of contemporary sources, ranging from chronicles and

---

[1] Huguet, *loc. cit.*, p. 634.

documents to student songs and literary reminiscences, like this couplet from the *Roman de la Rose*, quoted by the irrepressible Jehan Frollo:

> Que je ne beuvrai de piment
> Devant un an, si je cy ment
> (vol II, p. 238)[1]

When an isolated archaism appears in the narrative itself, Hugo sometimes has to explain it, contriving at the same time to underline its expressive quality:

. . . cette charpente prodigieuse, si touffue qu'on appelait *la forêt* (vol. II, p. 255).

C'était une de ces fameuses cages à prisonniers d'état qu'on appelait *les fillettes du roi* (vol. II, p. 281).

Elle n'en sortait que pour le gibet ou le bûcher. Quelquefois elle y pourrissait. La justice humaine appelait cela *oublier* (vol. II, p. 109).

In most cases, no special explanation is offered; the obsolete terms are either self-explanatory or clarified by the context:

. . . c'était la couleur dont le bourreau brossait les édifices *scélérés* (vol. I, p. 167).

Une fruitière me donnait une prune par-ci, un *talmellier* (baker) me jetait une croûte par-là (vol. I, p. 160).

Relatively few archaisms occur in isolation; usually, several terms are combined to give a vivid impression of a scene or a social milieu: a court of justice, a torture chamber, the Parisian underworld, etc. Such combinations are particularly effective when they take the form of an *enumeration*, one of the favourite devices of Hugo's rhetoric:

Les grands-blancs, les petits-blancs, les targes, les liards-à-l'aigle pleuvaient (vol. I, p. 102).

. . . d'où se dégorgeaient en foule haches, épées, bassinets, cottes de mailles, platers, fers de lance et d'archegayes, sagettes et viretons, comme pommes et raisins d'une corne d'abondance (vol. II, p. 233).

Here we have what Spitzer has called a 'chaotic enumeration': physical confusion graphically rendered by the accumulation of bizarre and half-understood old vocables. This device is admirably suited to the description of scenes like the beggars' march:

[1] Cf. Huguet, *loc. cit.*, pp. 67f.

Ainsi défilaient . . . les courtauds de boutanche, les coquillarts, les hubins, les sabouleux, les calots, les francs-mitoux, les polissons, les piètres, les capons, les malingreux, les rifodés, les marchandiers, les narquois, les orphelins, les archisuppôts, les cagoux; dénombrement à fatiguer Homère (vol. i, p. 106).

A modern critic has rightly spoken here of 'ivresse verbale';[1] yet it is interesting to reflect that the enumeration was taken over almost bodily from Sauval, though Hugo has inverted the order of the procession.[2]

The linguistic elements brought into play in the evocation of the past are extremely varied: they are drawn not only from the vocabulary but from every part of language. Some archaisms are merely phonetic or graphic. Archaic modes of spelling give words like *haulteur* (vol. i, p. 169) and *loyaultez* (vol. i, p. 58) an old-fashioned appearance. Some words are transcribed as they were pronounced in Middle French: *élabourées* (vol. ii, p. 22), *madamoiselle* (vol. i, p. 113 and elsewhere), *pourtraicts* (vol. i, p. 90); the last word is also a grammatical archaism as it is used here as a past participle. Obsolete word-forms like *drapels* (*ibid.*) for *drapeaux*, and *bourrel* (vol. ii, p. 225) for *bourreau*, produce a similar effect.

Lexical archaisms include a multiplicity of technical terms from the most diverse spheres. In the centre of the picture is the complicated system of public administration. Words like *présidial* (vol. i, p. 301), *queux-le-roi* (vol. i, p. 320), *sergent fieffé* (vol. i, p. 291), *tru* 'tax, duty' (*ibid.*), *hart* 'rope' (vol. i, p. 300),[3] abound in the novel and are sometimes found in heavy concentrations (e.g. Book x, ch. 5). The Church and the world of learning are another prolific source of technical terms: *officialité* (vol. i, p. 245), *machicots* 'a kind of lower clergy' (vol. i, p. 239), *artiens* (vol. i, p. 242), *doctorerie* (vol. i, p.221), *astrologien* (vol. i, p. 222), and many more. Medieval medicine is evoked by *navrure* 'wound' (vol. i, p. 221), *maladrerie* 'leper-house' (vol. ii, p. 167), 'les *pharmacopoles* et les maîtres *mires*' (vol. i, p. 257), and others.

---

[1] P. Berret, *Victor Hugo*, Paris (1927), p. 342.

[2] Huguet, *loc. cit.*, p. 633. On Hugo's use of archaisms in enumerations, cf. G. Lanson, *L'Art de la prose*, Paris (1909), pp. 228 ff.

[3] See on this word G. Tilander, *Studia Neophilologica*, xxi (1949), pp. 131–40.

There is a full gallery of medieval types and occupations, from military units (*voulgiers* 'halberdiers', *cranequiniers* 'crossbowmen', vol. II, p. 76) and civilian trades (*talmelliers; haubergiers* 'makers of hauberks', vol. I, p. 296) down to the underworld of the Cour des Miracles, of which we have already seen some specimens. Hugo also delights in the description of old-fashioned dresses (*jaques* 'jerkins', vol. II, p. 76; *gonelle*, vol. II, p. 217), arms and accoutrements (see above, p. 68), musical instruments (*rebec*, vol. I, p. 107), coins (*sol parisis*, vol. I, p. 153; *teston*, vol. II, p. 10; cf. above, p. 68), and games ('les joueurs accroupis sur les billes, sur les merelles, sur les dés, sur les vachettes, sur le jeu passionné du tringlet', vol. II, p. 233).

Apart from this panorama of contemporary life and customs, Victor Hugo also uses some archaisms of a more general kind. He revives obsolete nouns like *noise* ('j'ai eu *noise* avec Mahé Fédy', vol. II, p. 141) and *pourchas* (vol. II, p. 313), both of which have survived in English, and old derivatives like *historieur* (vol. I, p. 85) and *mahomerie* (vol. II, p. 33). Other word-classes are also represented, as in the adjective *gigantal* (vol. II, p. 143), copied from Sauval;[1] the verb *maugréer* ('*maugréer* un peu le nom de Dieu', vol. I, p. 55);[2] and the adverb *moult* (vol. I, p. 16; vol. I, p. 57). Some words are used in an old meaning which has since disappeared: *oublier* and *forêt*, which we have already seen; *plaidoyer* in the sense of 'court-room' (vol. I, p. 94); *désappointer* in the sentence: '. . . *désappointait* Pierre Puy de la charge de maître des requêtes' (vol. I, p. 290). The exact value of titles and forms of address is also noted: 'Ce n'est pas un clerc, c'est un laïque; il ne faut pas dire *maître*, mais bien *messire*' (vol. I, p. 38); 'les trois *damoiselles* (car le nom de *dames* était réservé alors aux femmes nobles)' (vol. I, p. 313).

The archaic flavour of the novel is further increased by the use of some obsolete grammatical forms and constructions. There are one or two cases of archaic gender and agreement: '*ce grand image* de saint Christophe' (vol. I, p. 213; *image*, which means 'statue' in this context, could then be either masculine or feminine); *la plus belle comté* (vol. II, p. 287; cf. *la Franche-Comté*) ; *souventes fois* (vol. I, p. 241; this phrase is now con-

---

[1] Huguet, *loc. cit.*, p. 648.
[2] On the meaning of this verb see Orr, *op. cit.*, p. 193.

sidered archaic and regional). Some old particles are also employed: the preposition *emprès* (vol. ii, p. 279), the pronominal adverb *céans* (vol. i, p. 378; vol. ii, p. 263), and, in legal contexts, the fuller forms of the demonstrative pronoun *celui* (*icelle*, vol. ii, p. 280; *iceux*, vol. ii, p. 380; cf. *icelui* in Racine's *Plaideurs*, Act iii, sc. 3). The vigesimal system of counting is used in ' *Six-vingts* livres, pas même parisis' (vol. i, p. 253) and in 'un des *sept-vingt-un* seigneurs' (vol. i, p. 219). There are also examples of antiquated sentence-structure: 'c'est un mien chat' (vol ii, p. 52); 'je ne m'attendais pas à si honorable visite' (vol. i, p. 252). Archaisms of this type usually appear either in direct speech or in more or less modernized quotations from old documents.

Outside the system of organized language proper are interjections, swear-words and the like, in which the Middle Ages were particularly rich. Hugo makes free use of them because of their emotional force and graphic quality. They range from harmless exclamations like *Or çà!*[1] (vol. i, p. 378) to oaths invoking the name of God (*Bédieu!*, vol. ii, p. 27; *Pasque-Dieu!*, vol. ii, p. 299; *Gueule-Dieu!*, vol. ii, p. 263; *Corne-Dieu!*, *ibid.*, etc.) and the Holy Virgin ('Par les corbignolles de la sainte Vierge!', vol. ii, p. 27), or the devil (*Bédiable!*, *ibid.*) and, strangest to modern ears, Mohammed (*Pasque Mahom!*, vol. ii, p. 263; *Barbe-Mahom!*, *ibid.*, etc.). A number of these swear-words occur in the speech of the underworld leader Clopin Trouillefou, but other characters are also portrayed through their favourite expletives. Louis XI, for example, is particularly fond of *paillard*: 'il affectionnait ce mot, qui faisait avec *Pasque-Dieu* le fond de sa jovialité' (vol. ii, p. 299). Phoebus de Châteaupers swears with gusto, as befits a medieval cavalry officer:

'Sang-Dieu! ventre-Dieu! bédieu! corps de Dieu! nombril de de Belzébuth! nom d'un pape! corne et tonnerre!' (vol. ii, p. 54).

He finds an appreciative audience in young Jehan Frollo: 'Ma foi, capitaine Phoebus, vous sacrez avec une verve admirable' (vol. ii, p. 55).

This very selective survey, which could easily have been much longer, will perhaps give an idea of the vividness and

[1] Cf. Orr, *loc. cit.*, p. 195.

intensity of archaic colour in *Notre-Dame*. Naturally, the dosage will depend on the nature of the context. It is highest in what a recent critic has called the 'epic frescoes' and 'picturesque scenes'[1] through which Hugo tries to recapture the atmosphere of fifteenth-century Paris. It is lowest where he deals with timeless human situations, such as Claude Frollo's love for Esmeralda, which he does not want to tie down to a particular period.[2] But even where the archaic element is at its strongest, it is not excessive for a novel of this type, and the skill with which it is worked into the story is in marked contrast to the clumsiness of some of Hugo's contemporaries.

Two main criticisms have been directed against local colour in *Notre-Dame*. It has been suggested that the portrayal is purely external and is not matched by a similar effort to achieve internal verisimilitude.[3] This is undoubtedly true, but does not affect linguistic colour as such. The weakness in psychological motivation is quite unconnected with the lavish use of archaisms; there is no cause and effect relation between the two.

The second objection is more pertinent; it contends that Hugo's display of erudition is pedantic and has no real place in a work of art. 'Il a le désir de nous étonner, de nous éblouir', writes André Bellessort. 'Les chapitres intitulés *Coup d'oeil impartial sur l'ancienne magistrature* et *le Retrait où dit ses heures Monsieur Louis de France* sont hérissés de détails aussi faciles à se procurer que fastidieux. Nous le savons, il s'est consciencieusement documenté . . . Ce n'est pas sa documentation qu'on regrette, c'est l'intempérance avec laquelle il l'a déversée dans son livre, sans égard à notre fatigue.'[4]

No reader of the novel will dispute these conclusions, and linguistic colour has to bear part of the blame, even though it avoids some of the cruder excesses of *Walterscotterie*. But if Hugo's archaisms are not always free from pedantry, they are

---

[1] 'Le thème historique donne lieu à deux effets différents: d'une part, une fresque épique où se développe la vie secrète et passée de la cathédrale (notamment l'assaut des truands et l'incendie); d'autre part, des descriptions et des scènes pittoresques (la Fête des Fous, la Cour des Miracles), dont la truculence évoque Rabelais ou les peintres flamands' (J.-B. Barrère, *Hugo, l'homme et l'oeuvre*, Paris (1952), p. 64).

[2] Cf. Huguet, *loc. cit.*, p. 62.

[3] 'Des deux couleurs locales, l'intérieure manque ou à peu près, et l'extérieure est trop généreusement prodiguée' (L. Maigron, *Le Roman historique à l'époque romantique*, Paris (1912), p. 181).

[4] A. Bellessort, *Victor Hugo. Essai sur son oeuvre*, Paris (1930), p. 80.

redeemed by his verve and gusto and by his genuine fondness for the old language. To quote again M. Bellessort,

> . . . il aime l'érudition moins comme savant qu'en collectionneur et en artiste; il en poursuit les bizarreries qui en sont comme les orchidées; elles ont des sons, une forme, une figure qui enchantent son imagination.

He delights in the quaint old words, locutions and turns of phrase, not merely because they are part of the mediaeval scene, but also because of their picturesque quality and expressive force. In the last analysis, the novel owes its astonishing vitality to the grandiose evocation of the past, and archaism plays a significant part in that process.

3. PORTRAYAL OF COUNTRY LIFE

George Sand, *La Mare au Diable*

Realism in dialogue raises some delicate problems for the novelist and the dramatist. Even the speech of educated people is not easy to transcribe, with its inflexions, colloquialisms and inconsistencies, and its overtones of emphasis and emotion. But it is the language of the uneducated which presents the chief difficulty. If it is accurately reproduced, it may be unintelligible to the ordinary reader, or may at least irritate him and place a heavy strain on his patience. Some vulgarisms may appear improper and offensive to good taste. The discrepancy between the author's own style and that of his characters may produce a jarring effect and disturb the harmony of the work. On the other hand, if the characters are made to speak in a language out of tune with their personality and their background, it will be difficult to produce that illusion of reality which is the prime purpose of dialogue in literature.

In spite of all the difficulties, realism in the portrayal of vulgar speech has a long tradition going back to Roman times. In the comedies of Plautus and in the famous banquet scene of Petronius's novel *Satyricon*, the *sermo vulgaris* is accurately and vividly presented; works of this type are among our most valuable sources of information about the way the lower classes actually spoke at the time. In modern literature, some measure of linguistic realism has become almost compulsory, except in writers like D'Annunzio or Claudel who aim at a different level of style. There are even cases where changes in the language of a character are an essential element in the plot, as a barometer of changes in his social status; we shall see an example of this in *Splendeurs et misères*. At the same time, some writers shrink from absolute realism where this would limit their range and cramp their style. This is particularly so in novels told in the first person singular. Chateaubriand was faced with a similar dilemma in *Atala* where the narrator is the Red Indian Chactas. In the preface he explained the compromise which he had had to adopt:

> C'est un sauvage qui est plus qu'à demi civilisé, puisque non seulement il sait les langues vivantes, mais encore les langues mortes de l'Europe. Il doit donc s'exprimer dans un style mêlé, convenable à la ligne sur laquelle il marche, entre la société et la nature. Cela m'a donné quelques avantages, en le faisant parler en sauvage dans la peinture des moeurs, et en Européen dans le drame de la narration. Sans cela il eût fallu renoncer à l'ouvrage: si je m'étais toujours servi du style indien, *Atala* eût été de l'hébreu pour le lecteur.

With the progress of Romanticism, the problem of speech-reporting became more acute. The widening of literary horizons and the social sympathies of the Romantics brought the lower classes, urban as well as rural, within the orbit of fiction. Balzac was faced at quite an early stage with the problem of dialect in literature. After some experiments in *Les Chouans* (1829), he made a more sustained effort fifteen years later, in *Les Paysans*, to reproduce the speech of the peasantry. But he was not sufficiently familiar with their language; his technique was uncertain, and he failed to distinguish between dialect and argot. In the words of Professor Bruneau, 'les Paysans de Balzac parlent et agissent trop souvent comme des repris de justice'.[1] It fell to George Sand to evolve a linguistic medium which would serve as a vehicle for a new *genre*, the 'roman champêtre'.

George Sand started with one great asset: she had a thorough first-hand knowledge of the Berry region, which is the scene of her rustic stories, and of the local dialect. Her family came from that area, and although she was born in Paris, she moved there

---

[1] *Histoire de la langue française*, vol. XII, p. 426.

at the age of four and spent there most of her childhood and youth, and much of her later life.[1] Yet she did not find it easy to develop a rustic style to her own satisfaction.[2] Her first experiments (*Valentine*, 1832) were still rather timid. It was not till twelve years later, in the novel *Jeanne*, that she set herself in all seriousness to reproduce the dialect spoken by her characters. In the intervening period, she had acquired progressive social views and had become associated with the so-called 'proletarian' movement in literature, centred on Pierre Leroux's *Revue Indépendante*. Under the influence of Rousseau and Leroux, she had formed an ideal picture of the peasant who had remained free from the debasing and corrupting effects of urban civilization. Her enthusiasm extended to the speech of the countryside; in the foreword to *François le Champi* she wrote:

Leur langage . . . est plus expressif, plus énergique et plus logique cent fois que notre langue littéraire. C'est pour moi une cause de désespoir que d'être forcée d'écrire la langue de l'Académie, quand j'en sais beaucoup mieux une autre qui est si supérieure pour rendre tout un ordre d'émotions, de sentiments et de pensées.

In her admiration for local dialects, she found a powerful ally in Count Jaubert who brought out in 1842 his *Vocabulaire du Berry et de quelques cantons voisins*, where he echoed Nodier's views about the purity of the patois and the hybrid and corrupt nature of Standard French.

The mood of naive enthusiasm in which *Jeanne* was written accounts for the extravagant use of linguistic colour in the novel. Here is a sample of direct speech:

Alle a ce qu'il faut, et *alle* sait les paroles de la *chouse*. Faut la laisser; vous voyez ben que ça li ficherait malheur *por el* restant de ses jours, de laisser consommer les *ous* de sa mère. *Alle saillera d'élà* aussi nette qu'*alle* y entre, foi d'*houme*! vous allez *voère*! Souffrez pas! Faut pas vous fâcher. On *z'ou* fait pour *vot'* bien; on veut pas vous offenser. Vous la feriez brûler si vous *alliège anvec-z-elle*. Faut pas *contreyer* l'ouvraige aux Fades.[3]

[1] Cf. L. Vincent, *George Sand et le Berry*, Paris (1919), p. 26.

[2] The evolution of George Sand's rustic manner is outlined in Bruneau, *Histoire de la langue française*, vol. XII, Book VI, ch. 5. The most detailed monograph on the subject is L. Vincent, *La Langue et le style rustiques de George Sand dans les romans champêtres*, Paris (1916). Cf. also R. Zellweger, *Les Débuts du roman rustique: Suisse, Allemagne, France*, Paris (1941), ch. IV, esp. pp. 133f.

[3] Quoted after Vincent, *La Langue et le style*, pp. 99f.

Such an extraordinary style could hardly commend itself to the common reader. The author herself was not happy about it; she felt in particular that the way her heroine spoke was out of harmony with her idealized portrait and also with the style of the narrative itself: 'Ton sentiment et ton langage font avec les siens un effet disparate comme la rencontre de tons criards dans un tableau.'[1] She therefore promptly abandoned this manner; in *La Mare au Diable* (1846) and other stories from the same period, linguistic colour is considerably toned down, and no attempt is made to give an exact transcription of local speech. The characters talk in a kind of Basic French, with some dialect terms and grammatical peculiarities thrown in here and there to remind the reader of their background: 'Vous n'êtes pas *poumonique*?' (p. 69); 'Mes chiens ont *jappé à nuitée*' (pp. 102–3); 'Tiens, je *vas* prendre ta place' (p. 72); 'Vous n'êtes guère occupée, ma petite fille, *qu*'il lui dit; et trois moutons pour une *pastoure*, ce n'est guère' (p. 43).

Even this solution failed to satisfy the exacting taste of the author, and only a year later, she tried yet another manner in *François le Champi*, the novel which fascinated Proust in his childhood. In the foreword to that book, she declared that, while *La Mare au Diable* represented a certain progress over *Jeanne*, 'l'auteur y montre encore de temps en temps le bout de l'oreille; il s'y trouve des *mots d'auteur*'. She put her dilemma quite squarely:

Si je fais parler l'homme des champs comme il parle, il faut une traduction en regard pour le lecteur civilisé, et si je le fais parler comme nous parlons, j'en fais un être impossible, auquel il faut supposer un ordre d'idées qu'il n'a pas.

To solve this dilemma, and to safeguard the inner harmony of the story, she suggested a compromise:

Raconte-la-moi comme si tu avais à ta droite un Parisien parlant la langue moderne, et à ta gauche un paysan devant lequel tu ne voudrais pas dire une phrase, un mot où il ne pourrait pas pénétrer. Ainsi tu dois parler clairement pour le Parisien, naïvement pour le paysan.

Some of the rustic novels of this period (*François le Champi*, *Les Maîtres Sonneurs*) are actually told by peasant speakers, and

[1] *François le Champi*, Avant-propos, p. 19.

there is an obvious tendency to strengthen linguistic colour, lexical as well as grammatical.[1]

La Mare au Diable, then, represents a transitional stage, a trough between two crests, in George Sand's method of speech-reporting. But this does not mean in any way that the novel is lacking in local colour. There is a sprinkling of dialect terms and features throughout the story—some fifty in all, which is not inconsiderable in a book of this size. Many of them occur in the Appendix which is a study in local customs rather than an integral part of the narrative. Occasionally, several provincialisms are aligned to strengthen the effect. The heaviest concentration appears at the beginning of the Appendix:

Il invitait le maître de la maison et toute sa *compagnie*, c'est-à-dire tous ses enfants, tous ses parents, tous ses amis et tous ses serviteurs, à la bénédiction, *au festin, à la divertissance, à la dansière et à tout ce qui en suit*. Il ne manqua pas de dire:—Je viens *vous faire l'honneur* de vous *semondre* (p. 155).

Among dialect terms introduced as elements of local colour, there are naturally many relating to farming: 'son *areau* de forme antique, traîné par deux boeufs tranquilles' (p. 16); 'autour des *broyes* en mouvement' (p. 162); 'ce qu'on appelle des boeufs *fraîchement liés*' (p. 18); *chanvreur* (p. 157); 'chanvre en *poupées*' (p. 179); *brande* 'heather country',[2] and various others. Some of them are fully explained for the benefit of the urban reader: 'Si vos sabots sont fendus, vous pouvez chercher par terre; vous trouverez bien un brin d'oisil (d'osier) pour faire des *arcelets* (petites lames de fer en forme d'arcs qu'on place sur les sabots fendus pour les consolider)' (p. 166). Mlle Vincent, who has checked George Sand's provincialisms against contemporary usage on the spot, has been able to confirm the accuracy of this definition (*op. cit.*, p. 140).

Another side of rural life which is portrayed with great care is the complicated process of a village wedding. The wedding presents or *livrées* (p. 153) are described in full detail; they include, amongst other things, 'un beau *devanteau* (tablier), de beaux rubans, un habit de drap . . . et jusqu'à *un cent d'épingles*' (p. 177). During the ceremony, the bridegroom places a

[1] Cf. Vincent, *ibid.*, pp. 35–40.

[2] *Brande* 'heather' is an old word preserved in modern dialects; it was already used by Chateaubriand and later by Vigny; cf. Wartburg, *Evolution et structure de la langue française*, p. 241.

treizain, i.e. thirteen pieces of silver, in the hands of the bride (p. 189). A further phase of the wedding is the game of the cabbage (*chou*), a kind of morality play, in which the bridegroom appears under various names: 'le *pailloux*, parce qu'il est coiffé d'une perruque de paille ou de chanvre', 'le *peilloux*, parce qu'il est couvert de *peille* (de guenilles),' and 'le *païen*, parce qu'il est censé, par son cynisme et ses débauches, résumer en lui l'antipode de toutes les vertus chrétiennes' (pp. 192f.). It is easy to see how these words have been brought together by 'popular etymology', through various associations of sound and sense.[1] All these dialect terms are designed to underline the authenticity of the author's excursion into folklore.

In some of the examples already quoted, Standard French words are used in the patois with a different meaning. There are a number of similar cases: *exploit* in the sense of invitation (p. 155), *fin* in the locution 'un *fin laboureur*' (p. 21), etc. The etymological link between *arriver* and *rive* (Latin *arripare* and *ripa*) is still clearly visible in the phrase: 'Quand le chanvre est *arrivé* à point, c'est-à-dire suffisamment trempé dans les eaux courantes et à demi séché à la *rive* . . .' (p. 158). Some abstract words are used in a concrete sense : 'J'ai cru que c'était une *honnêteté*' (p. 132); 'je ne suis pas d'avis que tu prennes une *jeunesse*' (p. 29). This is interesting as the counterpart in popular speech of an impressionist tendency which will be examined in a later chapter.[2]

George Sand is particularly anxious to record some pithy and graphic expressions which reflect the French peasant's turn of mind and his characteristic form of humour. The back street in a village is known as 'le chemin des *affronteux*' because 'les gens qui craignent de recevoir quelque affront mérité le prennent pour éviter d'être vus' (p. 131).[3] When one inquires politely about the purpose of a visit, the appropriate formula is: 'Vous êtes donc venu vous promener par ici ?' (p. 106). Peasant mentality is effectively portrayed through certain images and idioms which could only have arisen in this milieu:[4]

---

[1] '*Pailloux, peilloux* ou *payen* signifient de paille à Nohant et environs' (Vincent, *op. cit.*, p. 217).

[2] Other examples in Vossler, *Frankreichs Kultur und Sprache*, pp. 379f.

[3] At La Châtre, a village near George Sand's home at Nohant, there is still a *chemin des affronteux* (Vincent, *op. cit.*, p. 139).

[4] Examples from other novels are given in Vincent, *op. cit.*, pp. 74ff.

Elle est faite comme une petite caille et légère comme un petit pinson (p. 90).

Il était de noce, chantait comme une grive et sautait comme un cabri (p. 190).

Il ne songea qu'à *faire l'homme* avec les boeufs et les chevaux (p. 137).

. . . traîné par deux boeufs . . . qu'une longue habitude a rendus *frères*, comme on les appelle dans nos campagnes (p. 16).

Some of George Sand's provincialisms are, by their very nature, confined to direct speech. Such are, for example, certain forms of address as well as local expressions for family relationships: 'mes pauvres *mondes* (mes pauvres gens)' (p. 194); '*l'homme et la femme de chez nous* (désignant ainsi, selon l'usage, les chefs de famille)' (p. 146); 'ma pauvre chère femme de mère' (p. 52). Grammatical provincialisms, too, are restricted to direct speech. In *La Mare au Diable*, they are much less frequent than in *Jeanne* or in the later novels. There are one or two peculiarities in inflexion: *j'ons* occurs in the text of an old song, and *je vas* is repeatedly used in dialogue (p. 42 etc.). This form is still current in the region, even among educated people; it was the one George Sand would normally employ in conversation, and is found even in her correspondence.[1] The preposition *à* is used in some cases where Standard French would have a different construction: 'la petite Marie *à* la mère Guillette' (p. 45); 'on voit *à* se conduire' (p. 93).[2] It commonly replaces *de* in possessive phrases, as in the title of the novel and in constructions like 'le jardin *à* monsieur le curé' (p. 88). Some uses of the conjunction *que* are also dialectal: 'Vous n'êtes guère occupée, ma petite fille, *qu'*il lui dit' (p. 43); 'Oui, *qu'*il est gentil' (p. 49); 'au lieu *que*' (p. 97); 'à cause *que*' (p. 144). Two obsolete particles preserved in the patois also occur in our novel: the pronominal adverb *mêmement* (p. 168) and the negative *nenni* (p. 169).[3] Some of these features are not peculiar to

---

[1] Cf. Vincent, *op. cit.*, p. 236. The form *je vas* first appears during the Renaissance; in the seventeenth century, it was, according to Vaugelas, current in Court usage, whereas *je vais* was regarded as provincial or popular. The position was soon reversed, but La Fontaine still wrote in *Le loup et l'agneau*: 'Je me *vas* désaltérant.' Cf. Nyrop, *Grammaire historique*, vol. II, p. 90.

[2] This phrase is still found in local usage (Vincent, *op. cit.*, p. 278).

[3] Cf. Brunot, *La Pensée et la langue*, pp. 494 and 721.

the Berry region: they are common to various dialects or are current in uneducated speech throughout France.

One interesting aspect of George Sand's provincialisms is that many of them have a strong archaic flavour. They are old expressions or grammatical forms which have fallen into disuse in Standard French, but have been preserved in the more conservative patois.[1] Some of these archaisms have already been mentioned; others include the nouns *cueille* (p. 161), *déshabillé* (p. 188), *us* (p. 157), *pertuis*[2] (p. 169), the verb *lutiner* (p. 183), and the adverbs *oncques* ('Je ne vis *oncques* si gentille fiancée', p. 154) and *céans* ('Vous n'entrerez point *céans*', p. 168). The purity and antiquity of French dialects had been strongly emphasized by Nodier and Jaubert, and George Sand was echoing the same views when she wrote in the appendix to *La Mare au Diable*:

> Ces gens-là parlent trop français pour nous, et, depuis Rabelais et Montaigne, les progrès de la langue nous ont fait perdre bien des vieilles richesses. Mais c'est encore un plaisir d'entendre ces idiotismes pittoresques régner sur le vieux terroir du centre de la France; d'autant plus que c'est la véritable expression du caractère moqueusement tranquille et plaisamment disert des gens qui s'en servent (pp. 151–2).

La Mare au Diable is a simple, unpretentious story, hardly a novel at all. The vivid colours and strong contrast effects of a *Carmen* or a *Notre-Dame* would have been quite out of place in such a stylistic milieu. Discouraged by her previous failures, George Sand was aiming at a style which would be in harmony with the general tone of the narrative and with the mentality of the people portrayed. Hence the sparing use of linguistic colour; hence also the protest in the preface: 'Je n'ai voulu ni faire une nouvelle langue, ni me chercher une nouvelle manière.' The result was a somewhat diluted form of regionalism which would be acceptable both to the local and to the general reader. At the same time, there is sufficient local colour in the novel to evoke the idyllic and old-world atmosphere of the countryside

---

[1] See Vincent, *op. cit.*, Appendix II, ch. 1. The connexion between archaism and provincialism is discussed in W. v. Wartburg, 'Archaismus und Regionalismus bei Chateaubriand', *Festschrift für Tappolet*, Basle (1935), pp. 275–8.

[2] *Pertuis* was already regarded as obsolete in the seventeenth century; cf. Brunot, *Histoire de la langue française*, vol. IV, pt. 1, p. 260.

as George Sand saw it, to give the story an air of authenticity, and to show that the author was thoroughly familiar with the dialect and genuinely fond and proud of it.[1]

4. PORTRAYAL OF THE PARISIAN UNDERWORLD

Balzac, *Splendeurs et misères des courtisanes*

The use of argot in Romantic literature had a curious history.[2] Its vogue began with the publication, in 1828–9, of the *Mémoires* of Vidocq, the ex-convict who had joined the police and had become head of the Sûreté. There had been sporadic interest in argot before Vidocq, including some dictionaries one of which had appeared as early as 1725. But it was Vidocq's influence which focused the attention of writers on the underworld and its jargon. Even before he published his memoirs, Balzac and other writers had begun to turn his legend to literary use. Hardly a month after the appearance of the book, Victor Hugo set pen to his novel, *Les derniers jours d'un condamné* (1829), the first major literary work to use argot on a significant scale. Hugo's interest in argot has been aptly described as 'teratological'.[3] It intrigued him as a repellent and yet strangely fascinating monstrosity. His imagination was caught by the expressiveness and crude humour of these 'bizarre' and 'ugly' words which reminded him of toads and spiders; the language itself he visualized as 'entée sur la langue générale comme une espèce d'excroissance hideuse, comme une verrue'. Many years later, he reverted in *Les Misérables* to a detailed study of argot. Meanwhile, the device had spread rapidly among the Romantics; the untapped resources of argot were bound to appeal to their taste for the expressive, the exotic and the grotesque. They were used by Gautier, Gérard de Nerval

---

[1] George Sand was a great collector of dialect terms; a manuscript in her own handwriting, containing nearly 600 local expressions, has recently been published by M. Parent in *Bulletin de la Faculté des Lettres de Strasbourg*, May-June 1954.

[2] See esp. L. Sainéan, *Les Sources de l'argot ancien*, vol. II, Paris (1912); Bruneau, *op. cit.*, vol. XII, book VI, ch. 3; Matoré, *Le Vocabulaire et la société*, pp. 178–85; P. Guiraud, *L'Argot*, Paris (1956). A detailed lexicographical analysis of Balzac's use of argot was given recently by R. Dagneaud, *Les Eléments populaires dans le lexique de la Comédie Humaine d'Honoré de Balzac*, Quimper (1954), ch. V.

[3] Matoré, *op. cit.*, p. 179, n. 6.

and other writers, and became popular in the vaudevilles played at the Variétés. A new phase in the progress of argot was marked by Eugène Sue's *Mystères de Paris* (1842–3), whose success was quite out of proportion to its literary merits. A special dictionary was compiled to facilitate the reading of this novel, and, as one critic acidly remarked, its continued popularity might have made it necessary to establish a chair of argot in the Collège de France.[1]

Balzac's interest in argot was part of the strange fascination which one of the most powerful figures of the *Comédie humaine*, the ex-convict Vautrin, exercised on his maker.[2] The author himself admitted that he had drawn this character with exceptional warmth. Vautrin plays a prominent part in half a dozen novels as diverse as *Le Père Goriot* and *Splendeurs et misères*, and he is even the hero of an ill-starred excursion into drama. He may have had Schiller's *Robbers*, Byron's *Corsair* and other idealized outlaws among his literary ancestors, but the peculiar spell he cast was due to different reasons: to the sheer force of his will-power, the quickness of his intelligence, and his irrepressible vitality, and also to a quality which Balzac has described in Baudelairean terms: 'C'est la plante vénéneuse aux riches couleurs qui fascine l'enfant dans les bois. C'est la poésie du mal.'[3]

A very similar fascination emanates, in Balzac's view, from the 'affreuse poésie' of argot. He enlarges on the theme in the 'Dernière incarnation de Vautrin', which forms Part IV of *Splendeurs et misères*:

> Il n'est pas de langue plus énergique, plus colorée que celle de ce monde souterrain qui, depuis l'origine des empires à capitale, s'agite dans les caves, dans les sentines, dans le *troisième dessous* des sociétés. . . . Chaque mot de ce langage est une image brutale, ingénieuse ou terrible. . . . Tout est farouche dans cet idiome.

And he goes on to give some examples of this terrifying imagery:

---

[1] *Ibid.*, p. 182. It has even been suggested that Eugène Sue's financial success may have been one of Balzac's reasons for trying a similar experiment in *Splendeurs et misères* (Dagneaud, *op. cit.*, p. 176).

[2] See P. Vernière, 'Balzac et la genèse de "Vautrin"', *Revue d'Histoire Littéraire de la France*, vol. XLVIII (1948), pp. 53–68.

[3] Cf. Vernière, *loc. cit.*, p. 53, n. 3.

Les syllabes qui commencent ou qui finissent les mots sont âpres et étonnent singulièrement. Une femme est une *largue*. Et quelle poésie! la paille est *la plume de Beauce*. Le mot minuit est rendu par cette périphrase: *douze plombes crossent!* Ça ne donne-t-il pas le frisson? *Rincer une cambriole*, veut dire dévaliser une chambre. Qu'est-ce que l'expression se coucher, comparée à se *piausser*, revêtir une autre peau? (pp. 399–400)

In the same passage, Balzac also dwells on the antiquity of argot. He claims that it contains 'un dixième de mots de la langue romane, un autre dixième de la vieille langue gauloise de Rabelais', and quotes several picturesque vocables in support (*otolondrer* 'ennuyer', *fouillousse* 'poche' etc.). His philology may have been somewhat fanciful, but it had a direct bearing on his general attitude to argot and to its use in literature.

For information about the criminal classes and their speech, Balzac relied on no less authoritative a source than Vidocq himself. Not only did he use his printed works, but he knew the man himself and was able to draw on his experience. He first met him at the house of a well-known philanthropist and prison reformer, Benjamin Appert, whose parties also included Dumas, Liszt and other celebrities, as well as the executioner of Paris, Sanson.[1] Later on, friendly relations developed between Balzac and Vidocq, and the policeman paid repeated visits to the writer. Léon Gozlan has given a graphic account of one of these little parties in the rue Basse at Passy, with Vidocq trying to suggest subjects for novels to Balzac, and his host replying, with amiable superiority: 'C'est nous qui la faisons, la réalité.'[2] This conversation took place in 1844, two years before the publication of the last two parts of *Splendeurs et Misères*. To complete his documentation, Balzac visited the Conciergerie prison before giving final shape to his novel, and spent a whole morning inspecting the cells.

Splendeurs et misères, 'ce Saint-Gothard de la *Comédie Humaine*, où Balzac donne à la fois son meilleur et son pire',[3] is Balzac's only novel where argot is used on a major scale. Even here, there is very little argot proper until we reach Part IV where

---

[1] See Vernière, *loc. cit.*, pp. 58f., and M. Bouteron, 'En marge du "*Père Goriot*"': Balzac, Vidocq et Sanson', *La Revue*, January 1948.

[2] See A. Billy, *Vie de Balzac*, vol. II, Paris (1944), pp. 161ff.

[3] André Gide, *Journal*, Paris (1939), p. 1225.

Vautrin, disguised as a Spanish priest, meets his former fellow-criminals in the courtyard of the Conciergerie. The conversations which follow are interlarded with argot terms many of which have to be explained by the author. Here is a short specimen of these dialogues which cover several pages, though the explanations tend to become fewer as the same limited vocabulary recurs all the time:

—N'y a-t-il pas ici des *cuisiniers*? *Allumez vos clairs et remouchez* (voyez et observez)! *Ne me conobrez pas, épargnons le poitou* et *engantez-moi en sanglier* (ne me connaissez pas, prenons nos précautions et traitez-moi en prêtre), ou je vous *effondre*, vous, vos *largues* et votre *aubert* (je vous ruine, vous, vos femmes et votre fortune).

—*T'as donc tafe de nozigues* (tu te méfies donc de nous)? dit Fil-de-Soie. Tu viens *cromper ta tante* (sauver ton ami).

—Madeleine est *paré* pour la *placarde de vergne* (est prêt pour la place de Grève), dit la Pouraille (p. 412).

As can be seen from this extract, the criminals' jargon is a mixture of various elements: words unknown to the standard language (*largue*); ordinary words modified in form (*conobrez* for *connaissez*, *nozigues* for *nous*[1]) or in meaning (*tante* in the sense of 'ami'); periphrases (*allumez vos clairs* = 'voyez'). Many argot terms and locutions have a figurative turn and are tinged with a macabre humour (*effondrer* 'ruiner'; *paré pour la placarde de vergne* 'prêt pour la place de Grève'). Balzac, like other Romantics, had been profoundly influenced by Nodier's ideas on language, and he was impressed by the creative resources of argot and by the psychological interest of some of these expressions: 'Quand on songe que le bagne se nomme le *pré*, vraiment ceux qui s'occupent de linguistique doivent admirer la création de ces affreux *vocables*, eût dit Charles Nodier' (p. 401).

The argot terms used by Balzac refer to a limited range of subjects which bulk large in the criminals' activities and which it is particularly advisable to conceal from the uninitiated. There is first of all the hierarchy of the underworld. The rank and file are called *fanandels*, which means brothers, friends and comrades (p. 403). They are led by the *grands fanandels* who form the *haute pègre*, the élite of criminal society (*ibid.*). A

[1] Cf. Dagneaud, *op. cit.*, p. 180.

hardened criminal is known as an *ami* (p. 397); if he returns to prison, he is welcomed as a *cheval de retour* (p. 406); if he becomes a police spy, he is written off as a *mouton* (p. 397). At the top of the pyramid is the *dâb* (p. 412), who is no other than Vautrin himself. There is an equally fine mesh of terms for the forces of the law. Gendarmes are known by various names: 'quand il poursuit le voleur, c'est un *marchand de lacets*; quand il l'escorte, c'est une *hirondelle de la Grève*; quand il le mène à l'échafaud, c'est un *hussard de la guillotine*' (p. 407). The police is called *la raille* (p. 412), the law-courts la *cigogne* (p. 413), and the executioner is nicknamed *Charlot* (p. 428).[1]

A third group of argot terms refer to the criminal acts themselves and to their consequences. The following list epitomizes the main phases of the process: *nourrir le poupon* 'préparer le crime' (p. 426); *goupiner* 'voler' (p. 416); *refroidir* 'tuer' (p. 432); *enflacquer* 'emprisonner' and *serrer* 'mettre en prison' (p. 405); *gerber à la passe* 'condamner à mort (p. 413); *l'abbaye de Monte-à-Regret* 'guillotine' (.p 401; a man sentenced to death is a *Chanoine*, viz. *chanoine de l'abbaye de Monte-à-Regret*, p. 409); *faucher* (p. 401) and *terrer* (p. 411) 'guillotiner'.

There are also argot terms belonging to other spheres: nouns like *sorbonne* 'tête' (p. 401), *gourganes* 'haricots destinés à la nourriture des forçats' (p. 406), *fafiot* 'banknote' (p. 401; a thousand franc note is a *fafiot mâle*, a five hundred franc note a *fafiot femelle*); adjectives like *sinve* 'simple' (p. 414); verbs like *morfiler* 'manger', *se dessaler* 'boire' (p. 416); locutions like 'sans *raisiné* dans les *vermichels*' 'sans sang dans les veines' (p. 440), and many more.[2]

Apart from argot proper, the criminals also need private codes; Vautrin and Asie, his aunt and chief accomplice, communicate for example in a secret language based on the simple device of adding *-ar*, *-or*, or *-al*, *-i* to ordinary and argot words (p. 435).

In the final section of *Splendeurs et misères*, argot is used not

[1] Balzac says that this sobriquet was invented during the Revolution; but it was already used by Vadé in 1748, and may go back to the seventeenth century; cf. Dagneaud, *op. cit.*, pp. 11 and 21.

[2] Some of the words listed above also occur elsewhere in the *Comédie humaine*: *raisiné, sorbonne, terrer* in *Le Père Goriot*, *hussard de la guillotine, mouton, pré, serrer* in other novels. The relevant passages are printed in Dagneaud, *op. cit.*, Index I.

merely for its own sake, but as a factor of some importance in the *dénouement* of the novel. Vautrin, imprisoned in the Conciergerie, is playing a double game. He has to convince the authorities, who suspect his identity, that he is a Spanish diplomat, the abbé Carlos Herrera; at the same time he must make himself known to the other convicts and warn them not to give him away. Argot plays a significant part in this complicated manoeuvre. In the prison yard, he whispers to his neighbours, whilst outwardly maintaining the manner of a priest: '*Ne fais pas de ragoût sur ton dâb* (n'éveille pas les soupçons sur ton maître)!' (p. 412); and they continue to communicate in argot whenever there is an opportunity. In his dealings with the law, he disclaims all knowledge of argot (p. 414) and adopts the kind of language which befits his alleged status. When, towards the end of the novel, this pretence breaks down and he goes over to the police, there is no further need for this linguistic mimicry, and he will even risk argot words when talking to the Procureur Général: 'Vous n'avez donc à me gracier que pour les aggravations de peine que j'ai empoignées au *pré* . . . (pardon! au bagne)' (pp. 492–3). Later he does not even apologize for using argot: '*Je le paumerais marron* (je le prendrais en flagrant délit)' (p. 496). In this way, the use of argot is fully integrated into the plot and has a psychological motivation.

Argot is only one aspect of the complex technique of linguistic portrayal in *Splendeurs et misères.* Throughout the novel, as elsewhere in Balzac, the characters—except those belonging to the upper classes—are made to talk in a language consistent with their social and cultural background, their occupation, and, in the case of the fully individualized ones, with their personality. Once again, Vautrin's way of speaking is studied with great care and acuteness. His ordinary conversation is at once vulgar, terse, graphic and forceful: 'Satanées[1] farceuses!' (p. 57); 'Allons, je suis cuit, ils y sont' (p. 210); 'Quand le baron t'aura donné le droit de lui frapper sur le ventre en l'appelant: "Gros corrompu!" . . .' (p. 140); 'pincer un million' (p. 185), etc. He has a natural liking for pungent and picturesque expressions with a slangy flavour: 'trouvé sa fortune en cardant vos matelas' (p. 184); 'Nous avons un taon sur le dos' (p. 203); 'Tu feras encore *cracher* cent cinquante mille francs à notre ponte' (p. 157).

[1] See on this word Dagneaud, *op cit.*, pp. 19 and 41.

To him, the worst human weakness of all is prudery. He has a special word for it: *bégueulisme*: 'Carlos appelait *bégueulisme* cette défense si naturelle' (p. 182; cf. p. 157). In the scene of his interrogation by the examining magistrate, there is an amusing contrast between the coarseness of his inner speech and the dignified tone which he has to adopt in his assumed role of a priest and a diplomat. At one point he almost gives himself away by an involuntary gesture:

—Vous avez été promptement guéri? dit Camusot.
—Je suis pincé, pensa Jacques Colin.
Puis il répondit à haute voix:
—La joie, monsieur, est la seule panacée qui existe ... (p. 339).

The speech of Vautrin's feminine counterpart, Asie, is also carefully portrayed. In resourcefulness, alertness and histrionic ability, she is a match to her nephew, though ultimately she is a mere tool in his hands and lacks his intellectual brilliance. Her mentality is reflected in her language which is of a coarser fibre than Vautrin's. Occasionally, she lapses into argot proper: 'Ils ont soif, *et il y a gras!*'[1] (p. 155; cf. p. 307); 'Ne vas-tu pas m'écraser, hussard de la guillotine!' (p. 278). When speaking to people of her own type, her language is full of expressive and idiomatic vulgarisms. These are her instructions to a shady dressmaker who is to transform her into a fashionable lady;

Ma fille, il s'agit de me ficeler. Je dois être au moins une baronne du faubourg Saint-Germain. Et bricolons tout *pus vite que ça!* car j'ai les pieds dans l'huile bouillante! . . . En avant le pot de rouge; Trouve-moi des dentelles *chouettes*,[2] et donne-moi les plus reluisants *bibelots* (p. 307).

She is particularly coarse in her dealings with Nucingen— the Alsatian banker whose quaint French is in itself a study in local colour—where she plays the traditional part of a servant turned into procuress. Here the modern reader has the impression that Balzac has gone too far and that linguistic realism changes into caricature; a woman as shrewd and calculating as Asie would hardly talk this way to a millionaire. She calls him *mon gros farceur* (p. 144), *grosse bête* (p. 146), and seems to go out of her way to humiliate him:

[1] Described as studio slang in *Pierre Grassou* (Dagneaud, *op. cit.*, p. 158).
[2] Cf. *ibid.*, p. 75.

Vous avez fait aller les autres, papa, la petite vous tient et vous *polissonne* . . . ces créatures aiment à *flamber*[1]. . . . Vous êtes gros comme Louis XVIII, et un peu bêta . . . des femmes pour qui l'on a craché sa tête dans un panier. . . . Vous avez été rincé comme ça . . . (pp. 179f.).

As Balzac himself explains, the price one has to pay to such women is 'la familiarité la plus déshonorante'; they drag down their client to their own level (p. 144). This is no doubt true, but one wonders whether the author has not overdone it.

Among the social types portrayed through their speech, the courtesans and the police are given special attention. Balzac notes some typical expressions of what was soon to be known as the *demi-monde*:[2] *femme à pied* (p. 197; cf. p. 193); 'heureux comme *un coq en plâtre*' (p. 215); '*Fait-elle sa tête*! s'écria madame de Val-Noble en se servant d'une admirable expression du vocabulaire des filles' (p. 192).[3] There. is also the amusing malapropism *de caraïbe en syllabe* (p. 194).[4] Esther Gobseck is fond of slang terms like *chouchouter* (p. 219), 'faire des *noirs* en dormant' (p. 332) and others. The way she addresses her two lovers is characteristic. She calls Nucingen, whom she abhors, *gros monstre* (p. 219), *vieux fat* (p. 217), *mon gros éléphant* and *animal bête*, with the banker feebly protesting, in his Alsatian brogue: '*Hânimâl édait azez*' (p. 190). Lucien de Rubempré, on the other hand, is addressed as *mon chat, mon nini, mon mignon* (pp. 332f.). The crucial event in Esther's story is her renunciation of religious ideals—what Vautrin calls her *bégueulisme*—and her return to her former way of life. She succumbs to Vautrin's pressure, sacrifices her purity to her love for Lucien, and, with almost hysterical abruptness, relapses at once into the language of the courtesan. Even her cynical chambermaid cannot conceal her surprise at the suddenness of the change:

—J'aurais voulu que Lucien me vît ainsi, dit-elle en laissant échapper un soupir étouffé.—Maintenant, reprit-elle d'une voix vibrante, *blaguons* . . .

[1] See *ibid.*, p. 77.
[2] The term *demi-monde* was first used by Dumas Fils in 1855, in the title of a play.
[3] Cf. Dagneaud, *op. cit.*, pp. 76f.
[4] On Balzac's puns, see Bruneau, *op. cit.*, vol. XII, p. 375, and G. Mayer, *La Qualification affective dans les romans d'Honoré de Balzac*, Paris (1940), pp. 368ff.

En entendant ce mot, Europe resta tout hébétée, comme elle eût pu l'être en entendant blasphémer un ange.

—Eh bien, qu'as-tu donc à regarder si j'ai dans la bouche des clous de girofle au lieu de dents? Je ne suis plus maintenant qu'une infâme créature, une fille, une *voleuse*, et j'attends milord . . . (p. 186).[1]

Her moral metamorphosis is accompanied by a sudden transition to a different level of style. Once again we see the dynamic role played by language in the inner movement of Balzac's novels.

The speech of police-officers is also studied with meticulous care. Here there is no dramatic duel between two personalities, as in *Les Misérables* between Javert and Jean Valjean; some of the most experienced policemen of France are on the tracks of Vautrin who outwits them all. In this curious world where ex-convicts rise to the highest ranks of the police force, it is not surprising to find policemen using argot. It comes quite naturally to Bibi-Lupin, head of the Sûreté, whose career has been similar to Vautrin's (and Vidocq's): 'Vous verrez une terrible danse au préau, pour peu qu'il y ait des *chevaux de retour*' (p. 304). But other police officers also use argot terms: 'Le préfet m'*otolondre* toujours' (p. 209); 'ceux qui se livrent à ce *chantage*' (p. 213).[2] Naturally, the police have their own professional jargon where, for example, *la maison* means 'la préfecture' (p. 114). Like the criminals, policemen sometimes have their private code (p. 116); like them, they have to assume false identities which may entail adopting a special type of speech; thus, when Peyrade poses as an old man from Vaucluse, he used dialect forms like *estatue, espécialle, le peuble*, and *ture* for *turc* (p. 100). The ordinary conversation of a policeman has a sprinkling of vulgarisms and is not so very different from that of Vautrin: 'ils ont d'autres chats à fouetter' (p. 91); 'Contenson vous a *carotté* un billet de mille' (p. 92);[3] 'ne me graisse pas la patte' (p. 99); 'vous aviez reçu des giroflées à la préfecture' (p. 133).[4]

It would be easy to continue this catalogue of portrayal through language and to show how Balzac presents the speech

---

[1] On the exact value of some of these words, see Dagneaud, *op. cit.*, pp. 98f. (*blaguer*); p. 81 (*voleuse*); p. 86 (*milord*).

[2] On *chantage* 'blackmail' and its family, cf. Dagneaud, *op. cit.*, pp. 188ff.

[3] *Ibid.*, p. 110.   [4] *Ibid.*, p. 116.

of dandies, journalists, magistrates, and other social classes. Balzac was deeply interested in language, both in its general and in its specific aspects. In *Louis Lambert* he has spoken of the 'incroyables délices' which the study of dictionaries can provide, and of the intriguing problems raised by the history and 'physiognomy' of words. Under Nodier's influence he evolved, in the same novel, a theory about a mysterious correspondence, a recondite harmony, between sound and sense.[1] There are some echoes of these speculations in *Splendeurs et misères*; the argot word for banknote, *fafiot*, strikes him for example as particularly apposite: 'Fafiot! N'entendez-vous pas le bruissement du papier de soie?' (p. 401). However naive some of these ideas may be, there can be no doubt that they heightened Balzac's sensitivity to word values. But he was equally interested in the linguistic problems of his own day, in the changes through which the vocabulary was passing, and in the various forms and levels of language corresponding to the new structure of society. His novels are full of shrewd remarks on these points, and his essay 'Des mots à la mode', published in 1830, has been of great value to modern lexicography. In the *Comédie humaine* he was faced with a linguistic problem on an unprecedented scale: to make each class, each group and profession speak in its own characteristic way, and even to individualize the major figures through their language. In this task he could never have succeeded had he not been, by inclination and experience, an acute observer of linguistic processes.

Ever since Sainte-Beuve it has been customary, and has become almost a cliché, to say that Balzac had a poor style or, even worse, no style at all. On this view, Balzac would be an anomaly in the history of French literature: the only major classic who was not a great master of language. From a strictly aesthetic point of view, there is a certain amount of truth in these statements. But there is another side to the picture. Balzac once proudly declared: 'Nous sommes trois à connaître notre langue, Hugo, Gautier et moi.' We know now that this was no empty boast: he had in fact an unrivalled grasp of concontemporary French in all its complexity and social stratification. Anatole France has marvelled at his ability to shape the lives of so many figures without ever losing any thread. 'Il

[1] *Louis Lambert*, pp. 3–4 (*Oeuvres Complètes*, ed. M. Lévy, Paris (1870)).

est inconcevable', he wrote, 'qu'un homme ait suivi, sans les brouiller, les fils de tant d'existences.'[1] It is hardly less astonishing that he should have been able to play on so many different linguistic registers. In recent years, there have been signs of a reappraisal of Balzac's style,[2] and his success in portraying a complex and changing social structure through language is bound to weigh heavily in the balance.

Half a dozen novels provide no basis for general conclusions or even for comparison. Nevertheless, one or two points emerge quite clearly from the material discussed in this chapter.

It should be remembered, first of all, that in the matter of linguistic colour—whether foreign, historical, regional or social —the Romantics were pioneers, with no coherent doctrine or tradition behind them. Their success or failure must be judged in this light. The fallacy of projecting modern reactions into the interpretation of older texts should once again be guarded against. In the matter of argot, for example, our palates have become somewhat jaded after Zola, Barbusse, Sartre and many others; yet we must make an effort to replace the early experiments of Hugo and Balzac in their historical context. Even so, some of the writers studied were clearly more successful than others. Hugo, Mérimée and Balzac stand out by their verve and by the boldness and complexity of their method; Mérimée and Balzac, but especially the latter, achieved the highest degree of integration between linguistic colour and other elements of the novel. But whatever the measure of their success, they were all engaged in forging a new tool, a new technique in narration and speech-reporting.

Another feature which the six authors have in common is their intense interest in language. It is no accident that four of the novels examined contain substantial digressions on some philological problem: Vigny on Middle English, Mérimée on Romany, Balzac on argot, and George Sand on the terminology and folklore of a village wedding. Linguistic interests are also very conspicuous in *Notre-Dame*, and the handling of Italian

[1] *La Vie littéraire*, vols. I–II, p. 140 (*Oeuvres Complètes*, ed. Calmann-Lévy, Paris (1926)).

[2] See esp. M. Roques, 'La langue de Balzac', in *Balzac: Le Livre du Centenaire*, Paris (1952), pp. 246–57; Cressot, *Le Style et ses techniques*, Appendix I; Bruneau, *op. cit.*, vol. XII, book V, ch. 5; Dagneaud, *op. cit.*, pp. 196f.

words in the *Chartreuse* shows how keenly alive Stendhal was to their nuances and overtones. This attitude to language is one of the distinctive traits of the Romantic movement. The name of Charles Nodier has been repeatedly mentioned in this chapter, and there can be no doubt that he exerted a decisive influence on the ideas of his fellow-Romantics about language. Some points of his doctrine were erroneous and unscientific,[1] but he certainly helped to make his generation aware of the problems and implications of human speech. He acted as a catalyst of ideas which were then current all over Europe. The Romantics' absorption in history, folklore and mediaeval literature aroused everywhere keen interest in language and created a climate where the new discipline of historical linguistics could take shape.[2] Hugo's and Vigny's mediaevalism, George Sand's championship of dialects, Mérimée's taste for the exotic, the fascination which the low and the grotesque in language held for a Balzac and an Hugo, were different facets of the same Romantic enthusiasm for things linguistic.

Ever since the Classical period, French writers had given much thought and attention to their mother-tongue. Pascal, La Bruyère, Fénelon, Voltaire and other writers had made many astute comments on general and specific points; some, like Rousseau, had even speculated on the origin of speech. What was new about the Romantics was that they were the first to possess some kind of doctrine about language, a body of more or less coherent and systematic ideas about its structure and history. Since then, a measure of linguistic 'sophistication' has become part of the French literary tradition. Mallarmé's debt to Littré is well-known; the words 'Donner un sens plus pur aux mots de la tribu'[3] sum up one of the deepest aspirations of his aesthetic. Proust had, as we shall see later, his own theory of proper names, and it is symptomatic that Valéry wrote a review of Bréal's *Essai de sémantique*,[4] and that Gide impro-

---

[1] For a summary of Nodier's doctrine, see Bruneau, *op. cit.*, vol. XII, pp. 212ff.; cf. also pp. 544ff.

[2] In *Louis Lambert*, p. 4, Balzac even foresaw the possibility of a new science on the lines of modern semantics: a science which would study the structure and development of words. His ideas on the subject were, however, vitiated by his acceptance of Nodier's theory of onomatopoeia.

[3] *Le tombeau d'Edgar Poe.*

[4] F. H. Scarfe, *The Art of Paul Valéry*, London (1954), pp. 56f.

vised in his *Journal* a conversation between Racine and the grammarian Bouhours on a fine point of language.[1] At the same time, these interests were bound to colour the writer's whole approach to style. For the Romantics, words had a lustre and significance of their own; they delighted in their shape and their suggestive power and put a collector's pride into the hunt for linguistic curios. The Romantic cult of local colour was the first large-scale manifestation of this new attitude to language.

[1] Pp. 662f.

CHAPTER II

REPORTED SPEECH AND INTERNAL MONOLOGUE IN FLAUBERT

1

Un homme qui par l'usage entièrement nouveau qu'il a fait du passé défini, du passé indéfini, du participe présent, de certains pronoms et de certaines prépositions, a renouvelé presque autant notre vision des choses que Kant avec ses Catégories, les théories de la Connaissance et de la Réalité du monde extérieur . . .

These words about Flaubert were not written by a linguist who might be professionally inclined to overestimate the importance of grammar. They were written by Proust, in a provocative essay published in 1920 in the *Nouvelle Revue Française*.[1] Proust frankly confessed that he was out of sympathy with Flaubert's way of writing; in his view, metaphor was the hall-mark of great style, and Flaubert's metaphors were unimpressive: 'il n'y a peut-être pas dans tout Flaubert une seule belle métaphore.' But he recognized that Flaubert had revolutionized and revitalized French literary syntax. One of his major innovations was the 'eternal Imperfect', in particular when used in a new type of indirect speech which merges into the narrative. In a series of images typically Proustian in their density and intricacy, he summed up the importance of Flaubert's discovery:

Cet imparfait, si nouveau dans la littérature, change entièrement l'aspect des choses et des êtres, comme font une lampe qu'on a déplacée, l'arrivée dans une maison nouvelle, l'ancienne si elle est presque vide et qu'on est en plein déménagement.

Proust's remarks had been prompted by an article by A. Thibaudet, and Thibaudet replied to some of Proust's points in the same journal.[2] On the general issue, he refused to rate style

---

[1] 'A propos du "style" de Flaubert', *Nouvelle Revue Française*, vol. XIV, 1 (1920), pp. 72–90.

[2] 'Réflexions sur la littérature. Lettre à M. Marcel Proust', *Nouvelle Revue Française*, vol. XIV, 1 (1920), pp. 426–41.

as high as Proust did. 'Mettons le style et, comme vous dites, la beauté grammaticale à leur place,' he wrote, 'mais sachons aussi les tenir à cette place.' As for the new Imperfect, or rather the new type of reproduced speech, Thibaudet was able to show that Flaubert had not been the first to use it: there were already some examples in La Fontaine.

The little discussion had one amusing aspect. Eight years earlier, Bally had discovered the existence of a special form of speech-reporting; he had given it the name of 'style indirect libre', and his initial article[1] had been followed by a brisk debate in philological journals.[2] Both Proust and Thibaudet were unaware of Bally's discovery. Yet the incident is significant in two respects. It is remarkable that Proust, unaided by any specialist knowledge, should have noticed a construction so unobtrusive that the grammarians had only stumbled on it a few years earlier. And it is no less remarkable that the first impression of both Proust and Thibaudet should have been fully confirmed by subsequent research; Flaubert was the decisive innovator in this field, and he had one great precursor, La Fontaine.

The essence of free indirect speech[3] can best be defined in stylistic terms. It is a classical example of the possibility of choice between quasi-synonymous modes of expression. According to traditional grammar, two alternatives are open to the narrator when reporting the speech of other people: direct and indirect style, 'oratio recta' and 'oratio obliqua'. In the former, the words are reproduced as they were uttered; in the latter, they are embedded in the narrative itself, in the form of a subordinate clause dependent on a verb like 'he said, he

---

[1] 'Le style indirect libre en français moderne', *Germanisch-Romanische Monatsschrift*, vol. IV (1912), pp. 549–56 and 597–606.

[2] An account of this controversy will be found in M. Lips, *Le Style indirect libre*, Paris (1926), pp. 220ff.

[3] There is a voluminous literature on the subject; see esp. Lips, *op cit.*, and E. Lerch, 'Ursprung und Bedeutung der sog. *Erlebten Rede (Rede als Tatsache)*', in *Hauptprobleme der französischen Sprache. Allgemeineres*, Braunschweig-Berlin-Hamburg (1930), pp. 91–138, where further references will be found; cf. also recently M. Cohen, 'Le style indirect libre et l'imparfait en français après 1850', in *Grammaire et style*, Paris (1954), pp. 99–107. On Flaubert's use of this device there have been various comments, but no systematic treatment; cf. Lips, *op. cit.*, pp. 186ff. and 'Le style indirect libre chez Flaubert', *Journal de Psychologie*, vol. XVIII (1921), pp. 644–53; A. Thibaudet, *Gustave Flaubert*, 13th ed., Paris (1935), pp. 228ff.; H. Guddorf, *Der Stil Flauberts*, Münster (1933), pp. 40ff.

exclaimed, he replied, he wrote'. The great change brought about by the advent of free indirect speech is that we can now choose between *three*, not two, forms of reporting.[1] The new construction stands half-way between the two orthodox types. This can best be shown on a concrete example. In the following passage from *Madame Bovary*, the discovery of one of the bills rashly signed by Emma threatens to cause a domestic crisis:

Elle eut assez de prudence pour mettre en réserve mille écus, avec quoi furent payés, lorsqu'ils échurent, les trois premiers billets; mais le quatrième, par hasard, tomba dans la maison un jeudi et Charles, bouleversé, attendit patiemment le retour de sa femme pour avoir des explications.

Si elle ne l'avait point instruit de ce billet, c'était afin de lui épargner des tracas domestiques; elle s'assit sur ses genoux, le caressa, roucoula, fit une longue énumération de toutes les choses indispensables prises à crédit.

—Enfin, tu conviendras que, vu la quantité, ce n'est pas trop cher (p. 378).

The sentence which I have italicized could have been formulated in three different ways. Of the three, the one which Flaubert chose had the advantage of being the most concise. Both direct and indirect speech would have required an introductory, or intercalated, verb. By boldly suppressing the connecting link, he achieved not only terseness but a certain shock effect: the syntax leads us at first to believe that the author himself is speaking, but the sense and the context make us suddenly realize that this cannot be so, that we have moved from the narrative plane to that of reported speech. In fact, the narrator has not only withdrawn into the background, disclaiming any responsibility for what is being said: he obviously disagrees with Emma's hypocritical excuses and reports them with ironical detachment. It is also worth noting that there are three distinct shifts from one plane to another in this extract: from the narrative we pass into free indirect style, then back into the narrative, finally into direct speech. There is a marked difference in vividness between these various modes of presentation; as Professor Spitzer has put it, when we switch from

[1] On the possibility of yet a fourth alternative, see above, p. 18, n. 2.

one form to another it is as if we were adjusting a telescope to closer or more distant vision.[1]

Free indirect style has some features in common with both of the orthodox types. With indirect speech it shares a delicate system of transpositions affecting verbs and pronouns. Verbs will conform to the rules which govern the sequence of tenses in subordinate clauses. If the narrative is told in the past tense, the following main types of transposition will arise in indirect speech:

Il répondit: 'Je *suis* prêt.'	Il répondit qu'il *était* prêt.
Il répondit: 'Je *suis arrivé* dimanche.'	Il répondit qu'il *était arrivé* dimanche.
Il répondit: 'Je *viendrai* bientôt.'	Il répondit qu'il *viendrait* bientôt.

Thus, the Present becomes Imperfect, the Past Indefinite changes to Pluperfect, and the Future is replaced by the Conditional which plays here the part of a Future-in-the-Past. Pronouns too are transposed: in the sentences just quoted, they are all changed from the first person to the third. On all these points, free indirect style agrees with ordinary indirect speech.

In other respects, however, it is closer to the syntax of direct reporting. There is no subordination: in free indirect speech, each sentence is an independent unit, not a subordinate clause. It is even more independent than a quotation proper, since it requires no governing verb in the narrative. Free indirect speech may stand completely isolated, as in the strongly elliptical passage quoted above, or there may be some kind of preparation in the context; but in neither case will there be a key verb on which it is syntactically dependent.

Free indirect style also agrees with direct speech in preserving various emotive elements which have to be sacrificed in indirect reporting: questions, exclamations, interjections; adverbs like *donc* and *sûrement*, which give the utterance a subjective colouring; colloquial, vulgar and slang terms which are expressive of the speaker's character and attitude. Flaubert shows great virtuosity in retaining these nuances without actually quoting the words as they were spoken. The whole vulgarity of the cloth-merchant Lheureux is glaringly revealed by the way he

[1] L. Spitzer, 'Pseudo-objektive Motivierung', *Zeitschrift für französische Sprache und Literatur*, vol. XLVI (1923), pp. 359–85, esp. p. 374.

STYLE IN THE FRENCH NOVEL

talks when he calls on the Bovarys after the death of Charles's father. While Charles and his mother are there, he is conventional and even unctuous: 'Il venait offrir ses services, *eu égard à la fatale circonstance*' (p. 348). The last few words are italicized to dispel any possible misunderstanding. But when Lheureux is left in tête-à-tête with Emma, who is already heavily in his debt, he drops all pretences and adopts an offensively familiar and vulgar tone:

> Dès qu'ils furent seuls, M. Lheureux se mit, en termes assex nets, à féliciter Emma sur la succession, puis à causer de choses indifférentes, des espaliers, de la récolte, et de sa santé à lui, qui allait toujours *couci-couci entre le zist et le zest*. En effet, il se donnait un mal de cinq cents diables, bien qu'il ne fît pas, malgré les propos du monde, de quoi avoir seulement du beurre sur son pain (p. 349).

Here only the cruder slang terms are italicized, to mark that they belong to a special level of language, and perhaps also to reinforce their effect. The use of free indirect style adds to the piquancy of the portrayal: Lheureux's vulgarisms are included in the narrative and contrast all the more sharply with the author's own style.

The origin of free indirect speech has often been debated. According to one school of thought,[1] it is a purely literary construction which arose in two different ways: through the omission of the subordinating *que*, and through ambiguous passages which could be attributed either to the narrator or to the speaker. Others[2] believe that it originated in the spoken language, and emphasize its mimetic and potentially ironical character. They quote the case of the sergeant-major reporting a private's application for leave: 'Sa soeur fait sa première communion.' Delivered with an ironical intonation, these words will carry the implicit comment: 'Ce carotteur prétend qu'il a droit à une permission parce que sa soeur fait sa première communion.' But even the advocates of this theory admit that there is a wide gap between such examples and the sudden vogue of the construction in nineteenth-century literature. Yet, even if there is no direct connexion, the new technique has certain obvious affinities with the spoken language: it avoids

---

[1] Bally, *loc. cit.*, pp. 604f.; Lips, *Le Style indirect libre*, ch. VI.
[2] Thibaudet, *op. cit.*, pp. 230ff.; Spitzer, 'Zur Entstehung der sog. "erlebten Rede"', *Germanisch-Romanische Monatsschrift*, vol. XVI (1928), pp. 327–32.

explicit subordination, retains the expressive elements of speech, and tries to imitate the inflexions and intonations of the speaking voice.

2

The history of free indirect style still has to be written, but the main phases of its development stand out fairly clearly.[1] As a method of speech-reporting, it exists in various languages. In English, Jane Austen already used it with considerable skill.[2] In French, it is as old as literature itself: it appears in the very first literary text, the Sequence of Saint Eulalia.[3] Old French poetry and prose provide a number of examples; the loosely organized syntax of the period obviously favoured this manner of reporting. There is an excellent instance of deliberate ambiguity and implicit irony at the beginning of the *Chanson de Roland* where Blancandrin advises King Marsile to send an embassy to Charlemagne, offering terms of surrender which he has no intention to keep:

> Vos li sivrez a la feste seint Michel,
> Si recevrez la lei de chrestiens,
> Serez ses hom par honur e par ben
> (Laisse III)[4].

The perfidiousness of Blancandrin's scheme is neatly adumbrated by his Orwellian 'double-speak'.

The somewhat inchoate free indirect style of the medieval period practically disappeared during the Renaissance when Latin influence imposed a subordinating mode of sentence-structure. Yet there are several examples in the freer syntax practised by Rabelais. The rule of grammatically and logically correct subordination was rigidly observed during the classical period, and there were only sporadic instances of free indirect

[1] See Lips. *op. cit.*, chs. VII–VIII.

[2] *Ibid.*, pp. 214f. The history of the device in English literature has been investigated in L. Glauser's monograph, *Die erlebte Rede ('the interior monologue') im englischen Roman des 19. Jahrhunderts. Von Scott bis Meredith*, Berne (1949).

[3] That at least is the most probable interpretation of the lines: 'Ell' ent adunet (or *aduret*) lo suon element; Melz sostendreiet les empedementz Qu'elle perdesse sa virginitét.'

[4] Cf. Lips, *op. cit.*, pp. 120f. These implications are lost in Bédier's translation of the passage: 'Mandez-lui . . . *que* vous l'y suivrez à la fête de saint Michel; *que* vous y recevrez la loi des chrétiens; *que* vous deviendrez son vassal en tout honneur et tout bien.'

speech. La Fontaine seems to stand completely isolated in the varied and skilful use he made of this method. He frequently reports both speech and thoughts in this way, and shows remarkable dexterity in alternating direct, indirect and free indirect style:

> Il met bas son fagot, il songe à son malheur.
> 'Quel plaisir a-t-il eu depuis qu'il est au monde?
> En est-il un plus pauvre en la machine ronde?
> Point de pain quelquefois et jamais de repos'
> > (*La mort et le bûcheron*).

> Le Pot de fer proposa
> Au Pot de terre un voyage.
> Celui-ci s'en excusa,
> Disant qu'il ferait que sage
> De garder le coin du feu;
> Car il lui fallait si peu,
> Si peu, que la moindre chose
> De son débris serait cause;
> Il n'en reviendrait morceau.
> 'Pour vous, dit-il, dont la peau
> Est plus dure que la mienne,
> Je ne vois rien qui vous tienne'
> > (*Le pot de terre et le pot de fer*).

It is clear from these and many other examples that La Fontaine was fully aware of the stylistic potentialities of this device.

In the eighteenth century there was no significant increase in the use of the construction. Some examples occur in Marivaux, Diderot and Marmontel; the latter even prides himself on omitting 'les *dit-il* et les *dit-elle* du dialogue vif et pressé. . . . Cette manière de rendre le récit plus rapide n'est pénible qu'au premier instant: dès qu'on y est accoutumé, il fait briller le talent de bien lire.'[1] But Marmontel's recipe was not generally followed; it is symptomatic that in the whole of *Paul et Virginie*, only two free indirect passages have been discovered.

After the turn of the century, examples become more frequent, although the subjectivism of the Romantics was hardly favourable to the spread of an essentially objective and impersonal

---

[1] Quoted by Lips, *op. cit.*, pp. 163f.

method of presentation. Among the novelists of the period, Dumas Père appears to have employed it most freely, but there are also examples in Balzac, Hugo, Vigny and elsewhere. Yet it was still far from being an integral element of literary style. When re-reading a number of Romantic novels for other chapters of this book, I was struck by the sharp contrast between their practice and the concentrated and systematic use which Flaubert made of this construction. It is in his hands that it first became a device of style in the proper sense of the term.

3

A stylistic innovation of such magnitude must have taken some time to mature. Though the main purpose of this chapter is to examine the device at work in Flaubert's major novels, it may not be without interest to follow its development in his early writings.

In the short novel *Novembre*, written in 1842, at the age of twenty-one, free indirect style is already in evidence, but in a tentative and undeveloped form. It is still very infrequent: an average of one example in five pages. The nature of the book was not of a kind to invite this method of reporting. It is told in the first person singular; the tone is highly subjective and lyrical; there are few dialogues. Such examples as occur are confined to the reporting of thoughts, feelings and reveries; the construction has not yet spread to the reproduction of spoken words. In a novel of this type, free indirect style can easily become ambiguous: since the narrator is also the chief protagonist in the story, it has to be decided in each case whether he is communicating his present thoughts or those he had at the time of the event. In some cases, the ambiguity remains unresolved; mostly, however, the context or the sense of the passage will decide which interpretation is correct:

> J'ai songé à tous ceux qui étaient venus là pour en finir. Combien de gens avaient passé à la place où je me tenais alors, courant la tête levée à leurs amours ou à leurs affaires . . .! (p. 87).
> Je sentais un besoin de volupté. . . . Oh! que ne pouvais-je presser quelque chose dans mes bras, l'y étouffer sous ma chaleur . . . (p. 195).

Such presentation is well suited to the evocation of hallucinatory states of mind where the borderline between imagination and reality is temporarily obliterated:

> Les duchesses, penchées sur les portières blasonnées, semblaient me sourire, m'inviter à des amours sur la soie; du haut de leurs balcons, les dames en écharpe s'avançaient pour me voir et me regardaient en me disant: aime-nous! aime-nous! (p. 197).
> Je le détachais de la croix et je le faisais descendre vers moi, sur l'autel, l'encens l'entourait, il s'avançait dans la fumée . . . (p. 217).

Novembre gives little more than a foretaste of the part which free indirect speech was to play in the style of Flaubert. An entirely different picture emerges from the author's first full-length novel, the unpublished *Première Education Sentimentale* (1845), which has nothing to do with the novel of the same title published a quarter of a century later. Numerically, there is no progress at all; if anything, the frequency of the device is somewhat lower than in *Novembre*. But there is a fundamental change in its range and quality. The most significant development is that free indirect style can now be used in both of its functions: it can report speech as well as thoughts. Spoken and written words are not very often related this way; it would indeed seem that at this stage Flaubert was not yet averse to the accumulation of *que*-s, judging by the following passage where free indirect speech only appears at the very end, to relieve the monotony of the syntax:

> Elle lui avait dit *que* tout était fini entre eux, *qu'*il n'y fallait plus songer, *qu'*il le devait comprendre, *qu'*en tout cas ce qui s'était passé n'avait jamais été qu'un jeu, qu'un enfantillage auquel il ne fallait pas se laisser prendre, elle connaissait ses devoirs, elle y voulait tenir—elle le disait du moins (p. 76).

That Flaubert was exercised by the problem of speech-reporting can also be seen from a semi-apologetic remark he makes at the end of a narrative recounted partly in free indirect style:

> Le lecteur imagine sans peine qu'il raconta ses chagrins en d'autres termes que nous ne l'avons fait (p. 93).

The author still interposes himself between his characters and the reader; he has not yet arrived at the Olympian impersonality prevalent in his mature novels.

Nevertheless, he does not hesitate to report spoken and written utterances in free indirect syntax:

C'était Morel qui lui annonçait cette nouvelle, on était à un mardi matin. Ils étaient partis de l'avant-veille, le samedi au soir, on ne savait où ils s'étaient enfuis (p. 196).

Henry écrivit à Jules une longue lettre expansive, où il lui parlait de sa solitude, de sa misère, de son amour trompé. Que faire désormais dans la vie? . . . le présent était triste, l'avenir pire encore, il voulait mourir, il l'embrassait et lui disait adieu (pp. 95–6).

One of the refinements of the device, the alternation of free indirect and direct speech in reporting a dialogue, appears for the first time in the *Première Education*:

Elle l'engageait aussi, depuis quelque temps, à parler plus souvent à M. Renaud et à reprendre avec lui les longues conversations de l'année passée; il fallait se faire aimer encore plus fort, et le circonvenir tout à fait, afin de le tromper plus facilement.
—M'abaisser à faire semblant d'être son ami, répondit Henry, jamais! (p. 152).

There are also some attempts at portrayal through free indirect speech. This may be done explicitly, by means of italics or quotation marks:

Quand les parents avaient vu cela, ils étaient ravis, leur enfant respirerait un *bon air* (p. 12).

Le troisième (*viz.* historien) enfin bénit la Révolution dans son principe et dans ses résultats, tout en déplorant 'les excès qui l'avaient souillée' (p. 278).

Elsewhere, the portrayal is purely implicit but no less effective. Compare for example the speech of the two lovers— Henry's:

Henry partit donc pour la Provence, non toutefois sans avoir promis à Emilie de se revoir bientôt et de lui écrire souvent: ces deux années passées loin d'elle n'étaient qu'une concession pénible, qu'il avait faite à ses parents pour se débarrasser de leurs criailleries et de leurs intrigues (p. 233);

and Emilie's:

Elle s'était mariée jeune à M. Renaud, qu'elle avait cru adorer, disait-elle, parce qu'il la trouvait jolie; mais bientôt, veuve de ses illusions, elle s'était trouvée dans une solitude affreuse. C'est alors

qu'un homme s'était présentée, un homme qu'elle ne nommait pas,
celui-là elle l'avait aimé, il était parti, elle n'y pensait plus, il y avait si
longtemps de cela! il y avait dix ans (p. 154).

The very inflexions of the feminine voice can be heard behind
this string of short, emotional sentences.

There is equal variety in the rendering of thoughts through
free indirect style. 'Thoughts' is actually too narrow a term,
for all kinds of mental processes can be exteriorized this way,
sometimes by hardening into words what had only been half-
formulated in the mind. Occasionally, the reflections reported
are purely practical:

> Henry comptait y vivre en donnant des leçons de français et de latin,
> en écrivant des articles dans les journaux, en faisant n'importe quoi;
> d'ailleurs les six mille francs qu'ils avaient maintenant les aideraient
> toujours pendant quelque temps (p. 177).

More often, however, the thoughts are tinged with emotion,
and free indirect speech becomes the vehicle of effusive and
lyrical meditations:

> Il se leva et il se sentit fort, assez pour renverser le monde à lui
> seul. Elle l'aimait! il s'aimait lui-même, il était grand, il était magnifi-
> que, il dominait tout, il pouvait tout, il aurait volé avec les aigles, il se
> fût jeté à la gueule des canons (p. 56).

Here the crescendo rhythm reflects the growing exaltation of
the young man. But this form of presentation can transcend the
limits of a passing mood and fix a more lasting vision:

> Ainsi qu'à travers des lunettes vertes on voit tout en vert, elle ne
> voyait rien qu'à travers cet amour, tout s'y fondait et en prenait la
> teinte. Il y avait dans l'univers un homme; derrière elle, au second
> plan, s'agitait le reste de l'humanité (p. 176).

The use of free indirect style to evoke hallucinatory states is
greatly developed in the *Première Education*. The anguish of the
jealous husband finds its natural expression in this medium:

> . . . dans le fond de son âme, humilié par ce maudit petit jeune homme
> qui était la cause de tout cela, et aussi par cette belle femme qu'il avait
> eue, qu'il aurait pu avoir encore, qui était bien la sienne cependant, et
> dont la large poitrine gonflée . . . peut-être alors, en ce moment
> même, se dilatait sous celle d'un autre (p. 204).

The heaviest concentration of free indirect passages occurs in the account of Jules's meeting with a stray dog and of the nervous crisis which ensues. The device is heightened here to a pitch of hysteria:

> Le chien le suivit encore; ce n'était pas lui cependant, ce n'était pas lui, celui-ci d'ailleurs était plus petit et sa tache noire sur le dos s'étendait plus en avant. Ah! l'horrible bête! (p. 249);
>
> Puis il se rappela qu'un jour—oh! qu'il y avait bien longtemps!—il était venu sur ce pont et qu'il avait désiré mourir. Était-ce là ce que voulait dire la bête funèbre qui tournait autour de lui? Qu'y avait-il donc de caché dans la rivière pour qu'elle en parcourût sans cesse le bord en se dirigeant toujours, il semblait, de la source à l'embouchure, comme pour montrer quelque chose qui aurait coulé dessus, qui serait descendu? N'était-ce pas Lucinde? grand Dieu! était-ce elle? serait-ce elle, noyée, perdue sous le torrent? si jeune! si belle! morte! morte! (p. 251).

After such passages, the author tends to resume the narrative with a sentence introduced by *et* . This is the famous 'dynamic' *et*, Thibaudet's '*et* de mouvement',[1] which usually indicates some kind of change, progression or climax:

> Pourquoi donc cette opiniâtreté singulière? est-ce qu'il l'avait déjà vue autrefois? mais où donc? avait-elle appartenu à l'un de des amis? *Et* il cherchait à la reconnaître . . . (p. 247).

The pattern may be further complicated by the intrusion of direct speech to give more immediate expression to a strong emotional tension:[2]

> . . .il la voyait avec sa robe blanche, sa longue chevelure blonde épandue, et les mains en croix sur la poitrine, qui s'en allait doucement au courant, portée sur les ondes; elle était peut-être là, à cette place, ensevelie sous l'eau froide, couchée au fond du fleuve, sur les cailloux verts! 'Est-ce là ce que tu veux dire, avec ta voix qui pleure comme si tu hurlais sur un tombeau? ' Et il se figurait son cadavre, la bouche entr'ouverte, les yeux fermés (p. 251).

The main forms and functions of free indirect style are all present in the *Première Education*, but they are still infrequent and somewhat experimental. With the exception of a few

---

[1] Cf. Thibaudet, *op. cit.*, pp. 245ff.

[2] Cf. Lips, *Le Style indirect libre*, pp. 190 f., and Spitzer, *Germanisch-Romanische Monatsschrift*, vol. xvi, pp. 331f.

passages, in particular the episode of the stray dog, the new technique has not yet become an important element in the architecture of the novel.

4

With *Madame Bovary*, our construction reaches full maturity as a device of style. The numerical data alone are significant. I have counted over 150 examples, roughly one in every three pages; but counting is made very difficult by the structure of the passages themselves: their length and also the way in which they alternate with direct and indirect speech. The new method has penetrated into the very fabric of Flaubert's style; the only element which remains largely impervious to it is description. Even there, natural phenomena are sometimes evoked through their impact on the mind:

> En face, au delà des toits, le grand ciel pur s'étendait, avec le soleil rouge se couchant. Qu'il devait faire bon là-bas! Quelle fraîcheur sous la hêtraie! Et il ouvrait les narines pour aspirer les bonnes odeurs de la campagne, qui ne venaient pas jusqu'à lui (p. 11).

But most of the descriptive details so dear to Flaubert could not be forced into this mould. This was the one great obstacle to the attainment of that attitude of artistic impersonality which was the corner-stone of his programme.[1]

Of the two basic types of free indirect style, it is the reproduction of *speech* which has made the most spectacular progress: it is now almost as frequent as the reporting of thoughts. Its range of application is very wide. It can be confined to a brief sentence, an incidental comment, prepared or completely isolated; by the time it is realized that somebody's words have been quoted, the narrative has moved on:

> Léon malgré lui, se récria. D'ailleurs il n'aimait que les femmes brunes (p. 387).
> On les regardait. Ils passaient et revenaient. . . . Elle savait valser, celle-là! Ils continuèrent longtemps et fatiguèrent tous les autres (p. 74).

Elsewhere, a series of sentences will be quoted in free indirect speech:

[1] On this problem see Lips, *Le Style indirect libre*, pp. 191ff.

Et, aussitôt, racontant l'histoire de la saisie, elle lui exposa sa détresse; car Charles ignorait tout, sa belle-mère la détestait, le père Rouault ne pouvait rien; mais lui, Léon, allait se mettre en course pour trouver cette indispensable somme . . . (p. 410).

In the example which follows, two groups of free indirect sentences are separated by a narrative passage; eventually, the story is resumed by the usual 'dynamic' *et*:

Elle se plaignait sans cesse de ses nerfs, de sa poitrine, de ses humeurs. Le bruit des pas lui faisait mal; on s'en allait, la solitude lui devenait odieuse; revenait-on près d'elle, c'était pour la voir mourir, sans doute. Le soir, quand Charles rentrait, elle sortait de dessous ses draps ses longs bras maigres, les lui passait autour du cou, et, l'ayant fait asseoir au bord du lit, se mettait à lui parler de ses chagrins: il l'oubliait, il en aimait une autre! On lui avait bien dit qu'elle serait malheureuse; et elle finissait en lui demandant quelque sirop pour sa santé et un peu plus d'amour (pp. 13–14).

The advantages of free indirect style come to the fore in the reporting of emotional speech which has its own syntax and choice of words:

Mais le marchand s'écria qu'elle avait tort; ils se connaissaient; est-ce qu'il doutait d'elle? Quel enfantillage! (pp. 272–3)

Free indirect style permits the use of a spontaneous and impulsive form of sentence-structure:

Le clerc se récria que les natures idéales étaient difficiles à comprendre. Lui, du premier coup d'oeil, il l'avait aimée . . . (p. 126).

It can accommodate expressive colloquialisms:

Il fallait attendre, au contraire, tâter ce gaillard-là (p. 377).

The use of free indirect style as a means of portrayal and parody is greatly expanded in *Madame Bovary*. Italics are frequently employed to strengthen the effect. Some of the features singled out are typical of a certain social milieu:

Il n'avait avec lui que sa *demoiselle*, qui l'aidait à tenir la maison (p. 17; the speaker is a peasant boy).
Tout le monde désira connaître ce tapis; pourquoi la femme du médecin faisait-elle au clerc des *générosités*? Cela parut drôle, et l'on pensa définitivement qu'elle devait être sa *bonne amie* (p. 138).
M. Boulanger lui présenta son homme, qui voulait être saigné, parce qu'il éprouvait *des fourmis le long du corps* (p. 177).

Emma's defiance of bourgeois conventions is summed up in the words:

Elle eut même l'inconvenance de se promener avec M. Rodolphe une cigarette à la bouche, *comme pour narguer le monde* (p. 266).

This challenge could not fail to antagonize her environment, including her mother-in-law, whose way of speaking is parodied by the same method:

. . . et cependant Mme Bovary mère semblait prévenue contre sa bru. Elle lui trouvait *un genre trop relevé pour leur position de fortune*: le bois, le sucre et la chandelle *filaient comme dans une grande maison* (p. 59).

Her husband uses a very different language:

D'ailleurs, *avec du toupet, un homme réussit toujours dans le monde* (p. 8).

Parody and caricature are at their most intense in the style of Lheureux and in that of Homais, the chemist. Homais's language is presented with great attention to detail. To take but two aspects of his personality; his anticlericalism and his snobbery:

Ce refus d'accepter un rafraîchissement lui semblait une hypocrisie des plus odieuses; les prêtres godaillaient tous sans qu'on les vît, et cherchaient à ramener le temps de la dîme (p. 105).

Il exposa sur les femmes des théories immorales. Ce qui le séduisait par-dessus tout, c'était le *chic*. Il adorait une toilette élégante dans un appartement bien meublé, et, quant aux qualités corporelles, ne détestait pas le *morceau* (p. 387).

We had already been told earlier that the chemist was apt to use slang terms 'afin d'éblouir . . . les bourgeois, disant *turne*, *bazar*, *chicard*, *chicandard*, *Breda-street* et *je me la casse* pour: Je m'en vais' (p. 386).

In these passages, especially where italics are used, free indirect style comes very near to direct speech, and one may indeed wonder why Flaubert preferred it to the latter if he was so anxious to make the language of his characters true to life. But he may have had several reasons for doing so. He may have wished to vary the form of presentation. He may have been unwilling to commit himself to a complete and faithful transcription of what had been said. He may also have felt that a more selective treatment, aided by italics, would bring out more forcefully the idiosyncrasies of the speaker. Italics play here the same role on the written page as intonation would in the spoken language, and we have already noted the close connection between intonation and the free indirect method.

In some of these examples, the portrayal was not entirely objective, but had an undertone of irony. A different kind of irony arises when a person speaks out of tune with his or her character. Thus it is clear to all readers that Emma Bovary is not a devoted mother; yet:

> Elle déclarait adorer les enfants; c'était sa consolation, sa joie, sa folie, et elle accompagnait ses caresses d'expansions lyriques, qui, à d'autres qu'à des Yonvillais, eussent rappelé la Sachette de *Notre-Dame de Paris* (p. 147).

Grammatically, 'c'était sa consolation, sa joie, sa folie' might be the author's own words, but the reader knows from the wider context that it is Emma, not Flaubert, who is speaking, and that she is not telling the truth.

Flaubert can obtain varied and delicate effects from the alternation of direct and free indirect style. In some cases, the shift occurs in the speech of the same person. The reporting starts in direct style and continues in free indirect, or *vice versa*:

> —Que vous seriez charitable, poursuivit-il en se relevant, de satisfaire une fantaisie!
> C'était de visiter sa maison; il désirait la connaître (p. 217).
> D'abord, elle se soulagea par des allusions. . . . D'où vient qu'il retournait aux Bertaux, puisque M. Rouault était guéri et que ces gens-là n'avaient pas encore payé? Ah! c'est qu'il y avait là-bas *une personne*, une brodeuse, un bel esprit. C'était là ce qu'il aimait: il lui fallait des demoiselles de ville! Et elle reprenait:
> —La fille au père Rouault, une demoiselle de ville! Allons donc! leur grand-père était berger . . . (pp. 23–4).

A passage in free indirect style may also be sandwiched between two direct quotations:

> —Nous nous sommes rapatriés, et je venais encore lui proposer un arrangement.
> C'était de renouveler le billet signé par Bovary. Monsieur, du reste, agirait à sa guise; il ne devait point se tourmenter, maintenant surtout qu'il allait avoir une foule d'embarras.

—Et même il ferait mieux de s'en décharger sur quelqu'un, sur vous, par exemple . . . (p. 350).

The formula of alternating direct and free indirect speech in dialogue is put to effective use in *Madame Bovary*:

Il se lança même dans une digression ethnographique; l'Allemande était vaporeuse, la Française libertine, l'Italienne passionnée.
—Et les négresses? demanda le clerc (pp. 387–8).
Enfin il perdit patience; on le poursuivait, ses capitaux étaient absents, et, s'il ne rentrait dans quelques-uns, il serait forcé de lui reprendre toutes les marchandises qu'elle avait.
—Eh! reprenez-les! dit Emma (p. 263).

The digression into the free indirect mode may be quite short and incidental; it may even be interrupted by direct speech:

—Oh! je m'imagine . . .
—Eh! non! car vous n'êtes pas femme, vous.
Mais les hommes avaient aussi leurs chagrins; et la conversation s'engagea par quelques réflexions philosophiques (p. 321).
Charles se récria encore une fois qu'il ne pouvait s'absenter plus longtemps; mais rien n'empêchait Emma . . .
—C'est que . . . , balbutia-t-elle avec un singulier sourire, je ne sais pas trop . . . (p. 318).

When both interlocutors are quoted in free indirect style, there may be a subtle to-and-fro movement gliding in and out of reported speech:

Avec un haussement léger de ses épaules, Emma l'interrompit pour se plaindre de sa maladie où elle avait manqué mourir; quel dommage! elle ne souffrirait plus maintenant. Léon tout de suite envia *le calme du tombeau*, et même, un soir, il avait écrit son testament en recommandant qu'on l'ensevelît dans ce beau couvre-pied, à bandes de velours, qu'il tenait d'elle (p. 324).

5

The transcription of 'inner speech' presents an equally varied picture. It ranges from fleeting thoughts to fully developed internal monologues. Sometimes it is no more than a brief inner question or exclamation interrupting for a moment the flow of the narrative:

Il la vit seule, le soir, très tard, derrière le jardin, dans la ruelle; dans la ruelle, comme avec l'autre! Il faisait de l'orage . . . (p. 358).

Il la regardait en face, d'une manière insupportable. Soupçonnait-il quelque chose? Elle demeurait perdue dans toutes sortes d'appréhensions (p. 350).

On chantait, on s'agenouillait, on se relevait, cela n'en finissait pas! Il se rappela qu'une fois, dans les premiers temps, ils avaient ensemble assisté à la messe (p. 465).

This method is carried one step further when the perusal of a legal document is punctuated by the reader's inner comments:

'En vertu de la grosse, en forme exécutoire d'un jugement . . .' Quel jugement? La veille, en effet, on avait apporté un autre papier qu'elle ne connaissait pas . . .
'Dans vingt-quatre heures pour tout délai.'
—Quoi donc? 'Payer la somme totale de huit mille francs.' Et même, il y avait plus bas: 'Elle y sera contrainte par toute voie de droit . . .'
Que faire? . . . C'était dans vingt-quatre heures; demain! (p. 404)

In longer passages, there are various possibilities of emotive modulation. Questions and exclamations are lavishly used, and the sequence of mental processes is accurately recorded:

Elle était à Tostes. Lui, il était à Paris, maintenant; là-bas! Comment était-ce, Paris? Quel nom démesuré! Elle se le répétait à demi-voix . . . (pp. 79–80).
Qui était-ce donc? Elle le connaissait. . . . La voiture s'élança et disparut.
Mais c'était lui, le Vicomte! Elle se détourna; la rue était déserte (pp. 412–13).

As in direct speech, emotional emphasis may lead to repetition:

Comment donc avait-elle fait (elle qui était si intelligente!) pour se méprendre encore une fois? . . . Et pourquoi? et pourquoi? (pp. 255–6).
Elle se rappela des soirs d'été tout pleins de soleil. Les poulains hennissaient quand on passait, et galopaient, galopaient (p. 239).

Word-order may be closely modelled on the free and impulsive movement of ordinary speech:

Il croyait entendre l'haleine légère de son enfant. Elle allait grandir maintenant; chaque saison, vite, amènerait un progrès (p. 270).

Some of the reflexions have a colloquial tone:

Voilà ce qu'on ne voudrait jamais croire! on allait rire, au contraire, clabauder! (p. 255).

La part de la barque n'excéda point mille écus. Elle avait donc menti, la bonne dame! (p. 25).

Il le trouvait bien un peu *gringalet*, et ce n'était pas là un gendre comme il l'eût souhaité (p. 32).

Free indirect style also provides a natural vehicle for reveries, lyrical effusions and self-analysis. In Flaubert, these processes are still extensively rationalized; he does not attempt to record faithfully the raw material of mental experience. This is not yet the 'stream of consciousness' technique which was to be practised by Joyce and other writers, though it is undoubtedly a significant step in that direction.[1] In another respect, too, the reporting is not entirely realistic: occasionally, the author is carried away by his own rhetoric and makes his characters think in a language which is obviously his, not theirs:

La série des mêmes journées recommença. Elles allaient donc maintenant se suivre ainsi à la file toujours pareilles, innombrables, et n'apportant rien! Les autres existences, si plates qu'elles fussent, avaient du moins la chance d'un événement. Une aventure amenait parfois des péripéties à l'infini et le décor changeait. Mais, pour elle, rien n'arrivait, Dieu l'avait voulu! L'avenir était un corridor tout noir, et qui avait au fond sa porte bien fermée (p. 87).

The author's intrusion may become so marked that the free indirect form will be no more than a façade:

N'importe! elle n'était pas heureuse, ne l'avait jamais été. D'où venait donc cette insuffisance de la vie, cette pourriture instantanée des choses où elle s'appuyait? . . . Mais, s'il y avait quelque part un être fort et beau, une nature valeureuse, pleine à la fois d'exaltation et de raffinements, un coeur de poète sous une forme d'ange, lyre aux cordes d'airain, sonnant vers le ciel des épithalames élégiaques, pourquoi, par hasard, ne le trouverait-elle pas? Oh! quelle impossibilité! Rien, d'ailleurs, ne valait la peine d'une recherche; tout mentait! Chaque

---

[1] Cf. Scarfe, *op. cit.*, p. 108, and G. Struve, '*Monologue intérieur*: The Origins of the Formula and the First Statement of its Possibilities', *Publications of the Modern Language Association of America*, vol. LXIX (1954), pp. 1101–11: p. 1109.

sourire cachait un bâillement d'ennui, chaque joie une malédiction, tout plaisir son dégoût, et les meilleurs baisers ne vous laissaient sur la lèvre qu'une irréalisable envie d'une volupté plus haute (p. 393).

The ideas are Emma Bovary's, but, with all her fondness for Romantic novels, she would never have thought of 'épithalames élégiaques', and the elaborate structure of the last sentence, the delicately balanced triple rhythm broadening into a more ample movement which leads up to the final climax, unmistakably bears Flaubert's own stamp.

As in the early novels, dreamlike and hallucinatory visions may acquire a spurious air of reality by being related in free indirect style:

. . . elle se réveillait en d'autres rêves. Au galop de quatre chevaux, elle était emportée depuis huit jours vers un pays nouveau, d'où ils ne reviendraient plus. Ils allaient, ils allaient, les bras enlacés, sans parler (p. 271).

Puis elle lui apparaissait morte. Elle était là, devant lui, étendue sur le dos, au milieu de la route. Il tirait la bride, et l'hallucination disparaissait (p. 463).

The alternation of direct and free indirect style is just as effective in the reporting of internal monologues as in the reproduction of speech:

—Advienne que pourra! se disait-elle.
Et puis, qui sait? pourquoi, d'un moment à l'autre, ne surgirait-il pas un événement extraordinaire? Lheureux même pouvait mourir (p. 415).
Alors elle voulut se calmer; elle se rappela la lettre; il fallait la finir, elle n'osait pas. D'ailleurs, où? comment? on la verrait.
—Ah! non, ici, pensa-t-elle, je serai bien (p. 284).

Direct and free indirect sentences may be embedded in a narrative passage:

Elle abandonna la musique: pourquoi jouer? qui l'entendrait? . . . Elle laissa dans l'armoire ses cartons à dessin et la tapisserie. A quoi bon? A quoi bon? La couture l'irritait.
—J'ai tout lu, se disait-elle (p. 88).

Thanks to the free indirect method, the internal monologue can develop into a kind of internal dialogue:

Puis, qu'elle avouât ou n'avouât pas, tout à l'heure, tantôt, demain

I   113

il n'en saurait pas moins la catastrophe; donc il fallait attendre cette horrible scène et subir le poids de sa magnanimité. L'envie lui vint de retourner chez Lheureux: à quoi bon? d'écrire à son père: il était trop tard; et peut-être qu'elle se repentait maintenant de n'avoir pas cédé à l'autre (p. 421).

In the last example and in many others, the dynamic *et* marks the transition from indirect style to the narrative plane.

The passages quoted above, which could easily be multiplied, will have given some idea of the diversity of the device, the variety of its uses and the intricacy of its structure. Many vital aspects of Flaubert's aesthetic are intimately connected with this technique, and it is no exaggeration to say that without it, *Madame Bovary* would be a very different novel.

6

There is no need to follow in detail the development of free indirect style in Flaubert's later works. By the time he had completed *Madame Bovary*, the new method had become an integral part of his way of writing, and it was bound to persist, and even to develop further, by its own momentum. In his next novel, *Salammbô*, free indirect style is frequently employed, though not on the same scale as in *Madame Bovary*; in the first seven chapters of the book, the density of the device is about the same as in the *Première Education*. This recession is hardly surprising, as neither the theme nor the narrative form were particularly suited to this type of reporting. Some of the characteristic patterns evolved in the preceding books are transferred into the very different stylistic climate of a historical novel; indeed it is almost paradoxical to find the words and thoughts of Carthaginians of the third century B.C. reported in the same way as those of the people of Yonville. There is once again the dynamic *et* rounding off an internal monologue:

Il se sentait misérable, chétif, abandonné. Jamais il ne la posséderait. Il ne pouvait même s'emparer d'une ville.

La nuit, seul, dans sa tente, il contemplait le zaïmph. A quoi cette chose des dieux lui servait-elle? et des doutes survenaient dans la pensée du Barbare (p. 124).

Emotive elements are preserved, as usual, in free indirect style:

114

Giscon haussa les épaules; son courage serait inutile contre ces bêtes brutes, exaspérées (p. 10).

We find again the alternation of direct and free indirect speech in dialogue:

Alors l'esclave lui parla de son père. On le croyait parti vers la contrée de l'ambre, derrière les colonnes de Melkarth.
—Mais s'il ne revient pas, disait-elle, il te faudra, puisque c'était sa volonté, choisir un époux . . .
—Pourquoi? demanda la jeune fille.
Tous ceux qu'elle avait aperçus lui faisaient horreur avec leurs rires de bête fauve et leurs membres grossiers (p. 60).

But it would be quite wrong to believe that the use of free indirect style had reached saturation point in *Madame Bovary*. Even a cursory glance at the next great realistic novel, *L'Education Sentimentale*, will show that this is not so. In this work, the construction is literally ubiquitous; its frequency seems to be not far short of one on every page. The numerical progress is not matched by progress in quality and in diversity, since all the main forms of the device were already present in *Madame Bovary*. Yet there are important developments in some directions, and the handling of the method is bolder and more suggestive. One or two brief indications will suffice to show the new nuances of free indirect speech.

Flaubert displays remarkable inventiveness in devising ever new combinations of direct and free indirect style in dialogue, in the speech of the same person, and in internal monologue:

—Ah! saprelotte. J'oubliais!
—Quoi donc?
—Ce soir, je dîne en ville!
—Chez les Dambreuse? Pourquoi ne m'en parles-tu jamais dans tes lettres?
Ce n'était pas chez les Dambreuse, mais chez les Arnoux.
—Tu aurais dû m'avertir, dit Deslauriers (p. 63).
—Mais, saprelotte, qu'est-ce que tu as?
Frédéric souffrait des nerfs. Deslauriers n'en crut rien. Devant une pareille douleur, il avait senti se réveiller sa tendresse, et il le réconforta. Un homme comme lui se laisser abattre, quelle sottise! Passe encore dans la jeunesse, mais plus tard, c'est perdre son temps.
—Tu me gâtes mon Frédéric! Je redemande l'ancien (p. 99).

There is shrewd psychology in the way the two forms

alternate in the speech of the same person. The emotional climax at the beginning and the end is expressed with the forcefulness which only direct speech can command; the explanation in between is given in free indirect style, which permits some abridgement of the details:[1]

—Eh bien, oui! s'écria Frédéric. Je ne nie rien! Je suis un misérable! écoutez-moi!

S'il l'avait eue, c'était par désespoir, comme on se suicide. Du reste, il l'avait rendue fort malheureuse, pour se venger sur elle de sa propre honte.

—Quel supplice! Vous ne comprenez pas? (p. 513).

The same emotional rhythm seems to govern the alternation of the two styles in some internal monologues:

Frédéric fut saisi par l'étonnement que l'on éprouve à voir une farce réussir: 'Il se moque de moi, pensa-t-il, si je remontais?' Deslauriers croirait, peut-être, qu'il lui enviait cet amour? 'Comme si je n'en avais pas un, et cent fois plus rare, plus noble, plus fort!' (pp. 108–9).

Another change in the device is that it tends to become more elliptical; transitions are often abrupt and unprepared, leaving it to the reader's ingenuity to supply the missing link. One chapter opens laconically with the words: 'Ruiné, dépouillé, perdu!' (p. 130). Such reticence intensifies the shock-effect and leaves full scope for irony and ambiguity. At one point in the novel, there is an ingenious case of double meaning. Frédéric asks his friend Hussonnet not to mention his failure at the examinations when they call on the Arnoux-s:

—Pas un mot de tout cela, chez eux, bien entendu!

Le secret était facile, puisque Arnoux, le lendemain, partait pour l'Allemagne (p. 88).

This sounds like a statement of fact by the author himself; actually, it is a piece of information given by Hussonnet, which subsequently turns out to be wrong, as Frédéric finds out at his own expense when he calls on Madame Arnoux and is received by the husband.

In spite of these and many other subtleties, one has the impression that, in the *Education*, free indirect style is over-

[1] See above, p. 109; cf. also M. Riffaterre, *Le Français Moderne*, vol. XXIII (1955), p. 315: 'le discours direct tranche soudain, vif éclat, sur le murmure du discours indirect libre'.

worked. When a construction of this type is found on nearly every page, and often several times on one page, it becomes mechanical and begins to pall. One is reminded of some uncharitable verdicts on the machine-like rhythm of Flaubert's style. Proust has compared it to the noise of an excavator and of a moving staircase,[1] and Thibaudet has spoken of 'le ronflement du même moteur'.[2] It is also true that the suppression of so many marks of subordination makes for a somewhat invertebrate syntax. Yet there can be no doubt that free indirect style contributes in no small measure to the finesse and austere elegance of the style, and to that quality of lightness and fluidity which is the distinguishing mark of the novel.

7

Free indirect speech is, as we have seen, an invaluable stylistic device which can be put to a multiplicity of uses. Most of these can be traced back to three sources:

1. The very existence of the construction makes for variety in style. The author can now choose between three different forms of reported speech and can alternate them in a number of ways.

2. Free indirect style combines the advantages of the two orthodox methods. The author is not committed to an exact reproduction of words or thoughts; yet he is able to dispense with explicit subordination and to retain the emotive and expressive features and the very inflexions of the spoken language.

3. Free indirect style is reported speech masquerading as narrative. It means a break in continuity and a certain shock to the reader. It is essentially an oblique construction and provides a discreet but effective vehicle for irony and ambiguity, and for the description of reveries, dreams and hallucinatory states.

All these advantages explain the rapid spread of the method once Flaubert had established it as a device of style.[3] They do

---

[1] Cf. M. Turnell, *The Novel in France*, London (1950), p. 20.

[2] *Op. cit.*, pp. 220f.

[3] On the use of free indirect style in Zola and other later writers, see Lips, *op. cit.*, ch. IV. The usage of a contemporary novelist has been examined in Sr. A. G. Landry's monograph, *Represented Discourse in the Novels of François Mauriac*, Washington (1953) (The Catholic University of America Studies in Romance Languages and Literatures XLIV).

not explain why it should have fallen to Flaubert to discover these potentialities and bring them to fruition.

There were several reasons why Flaubert should have been the first writer to exploit the free indirect method. Some were connected with his personal preferences and idiosyncrasies. His hyper-sensitive ear shrank from the accumulation of *qui*-s and *que*-s to which even the best stylists of the Classical period had remained indifferent. ' Je répète encore une fois', he wrote in his correspondence, 'que jusqu'à nous, jusqu'aux très modernes, on n'avait pas l'idée de l'harmonie soutenue du style, les *qui*, les *que* enchevêtrés les uns dans les autres reviennent incessamment dans ces grands écrivains.'[1] French lacks the ease with which subordinating conjunctions and pronouns can be omitted in English, but free indirect style goes a long way to remedy this weakness. On the positive side, Flaubert's well-known fondness for the Imperfect naturally prompted him to use a construction where this tense would play a prominent part and acquire delicate stylistic values.

But one must probe deeper into Flaubert's aesthetic to discover the real root of his preference for free indirect style. Much has been written on his doctrine of impassivity, on the objective and impersonal attitude which he adopted in his novels.[2] He himself reverted time and again to the problem, most pregnantly perhaps in an often quoted passage of his correspondence:

L'auteur, dans son oeuvre, doit être comme Dieu dans l'univers, présent partout et visible nulle part. L'Art étant une seconde nature, le créateur de cette nature-là doit agir par des procédés analogues. Que l'on sente dans tous les atomes, à tous les aspects, une impassibilité cachée et infinie. L'effet, pour le spectateur, doit être une espèce d'ébahissement. Comment tout cela s'est-il fait? doit-on dire, et qu'on se sente écrasé sans savoir pourquoi.

Free indirect style is the exact equivalent, on the linguistic plane, of this withdrawal of the author from his work.[3] He

[1] Quoted by Thibaudet, *op. cit.*, p. 226; cf. also *ibid.*, p. 230.
[2] See especially M. Bonwit, *Gustave Flaubert et le principe d'impassibilité*, University of California Publications in Modern Philology, Vol. 33, no. 4 (1950), pp. 263–420; a number of relevant quotations are given on pp. 276ff. Cf. also Lips, *op. cit.*, pp. 186f., and B. F. Bart, 'Aesthetic Distance in *Madame Bovary*', *Publications of the Modern Language Association of America*, vol. LXIX (1954), pp. 1112–26.
[3] The author's disappearance behind his characters could be regarded as an impressionistic tendency; cf. Lerch, *op. cit.*, p. 114, and O. Walzel, *Gehalt und*

prefers, as far as possible, not to intervene directly; he merely reports the words and thoughts of his characters, and even refrains from explicitly stating that he is doing so. Such discreet self-effacement will run the risk of being misunderstood: the half-formulated thoughts and day-dreams of the characters may be attributed to their maker. Indeed it has been suggested that, if the nature of internal monologue had been known at the time, this would have been a strong argument for the defence at the trial of *Madame Bovary*: some of the allegedly revolting passages imputed to the author were really Emma's thoughts expressed in free indirect style.[1]

Yet impersonality did not mean aloofness for Flaubert; it had as its complement a capacity for sympathetic self-identification with the protagonists of the story.[2] Flaubert himself has spoken of this 'faculté panthéiste', and while at work on *Madame Bovary*, he wrote to Louise Colet: 'C'est une délicieuse chose que d'écrire, que de n'être plus soi, mais de circuler dans toute la création dont on parle.' He also records in his correspondence that, when relating Emma's suicide, he actually felt the taste of arsenic in his mouth and had two attacks of indigestion. Free indirect style provided a congenial expression for this attitude: it is an essentially mimetic device and supersedes the borderline between narrative and inner speech, so that the two imperceptibly merge into one another.

The free indirect technique was not the only syntactical innovation started by Flaubert. It takes its place among other experiments: novel uses of the Imperfect, of the Present Participle, of certain conjunctions and pronouns, of the indefinite article,[3] and similar developments. By these changes, Flaubert initiated a large-scale reform of literary syntax which was followed up by other writers and is still in progress. These efforts to make syntax more flexible and more expressive were

Gestalt im Kunstwerk des Dichters, Berlin (1923), p. 382. On the wider implications of this attitude, see N. Friedman, 'Point of View in Fiction: The Development of a Critical Concept', *Publications of the Modern Language Association of America*, vol. LXX (1955), pp. 1160–84.

[1] Lerch, *op. cit.*, pp. 132f.

[2] *Ibid.*, pp. 130 ff.; cf. Bonwit, *op. cit.*, pp. 298f.

[3] A detailed account of these innovations will be found in Thibaudet, *op. cit.* On the last point, cf. also my article, 'Note sur la syntaxe de Flaubert: l'emploi de l'article indéfini avec des substantifs abstraits', *Le Français Moderne*, vol. XXIII (1955), pp. 257–9.

closely bound up with Flaubert's conception of style. The sentence, he proclaimed, must not only be perfectly orchestrated in itself; it must also be completely attuned to the idea which it expresses. Style is not something external, a mere garment of thought; in Flaubert's memorable simile, it must penetrate into the thought like a stiletto. This new vision of style has had a decisive influence on European literature, and a hundred years after *Madame Bovary*, its impact has scarcely weakened.

CHAPTER III

NEW PATTERNS OF SENTENCE-STRUCTURE IN THE GONCOURTS

In the preface to his novel *Pierre et Jean*, Maupassant made a scathing attack on the style of the Goncourts. He did not mention them by name, but his meaning was quite plain. His strictures were mainly directed against their vocabulary. He took exception to the 'vocabulaire bizarre, compliqué, nombreux et chinois qu'on nous impose aujourd'hui sous le nom d'écriture artiste',[1] and protested against vagueness of meaning, neologisms, preciosity, and pretentious archaisms unearthed 'au fond de vieux livres inconnus'. After expressing the hope that the genius of the language would know how to deal with these 'tentatives inutiles' and 'efforts impuissants', Maupassant concluded with a Parthian shot:

Ceux qui font aujourd'hui des images, sans prendre garde aux termes abstraits, ceux qui font tomber la grêle ou la pluie sur la *propreté* des vitres, peuvent aussi jeter des pierres à la simplicité de leurs confrères! Elles frapperont peut-être les confrères qui ont un corps, mais n'atteindront jamais la simplicité qui n'en a pas.[2]

In these lines, Maupassant laid his finger on one of the most striking idiosyncrasies of the Goncourts: the use of an abstract quality-noun in preference to an adjective. Even a perfunctory study of their writings will show that the criticism was justified. Though there may be scores of pages without any example of this construction, it recurs in certain contexts with the regularity of a mannerism. Nor was it in any way an isolated feature; it links up with a number of parallel tendencies. It is only one aspect of what has been called the 'nominal syntax' of the Goncourts, their marked preference for nouns where ordinary

[1] The term *écriture artiste* seems to have been used for the first time in 1879, eight years before Maupassant's attack, in the preface to Edmond de Goncourt's novel, *Les Frères Zemganno*; cf. G. Loesch, *Die impressionistische Syntax der Goncourt*, Nürnberg (1919), pp. 15f.

[2] On Maupassant's attitude to the Goncourts, see F. Sabatier, *L'Esthétique des Goncourt*, Paris (1920), pp. 569ff.

ld require some other part of speech. From a different
w, it is one of the various means by which the Gon-
ove to achieve impressionistic effects. Several impor-
ant works have been published on both problems,[1] but, as
usual, new perspectives are opened up and greater precision is
obtained by examining them within the context of a complete
work of art.

The material for the analysis which follows has been drawn
from two novels very different in theme and in style: *Renée
Mauperin* (1864) and *Manette Salomon* (1867). The former is a
short and straightforward narrative with relatively few descriptions and a high proportion of dialogue. The language is
already experimental in many ways, but less so than in the next
three novels, *Germinie Lacerteux, Manette Salomon* and *Madame
Gervaisais*, which represent the high watermark of the Goncourt
brothers' joint activity.[2] *Manette Salomon* is a long and complicated novel in which descriptive and analytical passages are
very prominent; it has also a special interest for the student of
impressionism as it is a book about painters, full of animated
discussions on painting and of detailed descriptions of pictures.

The Goncourts' preference for nominal syntax—'le style
substantif', as it is sometimes called—is shown most strikingly
by the way the noun encroaches on the traditional province of
two other parts of speech, the adjective and the verb.

NOUNS FOR ADJECTIVES

The replacement of an adjective by a noun[3] can have two main
forms. The adjective itself may be turned into a noun, or an

[1] On nominal syntax, the chief authority is A. Lombard, *Les Constructions nomi-
nales dans le français moderne*, Uppsala-Stockholm (1930). On impressionism in the
Goncourts, see esp. Loesch, *op. cit.*, and Sabatier, *op. cit.*, pp. 409ff. Various aspects
of impressionism in style are discussed in the volume, *El Impresionismo en el Lenguaje*, Buenos Aires (1936); cf. also Hatzfeld's *Bibliography*, esp. pp. 160ff. On the
Impressionist movement in the various arts, see R. Moser, *L'Impressionnisme français. Peinture, littérature, musique*, Genève-Lille (1952), esp. pp. 100–5 and pp.
124–32. Cf. also H. Hatzfeld, *Literature Through Art. A New Approach to French
Literature*, New York (1952), ch. VI.

[2] See Loesch, *op. cit.*, pp. 32ff. A detailed account of the two novels will be
found in R. Ricatte's recent book, *La Création romanesque chez les Goncourt, 1851–
1870*, Paris (1953), chs. V and VII.

[3] For a general discussion see Loesch, *op cit.*, pp. 46f.; Lombard, *op. cit.*, pp.
152ff.; Bally, *Impresionismo*, pp. 40ff.; A. Alonso and R. Lida, *ibid.*, pp. 202ff.

abstract quality-noun may be used in its place. The normal phrase *une main blanche* may thus become either *le blanc d'une main* or *la blancheur d'une main*. Both types are already in evidence in *Renée Mauperin*, but they become incomparably bolder, more varied and more frequent in the second novel.

The use of an *abstract quality-noun* placed before the term which it qualifies is one of the favourite devices of the Goncourts; it is the construction to which Maupassant referred in the passage quoted above. The following extract from *Renée Mauperin* will show very clearly how the transposition works:

L'obscurité venait. Toute la pièce s'assombrissait. Couchée sur sa chaise longue, *Renée disparaissait dans la vague blancheur de son peignoir*. Il arrivait un instant où l'on ne distinguait plus rien, et où la chambre se mêlait au ciel (p. 334).

This description is impressionistic in two different ways. It detaches the quality of whiteness from the object, sets it up as an independent substance, and thereby focuses attention on the white colour rather than on the dressing-gown. Thus colour will take precedence over the objects to which it belongs, in the same way as it does in the impressionist style of painting introduced by Monet, Manet and their group.[1] But the passage is also impressionistic in a different sense: it reproduces the actual sequence of events in the observer's mind, the psychological order of sense-impressions as they reach our eye and our consciousness.[2] In the dusk which is descending on the room, all that one sees at first is a patch of misty whiteness; only on closer inspection, or on reflection, is the whiteness connected with an object, Renée's dressing-gown. The progression of speech in time enables it to reproduce the sequence of impressions in their impact on the mind.

The effect will be somewhat weaker when the order in which two impressions were received is immaterial. Take for example the sentence: 'Une respiration visible et pénible courait

---

[1] Mlle Moser is quite right in pointing out that, at the time of writing *Manette Salomon*, 'les Goncourt n'avaient pas encore sous les yeux les oeuvres de la pleine époque impressionniste', but that the affinity is none the less unmistakable (*op. cit.*, pp. 222f.). Nor did the terms *impressionniste* and *impressionnisme* exist at that time; *impressionniste* was first used, with a derogatory connotation, in 1874 by the art critic Leroy, with reference to Monet's picture *Impressions* (cf. Loesch, *op. cit.*, p. 18, and Bloch-Wartburg).

[2] Cf. Cressot, *Le Style et ses techniques*, pp. 7ff.

sous la maigreur de ses côtes' (*Salomon*, p. 307). Here the question does not arise as to which came first to the mind, a general impression of thinness or a more precise awareness of thin ribs. What is still impressionistic is the predominance of a quality over the object in which it is vested. The pictorial element may vanish altogether when the quality itself is of an abstract nature: 'des femmes, glissant en barque sur des fleuves, nonchalamment *penchées sur la poésie et la fugitivité de l'eau'* (*Salomon*, p. 174); 'ces hommes en blouse, qui, au Jardin des Plantes, s'amusent à *cracher sur la beauté des bêtes et la royauté des lions'* (*ibid.*, p. 30). The sharp contrast between the concrete verbs *se pencher* and *cracher*, and the abstract qualities with which they are linked, is too unnatural to be convincing. Generally speaking, the more abstract the quality, the more artificial will the construction sound; a sentence like 'Et la *bêtise même des femmes* rêvait' (*ibid.*, p. 106), provides an extreme example.

Certain themes recur with great persistence in this class of transpositions. In the concrete type, which is far more common than the abstract, *blancheur* is a special favourite, both in the singular and in the plural: 'ce pan de mur d'en face reflétant la *blancheur* d'un ciel glacé' (*Salomon*, p. 380); 'Sa peau ferme et douce sortant de la *blancheur écourtée* de la toile' (*ibid.*, p. 352); 'mêlant leurs jupes, leurs dentelles, l'éclair de leurs diamants et la *blancheur* de leurs épaules' (*Mauperin*, pp. 149–50); 'deux statues de marbre blanc luisantes, au premier plan, des *blancheurs tièdes* de l'ivoire' (*Salomon*, p. 391); 'le matin . . . passait sur leurs veines de bois les *blancheurs polies* de la pierre' (*Salomon*, p. 242). It will be seen from these examples that the quality-noun is apt to attract to itself an adjective which would logically belong to another term: 'les *blancheurs polies* de la pierre' instead of 'les blancheurs de la *pierre polie'*. This is a so-called 'hypallage', a reversal of logical relations, which may even lead to an intermingling of different senses: in 'les *blancheurs tièdes* de l'ivoire', a visual impression is combined with a sensation of heat.

The pattern set by *blancheur* can be extended to allied expressions like *pâleur* and *transparence*: 'des lèvres pleines, un peu saillantes, et rouges dans la *pâleur* légèrement boucanée de son visage' (*Salomon*, pp. 145–6); 'ombrant d'une adorable pâleur des *diaphanéités* laiteuses de la chair' (*ibid.*, p. 184); 'Autour de ses yeux, sur ses tempes, jouaient des *transparences* de nacre' (*ibid.*, p. 351).

A second favourite theme is that of *nudité*. There is already a clear example in *Renée Mauperin*: 'le soleil le fouettait amoureusement comme il fouette les *nudités* d'enfant' (p. 317). In *Manette Salomon*, the theme becomes more insistent: 'dans l'atelier, sa *nudité* avait mis tout à coup le rayonnement d'un chef-d'oeuvre' (p. 183); 'dont l'une a sa superbe *nudité* peinte dans la Renommée . . . de Delaroche' (p. 31); 'fait lever de la *nudité* absolue de la femme la pureté rigide d'un marbre' (p. 181). Here too there are some variations: 'elle laissa tomber . . . sur la *virginité* de ses formes, le dessin de sa jeunesse, la *pureté* de son ventre, un regard . . .' (p. 318).

Among other concrete qualities which enter into these combinations, thinness and immobility recur several times: 'une de ces toilettes . . . qui enveloppent d'ordinaire la *maigreur* des trotteuses de magasin' (*Salomon*, p. 194); 'une sorte de vieillesse descendait dans le creux de l'*amaigrissement* de ses petits traits' (*ibid.*, p. 308); 'circulant autour de la sèche *immobilité* du motif' (*ibid.*, p. 268); 'il se recueillait sur son séant, dans des *immobilités* de vieux bronze' (*ibid.*, p. 141).

Although this is essentially a pictorial device, non-visual impressions can also be presented this way: 'doucement bercé dans la *mollesse* d'un bon fauteuil' (*Salomon*, p. 379); 'à demi enveloppées dans l'*ampleur* de leur robe' (*Mauperin*, p. 176); 'elle respirait son amant en baisant l'*odeur* de ses cheveux' (*ibid.*, p. 162).

The tendency to extend this construction to abstract qualities, which are basically unsuited to such treatment, becomes almost an obsession in *Manette Salomon*: 'Il chercha dans la *pauvreté* de ses nippes et le vide de ses meubles' (pp. 118–19); 'en levant leurs bois comme la *majesté* d'une couronne' (p. 440); 'il se mettait à suivre, pendant des heures, l'*originalité* d'une silhouette excentrique' (pp. 314–15); 'il se jeta dans ses bras, avec *une folie de joie qui le tutoya*' (p. 57).

The noun which usurps the functions of an adjective can also be placed *after* the term which it qualifies.[1] This construction has less expressive force than the one just discussed. When the Goncourts speak of '*un geste de tristesse*' (*Salomon*, p. 145), the

[1] Cf. Lombard, *op. cit.*, pp. 174ff., and Bally, *Impresionismo*, pp. 41ff.

emphasis on sadness is less strong than it would be in *la tristesse d'un geste*, though it is stronger than in the ordinary construction *un geste triste*. As Professor Lombard rightly points out, *un geste triste* implies that this quality is only one out of many, whereas *un geste de tristesse* means that sadness is the pre-dominant quality, the feature *par excellence* which characterizes the gesture.[1] In this sense one may speak here of a 'pregnant' use of the quality-noun. As always, the unusual appearance of such combinations will enhance their expressive value.

These transpositions, the vogue of which seems to have been started by Hugo[2] and widened by the Goncourts, are less frequent in our texts than the preceding type. Nevertheless, there are a number of examples, concrete as well as abstract, which deviate sharply from ordinary usage. *Blancheur* is no longer a key-word in this group; it only occurs once in this position: 'Cette flamme de *blancheur*' (*Salomon*, p. 210). Impressions of darkness are, however, suggestively evoked by this device: 'des têtes d'hommes . . . psalmodiaient sur de grands livres, avec des voix de *nuit*, des chants de *ténèbres*' (*ibid.*, p. 200); 'la campagne était de *feu*, et puis elle était *d'ombre*' (*Mauperin*, p. 322). A general impression of silkiness is also repeatedly conveyed this way: 's'amusant les doigts de ce chatouillement de *soie*' (*Salomon*, p. 38); 'écoutant complaisamment le cri de *soie* de son bas' (*ibid.*, p. 213); 'elle lui mit le baiser de *soie* de ses lèvres contre l'oreille' (*ibid.*, p. 210). Permanent characteristics can also be emphasized by this method: 'De la pâte humaine, on dirait qu'elle tire . . . des peuples de *laideur*' (*Salomon*, p. 183); 'collé sur le dos de cette bête de *graisse*' (*ibid.*, p. 227). Once again, the inherent fatness and ugliness of these beings is more forcefully brought out by nominal syntax than if the adjectives *laid* and *gras* had been used. In the moral sphere, the device plays the same role in phrases like 'un accent de *tristesse*' (*Salomon*, p. 392) and 'une nature de *paresse*, de *volupté*' (*ibid.*, p. 146). There is, however, little justification for 'une pensée *d'inquiétude*' (*Mauperin*, p. 233) or 'quelque

---

[1] *Op. cit.*, pp. 179f.

[2] Lombard quotes 'âme de malheur', 'cardinaux d'écarlate' and 'silence de terreur' (*op. cit.*, p. 179). The device is fairly common in the Parnasse poets (cf. Bruneau, *op. cit.*, vol. XIII, pt. 1, pp. 293ff.), and in Sainte-Beuve's novel *Volupté* ('nuit de magnificence', 'tapis de mollesse', etc.); cf. Y. Le Hir, *L'Originalité littéraire de Sainte-Beuve dans 'Volupté'*, Paris (1953), pp. 21f.

promenade de *solitude'* (*Salomon*, p. 410). As so often h₂
with the Goncourts, a figure of style which can be very eff
in certain situations is allowed to develop into a manneri:

Another basic form of nominal syntax in the Goncourts is the
use of a *substantivized adjective*: *le blanc d'une main* for *une
main blanche*. There is a subtle difference in connotation between this type and *la blancheur d'une main*. The quality-noun
is an abstraction and gives the whole sentence a slightly abstract air, whereas the substantivized adjective, if originally
concrete in meaning, will retain its concrete force. In other
respects, the two constructions have much the same stylistic
effect. Like the quality-noun, the substantivized adjective is an
impressionist device, directing attention to the quality by detaching it from its bearer, and reproducing the sequence of experiences as they are registered by the mind. It will arise, for
example, when someone is looking at a town or a landscape
from a distance and is trying to pick out objects from the jumble
of shapes and colours. Thus, *Manette Salomon* opens with an
evocation of Paris viewed from a vantage-point in the Jardin
des Plantes. The spectators see 'des toits pressés, aux tuiles
brunes, faisant des masses d'un ton de tan et de marc de raisin,
d'où se détachait le *rose* des poteries des cheminées' (p. 3).
Here both impressionist functions are brought into play: the
quality is isolated from the object and integrated into the general
colour-scheme, and the sequence of experiences is also accurately reflected: first we see patches of light red emerging from
a darker background, then we realize that they are chimneys.
Other accounts of vision at a distance follow the same pattern:

. . . au pied d'un petit kiosque vert et groseille, avec le *bleu* du
Bosphore dans le lointain (p. 44).
Arrivait le réveil, à l'heure où, dans le ciel pâlissant, le *blanc* doré
et lointain des maisons de Paris faisait monter une lumière d'éclairage
(p. 99).

In the examples just quoted and in many others, sensations of
colour are presented by means of a substantivized adjective.
In *Renée Mauperin*, there are already some timid experiments of
this kind: 'la phrase . . . mit sur le visage de celui-ci le *rouge*
du plaisir, à ses lèvres une mouillure de salive' (p. 25); 'Son

pied, dépassant sa jupe, chaussé d'un soulier découvert, laissait voir un peu du *blanc* de son bas' (p. 107). In *Manette Salomon*, the substantivized colour-adjective is an almost indispensable element in the descriptions and aesthetic analyses which fill the pages of the novel. Sometimes a number of different colours are placed side by side, much as a painter would lay them on a canvas:

Puis, sur des chaises groupées et semées, de petites sociétés ramassées faisaient ces taches de *pourpre* et de *blanc* . . . qui jettent leur vie et leur fête dans l'aveuglante et métallique clarté de ces paysages, sur le *bleu* dur du ciel, sur le *vert* glauque et froid de la Manche (p. 341).

The technique can be varied in a number of ways. Contrast effects can be obtained from a juxtaposition of colours:

. . . le *blanc* et le *noir* de monceaux de toisons étaient triés par des femmes (p. 287).

Çà et là une lanterne, un réverbère était un point de *feu* dans le *noir* de la rivière (p. 372).

The substantivized adjective may itself be further qualified by other colour-terms marking its subsidiary shades:

Des tons fins de teint de vieillard jouaient sur le *rose jaunâtre* et *bleuâtre* de sa peau de visage (p. 145).

The same colour can be repeated, as in the following passage where we have a real 'symphony in blue':

Il s'arrêtait à ces *bleus* d'azurite, d'un *bleu* d'émail chinois, à ces *bleus* défaillants des cuivres oxydés, au *bleu* céleste de la lazulite allant du *bleu* de roi au *bleu* de l'eau (p. 429).

Isolated colours are even more frequent, including some which are not normally substantivized in ordinary language:

. . . les bisons, absorbés, endormis dans leur passivité solide, laissant tomber de leur masse le *sombre* d'un rocher (p. 440).

Le *bleuâtre* du soir commençait à se mêler à la fumée des cigarettes (p. 135).

. . . la ménagerie où le *roux* des lions marche dans la flamme de l'heure (p. 442).

Occasionally, impressions belonging to other senses are recorded in the same way: 'des livraisons à quatre sous fourrées entre la couverture et le *froid* du mur' (*Salomon*, p. 382); 'Le *velouté* du potage!—reprenait Anatole, comme pour se faire passer sur la langue la friandise de l'expression' (*ibid.*, p. 112).

As elsewhere, a basically pictorial device is often transferred into the abstract sphere. Such constructions have some proto-types in ordinary usage where 'le *piquant* de l'affaire', 'le *bien-fondé* d'une réclamation' and similar turns are very common; but the Goncourts have greatly extended their range and have overworked them as a device of style. In many cases the con-struction sounds artificial and lacks any stylistic justification: 'appuyant sur elle le *sérieux* de son regard' (*Salomon*, p. 319); 'ce grand musée de Versailles, si fatal à la peinture par l'*officiel* de ses sujets' (*ibid.*, p. 13); 'avec tout ce *mauvais* d'une femme dont elle savait s'envelopper' (*ibid.*, p. 209); 'Il sondait et bat-tait de son bâton, au passage, l'*inconnu* de ces arbustes' (*ibid.*, p. 243). Elsewhere, several substantivized adjectives are aligned, one form setting off another by a kind of semi-auto-matic process:

. . . il s'était mis en chasse de l'*imprévu*, de l'*inattendu*, de l'*inconnu* féminin (*Mauperin*, p. 218).

Ce qu'il y voyait, c'était . . . le *débraillé* de la vie, le hasard, l'aven-ture, l'*imprévu* de tous les jours, . . . tout l'*inconnu* de volupté du modèle de femme (*Salomon*, p. 18).

. . . le *piquant* de sa tournure, la vive expression de sa coquetterie, l'*osé* de son costume, le *négligé* de sa robe et de sa grâce, l'espèce de *déshabillé* de toute sa personne (*ibid.*, p. 344).

Far less interesting is another class of substantivized ad-jectives: those used in absolute position.[1] In French, as distinct from English, adjectives can be turned freely into nouns, and the Goncourts have fully exploited this possibility. The aesthe-tic discussions in *Manette Salomon* are full of substantivized ad-jectives like *le beau*, *le moderne*, *le vrai* and even *l'invrai*, though the latter is italicized to show that it is a neologism: 'il avait au suprême point le sens de l'*invrai*' (p. 368). Many of these occur in the speech of painters and are part of their professional jargon: 'La bonne a du *blanc*, et le petit chien a du *rouge*' (p. 154); 'Oh! le *Beau*! . . . le *suprême* de l'*illimité* et de l'*indéfinis-sable*' (p. 438). The familiar snowball effect is again in evidence in these series. But the authors themselves are not immune from this professional tic: 'la révélation d'un *Beau* qu'on pour-

[1] Cf. Lombard, *op. cit.*, pp. 131ff.

rait appeler le *Beau* expressif . . . le retour du sauveur du *Beau* de Raphaël' (p. 16); 'toutes ces sévérités de l'automne se perdant dans la grandeur du *noir*' (p. 295). In the following sentence, three different forms of nominal syntax—a quality-noun and two kinds of substantivized adjectives—are combined to produce an impressionist sketch of the landscape:

Sur les coteaux, le jour splendide laissait tomber des *douceurs* de *bleu* velouté dans le creux des ombres et le *vert* des arbres (p. 99).

Interchange between nouns and adjectives is not a one-way process. In French, nouns can be used adjectivally by the simple device of placing them after the term they qualify: *robe marron, ruban arc-en-ciel, style Louis XV*. In recent years, such constructions have become particularly frequent, as they are in line with the modern tendency towards brevity and condensation.[1] In this field, the Goncourts were no great innovators; they did, however, obtain some striking effects from the bold and startling juxtaposition of two nouns: 'veux-tu mes impressions *femmes* ici?' (*Salomon*, p. 46; authors' italics); 'aux reflets *rose de feu* des bobèches de bougies' (*ibid.*, p. 201); 'c'est un mariage *moire antique*' (*Mauperin*, p. 178); 'des bonshommes *farces*' (*Salomon*, p. 43); 'Maman est si *pot cassé*' (*Mauperin*, p. 178); 'des gens qui sont *turquoise* ou *vermillon*' (*Salomon*, p. 43). Some of these examples occur in letters or in direct speech and have a distinctly colloquial flavour.

NOUNS FOR VERBS

The infiltration of the noun into the province of the verb is a more complicated process. Noun and adjective are close to each other both in form and in meaning, and there are many precedents in ordinary speech for interchange between the two classes. The verb, however, is totally distinct in meaning and has an inflexion of its own. More important, the adjective is not an essential part of the sentence, whereas the verb is an indispensable element without which no utterance can be grammatically complete in French.[2] The replacement of the verb by the

[1] Cf. M. Davau, *Le Français Moderne*, vol. XVII (1949), pp. 202ff., and Harmer, *op. cit.*, pp. 140ff.

[2] Cf. O. Jespersen, *The Philosophy of Grammar*, London (1929 reimpr.), p. 86.

noun will therefore raise delicate problems, and
teresting to see how, by means of what subterfuge.
courts tried to get round these difficulties.

The extreme limits of nominal syntax are reached in tʰ.
called *verbless sentence* where the verb is not even replaced ᵥ
altogether suppressed.[1] Excluding interjections and other inarticulate utterances, verbless sentences have two main types:
they can be either exclamatory or descriptive. Of the two, the
second is by far the more interesting. Verbless exclamations
are fairly common in the spoken language where the stress of
emotion frequently dislocates the sentence. In *Manette Salomon*,
they are conspicuous in the aesthetic tirades of Chassagnol and
other painters: '. . . des plis cassés d'un style! des chairs souf-
frantes . . . des lumières boréales. . . . Et Lippi, l'amoureux
des blondes . . . Masaccio . . . un grand bonhomme! le trait
d'union entre Giotto et Raphaël . . .' (p. 104).

In the descriptive variety, the Goncourts played a decisive
part in starting a fashion which has become widespread in
modern literature. The recording of impressions as such, without any attention to syntax, was a device particularly well
suited for sketches and brief notations. It is a kind of verbal
shorthand which fixes the essential features of a picture or a
scene in a notebook, and which can be expanded and developed
later. It has been suggested that Tacitus, for whom the Goncourts had great admiration, may have served as a model for
these elliptical sentences; but no special impetus was needed for
a development which was almost inevitable.[2] Verbless sentences
abound in the Goncourts' non-fictional writings, especially in
the *Journal*. In their joint novels, however, the construction is
rare, though it becomes rather more frequent in those written by
Edmond after Jules' death. I have found no example in *Renée
Mauperin*, and the only ones which occur in *Manette Salomon* are
contained in a letter of the painter Coriolis, giving an impressionist account of his travel to the East. Here are two typical
passages of this notebook in letter form:

En selle, à trois heures du matin, une escorte d'une douzaine
d'Albanais et de Turcs, et bien entendu mon fidèle Omar. D'abord des

[1] A detailed discussion will be found in Loesch, *op. cit.*, pp. 35ff.; cf. also Lom
bard, *op. cit.*, pp. 65ff. and 77ff.; Harmer, *op. cit.*, pp. 154ff.

[2] Cf. Loesch, *op. cit.*, p. 39; Lombard, *op. cit.*, p. 82.

sentiers, des chemins bordés de lauriers-roses et de grenadiers sau-
vages. . . . De là, dégringolade dans le plaine. Des villages dominés
par de grands cyprès, de la bonne bête de grosse verdure, comme en
Normandie; des vergers avec de l'eau sourcillante sous le pied de nos
chevaux (p. 76).

At one point, there is a string of such sentences running on for
eleven lines without a finite verb, except occasionally in a subordinate clause. Yet, in spite of their boldness in matters of style,
the Goncourts seem to have shrunk back, in their novels, from
this extreme form of impressionist syntax.

Short of suppressing the verb altogether, it is possible to replace it by a weak verb, a kind of semi-auxiliary, whilst the
verbal meaning proper will be concentrated in an action-noun.
The verb best suited for this function is *avoir*,[1] which, in the
course of its history, has been largely emptied of its independent
meaning and weakened to a mere grammatical tool. A passage
in *Renée Mauperin* shows the device in its purest form. Renée is
nearing the final stage of her fatal illness. A cupping operation
is performed by her father; when the cupping-glass is applied,
'Renée *eut un sifflement* de douleur' (p. 300). Here the normal
construction would have been '*siffla* de douleur'. Instead, the
verbal process is presented as if it were a substance; it is expressed by an action-noun which becomes the object of the sentence, while the role of predicate is taken over by the weak verb
eut. By employing *avoir*, which implies no action proper, the
passive and involuntary nature of the response is emphasized,
as against the active and dynamic *siffla*. Two pages further on,
the inertness of Renée's body, her loss of control over her movements, is conveyed by the same means: 'Elle *avait des étreintes*
qui s'accrochaient maladroitement, des *caresses* qui avaient perdu
la grâce.' In this sentence, one can also see a further advantage
in using a noun for a verb: the possibility of choosing between
singular and plural, according to whether the action is single or
repeated. This nuance can also be expressed by verbal forms
such as the Imperfect, but the use of the plural lays greater
stress on this aspect.

Among the numerous examples of this device, one or two
types are particularly frequent. In the physical sphere, movements are repeatedly described this way, which is somewhat

[1] See Loesch, *op. cit.*, pp. 43f., and esp. Lombard, *op. cit.*, pp. 200ff.

surprising as such experiences would be expressed more naturally in a dynamic than in a static form: 'elle *eut une étreinte*'
(*Mauperin*, p. 166); 'Ses jambes *avaient des allongements* de
cuisse de lièvre blessé à mort' (*Salomon*, p. 307). In some
cases, the construction has a precious and artificial air: 'il *avait*,
sur le front de sa danseuse, *des bénédictions* de main à la Robert
Macaire' (*Salomon*, p. 231).[1] Sound-impressions are also
found in this combination: 'L'église *avait comme un murmure*
de voix éteintes' (*Mauperin*, p. 304); 'sa bouche *eut* pendant une
seconde *le murmure* d'une prière' (*ibid*., p. 333). Occasionally,
the same formula is applied to colours: 'Sur sa fourrure brune
. . . il *avait des bleuissements* de poils rappelant des bleus
d'aponévrose' (*Salomon*, p. 144).

Physical and mental states, attitudes and reactions are also
frequently expressed by *avoir* and an action-noun: 'Aussi
avait-elle à la voir *un épanouissement*' (*Salomon*, p. 277); 'Il
avait l'étourdissement d'un homme qui tombe dans un rêve et qui
a *l'angoisse* de tomber toujours' (*Mauperin*, p. 284); 'il *eut
l'éblouissement de* la bête féroce lâchée dans un grand cirque'
(*ibid*., p. 252). In some cases, the object of *avoir* is a quality-
noun, not an action-noun: 'Aussi n'*eut-il* point de *tristesse*'
(*Salomon*, p. 119); 'Il n'*eut aucune jalousie* de cette victoire'
(*ibid*., p. 67); 'Anatole *eut un héroïsme* à la Gribouille' (*ibid*., p.
128).

Active mental processes are seldom presented this way, and
when they are, the result is not very satisfying: 'elle *avait eu
l'imagination* de ces nouveautés bizarres qui charmèrent le
goût de la Restauration' (*Salomon*, p. 16); 'elle *avait eu aussi
l'invention* des toilettes de féerie' (*ibid*., p. 17).[2]

In another common form of nominal sentences, the action-noun
appears as subject, accompanied by a weak predicate such as

---

[1] It is characteristic of the affected tone of this passage that a neologism, the
verb *gracieuser*, occurs in the next sentence: 'Il embrassait la place des pas de la
femme qui lui faisait vis-à-vis, il se *gracieusait*.' This verb, which had existed
earlier in a different meaning, is used several times in the *Journal*; cf. M. Fuchs,
Lexique du Journal des Goncourt, Paris (1912), p. 77.

[2] Lombard, *op. cit*., pp. 210f., gives a list of action-nouns and quality-nouns
found in this combination. This list does not claim to be complete, and a number
of action-nouns which appear in the above examples are not included in it (*épanouissement, étourdissement, angoisse, étreinte, caresse, sifflement, murmure*).

c'est or *il y a*.[1] Instead of saying: 'La physionomie de madame Mauperin s'épanouissait', our authors will write: '*Il y avait* dans la physionomie de madame Mauperin . . . *un épanouissement*' (*Mauperin*, pp. 255–6). This construction offers several advantages. Like the preceding type, it presents a process as if it were a substance. Unlike the preceding type, it enables the writer to omit the agent altogether if his identity is unknown or immaterial. There is an air of impersonality and vagueness in some of the sentences built on this pattern. They are particularly effective in evoking a chaotic multiplicity of processes difficult to sort out and to attribute to specific sources:

> C'étaient des *secousses*, des *tressautements*, des *étirements*, des *tortillements* inapaisables, des *élancements* (*Salomon*, p. 308).
>
> C'était, sur la zébrure des peaux, un *remuement* presque invisible, un travail sur place et qui semblait immobile, des *avancements* et des *retraites* des muscles à peine perceptibles, d'insensibles *inflexions* de contours, de lents *déroulements*, des *coulées* de membres, des *glissements* serpentins, des mouvements qu'on eût dit arrondis par le soleil (*ibid.*, p. 214).

In these passages we have, so to speak, the raw material of experience before it is analysed and classified by our intelligence. But even where there is no uncertainty about the agent, the nominal construction may be preferred because of its greater expressive force:

> Et dans sa tête, où des restes d'ivresse flottaient sur des mirages de commandes, *c'étaient* des *échafaudages* de fortune, des *emmanchements* de hasards, des *enfilades* de travaux, des *connaissances* de grands personnages, des *rêves* à la piste de millionnaires offrant des sommes fabuleuses . . . (*Salomon*, p. 369).

Occasionally, some other weak verb—*prendre*, *mettre*, *faire* etc.—may act as grammatical predicate, while the real verb will appear in the form of an action-noun: 'Les plus petits contre-temps . . . *prenaient* . . . le *grossissement* que leur attribuent trop souvent ces natures d'êtres agités' (*Salomon*, p. 349); 'Des branches pendantes et balayantes de saules *mettaient* parfois contre les joues des *chatouillements* de chevelure' (*ibid.*, p. 106); 'des esquisses qui lui *mettaient* brusquement le

---

[1] Cf. Loesch, *op. cit.*, p. 45, and esp. Lombard, *op. cit.*, pp. 224ff.

froncement d'un pli au milieu du front' (*ibid.*, p. 198); 'Il *se faisait* en lui comme *un écroulement* de ses dernières énergies' (*ibid.*, p. 371). In the great descriptive passage which closes *Manette Salomon*, a long series of action-nouns is introduced by the formula *rien que*:

> Anatole s'y attarde comme à une mare du paradis : *rien que* des *frissonnements*, des *frémissements*, des *ondulations*, des *ébats*, des *demi-plongeons*, le *lever*, le *bain* de l'oiseau, . . . les *contentements* gonflés, les *renflements* en boule, les *hérissements*, les *rengorgements* (p. 440).

There is yet another way in which a noun can take the place of a verb. The main predicate of the sentence may remain intact while a *subsidiary verb* is changed into an action-noun. In ordinary syntax, such a subsidiary verb would appear as an infinitive or a participle or as the predicate of a subordinate clause. In the description of the Jardin des Plantes in *Manette Salomon*, there occurs this curious sentence:

> . . . le chemin ardu du labyrinthe d'où roulaient des cerceaux de gamins fabriqués de cercles de tonneaux, et des *descentes folles* de petites filles faisant sauter à leur dos des cornets à bouquin peints en bleu (p. 2).

Instead of '*descentes folles* de petites filles', ordinary usage would prefer a subordinate clause: 'de petites filles qui *descendaient follement*'. The expressive force of this unusual combination is strengthened by two further devices: the juxta-position of the action-noun *descentes* and the concrete *cerceaux*, and the change of the adverb *follement* into an adjective qualifying *descentes*.

This construction is impressionistic in the same sense as some of the others noticed in the previous section. The agent is over-shadowed by the verbal process which is detached from him and presented as a substance. At the same time, the sequence of impressions is carefully preserved by the syntax. Once again, the view from the Jardin des Plantes provides a clear example of this technique. Seen from a high point in the distance, the remote parts of Paris will appear as 'une espèce de chaos perdu dans une nuit d'ardoise'; all that one sees is 'un *fourmillement* de demeures', while farther away, 'à la dernière ligne de l'horizon, . . . l'oeil devinait une sorte d'*enfouissement* de

maisons' (*Salomon*, p. 3). Here the construction is both effective and psychologically true: the naked eye merely sees some
objects 'swarming' in the distance and, on the fringes of the
horizon, other objects which look as if they were 'buried in the
ground'; then the telescope, or the human brain, identifies
these objects as houses.

This type of syntax is often employed in the description of
movements, and in particular of complex and chaotic processes
difficult to analyse:

> Imagine là-dessous l'eau, un bruit de sources chantantes, un *ser-
> pentement* de jolis ruisseaux clairs (*Salomon*, p. 77).
>
> . . .ces passes lentes, errantes, dont elle promenait le *chatouillement*
> sur sa gorge (*ibid.*, p. 342).
>
> Il sondait et battait de son bâton . . . ces genévriers . . . à l'*emmêle-
> ment* de chevelure noueuse et fileuse (*ibid.*, p. 244).
>
> D'autres marchaient lentement, . . . enveloppées les unes et les
> autres de ce *flottement* d'étoffes, de ce *voltigement* de rubans par der-
> rière (*ibid.*, pp. 340–1).

Sometimes the same device is used to evoke quiescent states:
'Lentement le repos de la nuit descendit en s'épandant sur le
sommeil du paysage' (*Salomon*, p. 105); 'il semblait qu'on fût
à côté du *sommeil* d'un petit dieu' (*ibid.*, p. 352); 'Elle trouvait
que le lit, l'*ensevelissement* du drap, lui donnait l'air malade'
(*Mauperin*, p. 313).

When abstract ideas are treated in the same way, the construction loses much of its force. It is legitimate if the idea is
translated into a metaphor: 'Et qu'est-ce que vous auriez fait
de tout cet argent-là?—Un *ruissellement* entre mes doigts,
simplement' (*Mauperin*, p. 211). But it sounds out of place
where there is no image: 'des profils vulturins penchés sur la
délibération des intérêts' (*Salomon*, p. 104).

As elsewhere, the Goncourts are apt to overwork the device
by excessive repetition:

> Il fixait d'un trait l'effort d'une attelée de maçons, la paresse d'un
> *accoudement* sur un banc de jardin public, l'*accablement* d'un sommeil
> dans des démolitions, le *hanchement* d'une blanchisseuse au panier
> lourd, le *renversement* d'un enfant qui boit au mufle de bronze d'une
> fontaine, la *caresse* enveloppante avec laquelle un ouvrier herculéen
> porte son enfant dans des bras de nourrice (*Salomon*, p. 315).

The impressionist approach is very evident in this passage: the artist is primarily interested in catching a fleeting movement or characteristic posture, and is only incidentally concerned with the individuals whom he happens to use as his models.

ABSTRACTIONS

The general impression left behind by this survey of nominal syntax is one of abstractness. There is at first sight something fundamentally paradoxical in this result. Having set out with the aim of emulating the painter and of transcribing sense-impressions with the maximum of fidelity, the Goncourts seem to have drifted towards a highly abstract mode of vision. But on closer inspection, the paradox is found to be inevitable and somewhat deceptive. There were two reasons why linguistic impressionism was bound to evolve an abstract form of style. Firstly, the movement in painting from which it derived, and which it tried to imitate, was itself inclined towards abstraction. The recording of subjective impressions, the predominance of colour over objects, and the consequent disintegration of the material world, were important steps towards an abstract conception of art which, in more revolutionary forms, has become prevalent in our own century. As Ortega y Gasset has put it, in impressionist pictures, '. . . figures begin to become unrecognizable. Instead of painting objects as one sees them, the act of seeing itself is painted. Instead of an object, an impression is depicted, that is to say, a heap of sensations'.[1]

Another factor making for abstractness in style was inherent in the nature of language itself. If qualities were to receive more emphasis than their bearer, and processes more than the agent, this could only be done by turning them into substances. This was the only way to confer fixity and solidity on them and to give them a place of prominence within the sentence.[2] But

[1] J. Ortega y Gasset, 'Sobre el Punto de Vista en las Artes', *Revista de Occidente*, February 1924; reprinted in the volume *Goethe Desde Dentro*, Madrid (1933), p. 117.

[2] It may be noted that, according to Jespersen's theory of 'ranks' in the sentence (*Philosophy of Grammar*, pp. 96ff.), the two nominal elements, subject and object, are primaries, whereas the adjective and the verb normally appear as secondaries. The changing of a verb or an adjective into a noun will therefore mean that it is promoted from secondary to primary rank.

the linguistic resources available to this end were abstract terms: quality-nouns and action-nouns. Nominal syntax is the necessary instrument of linguistic impressionism, and nominal syntax is abstract in its very essence.

At the same time, the Goncourts' fondness for abstractions was not confined to transferred verbs and adjectives. There are in their style many other symptoms of the same abstract streak. The frequency and accumulation of abstract terms is a distinctive feature of their prose, and certain recurrent patterns are clearly discernible in their use of such expressions.

Even a cursory study of the texts reveals the omnipresence of abstract terms in our two novels. They are hardly less numerous, though rather less strident, in *Renée Mauperin* than in *Manette Salomon*. Formations in -*ment*, which were also popular with other writers of the period,[1] seem to have been specially favoured by our authors, and they are often found in pairs and whole series:

> Cette grandeur, cette maigreur flottant dans des vêtements amples, donnaient à sa personne, à sa tournure, un *dégingandement* qui n'était pas sans grâce, une sorte de *dandinement* souple et fatigué (*Salomon*, p. 145).
>
> Il n'y avait plus le *bourdonnement*, le *voltigement*, le *sifflement*, le stridulant murmure d'atomes ailés (*ibid.*, p. 295).
>
> . . . pour résister au *casernement*, à l'*énervement* de ces cinq ans, à l'*embourgeoisement* et l'*aplatissement* de ce milieu (*ibid.*, p. 60).
>
> Il contrefaisait . . . les *gloussements*, les *cacardements*, les *roucoulements*, . . . il faisait sortir, comme d'une gorge de l'Atlas, le *rauquement* du lion, un *rugissement* . . . (*ibid.*, p. 26).

The Goncourts seem to have been indifferent to the monotony of two -*ment*- formations in the same possessive phrase: 'le *commencement* de l'*entraînement*' (*Salomon*, p. 297); 'l'*enivrement* du *mouvement*' (*ibid.*, p. 143); 'l'*effacement* d'un *commencement* de somnolence' (*ibid.*, p. 381). When there was no suitable abstract term available, they did not hesitate to invent one: 'frappé de l'*ensoleillement* de ce corps de femme' (*Salomon*, p. 215); 'Il allait, par un entraînement de son tempérament, à tous les rassemblements, à toutes les agrégations, à tous les

---

[1] Cf. Ch. Bruneau, 'Noms créés au moyen du suffixe -*ment*; contribution à l'étude de la néologie chez les écrivains "décadents"', *Studies in Romance Philology and French Literature Presented to John Orr* (Manchester), 1953, pp. 23–33.

enrégimentements' (ibid., p. 369).[1] It is estimated that they have enriched the language with some seventy-five words in *-ment*.[2]

Other abstract formations are sometimes aligned in the same way, and when they are subordinated to one another the effect is not very pleasing: 'avec l'explosion de son *éloquence* du soir allumée par l'*imprudence* des *confidences* de Coriolis' (*Salomon*, p. 253); 'les jeunes filles courtisaient avec la *vivacité* de l'*ingé-nuité* ravissante des *coquetteries* russes' (*ibid.*, p. 166). Here again, the authors had no qualms about using rare words and, on occasion, coining new ones: 'ce grand côté dédaigné de l'art: la *contemporanéité*' (*Salomon*, p. 15); 'le reste des *entre-mangeries* de races' (*ibid.*, p. 420).[3]

One of the most remarkable aspects of the Goncourts' use of abstractions is the ease with which they are put in the *plural*. This is a peculiarity of the French language in general,[4] but the Goncourts extended it to words which normally have no plural, and developed it into a figure of style by their usual technique of enumerative accumulation. The construction may be used in speech and may have a colloquial and even vulgar tone:

> Ah! elle est jolie, l'hygiène, avec la gargotte, les *embêtements*, les *échignements* pour les concours, les *éreintements* d'estomac (*Salomon*, p. 115).[5]

Usually, however, it appears on a different plane, in descriptive and analytical passages:

> . . . elle trempait dans des *effacements* de pastel (*Salomon*, p. 164).
> . . . de hautes herbes ondulantes de *glissements* furtifs et de *rampements* suspects (*ibid.*, p. 244).
> . . . il s'emparait de toute la femme en la formant à des *docilités*, en lui révélant des *ivresses* . . . (*Mauperin*, p. 161).
> Il tombait dans des *béatitudes* hébétées, des *extases* idiotes, des *ahurissements* abrutis, coupés de subites *démangeaisons* bestiales (*Salomon*, p. 213).

---

[1] Cf. Fuchs, *op. cit.*, pp. 58f., where both words are listed among neologisms in the *Journal*.
[2] *Ibid.*, p. xxii.
[3] Fuchs quotes one example of *contemporanéité* from the *Journal*. The word is already attested in 1798 (Bloch-Wartburg), but Bescherelle's dictionary (1843–6) describes it as 'peu usité'. *Mangerie*, according to Fuchs, is a revived archaism.
[4] Cf. Lombard, *op. cit.*, pp. 95ff.
[5] On these three words see Fuchs, *op. cit.*, pp. 49, 53, 62.

Ses yeux . . . embrassaient ces fugitives *transparences*, ces *tendresses* et ces *tiédeurs* de couleurs, . . . ces imperceptibles *apparences* d'un bleu, d'un vert (*ibid.*, p. 164).

The advantage of the plural lies here in its ability to convey the recurrence, diversity and multiplicity of these phenomena. At the same time, the construction is often at variance with the meaning of these abstract terms which cannot easily be conceived of as plural.

Another favourite device of the Goncourts is the juxtaposition of a concrete and an abstract term, designed to give a shock to the reader:

. . . tombant la tête dans la poitrine de son amie, y cacha la *honte de son âme* et la *rougeur de son front* (*Mauperin*, p. 187).

. . . enfonçant dans l'oreiller son *désespoir* et ses *larmes* pour les y étouffer (*ibid.*, p. 308).

. . . des visages brouillés, sur lesquels se mêlait la *coupe fière de profil* des peuples de désert à des *humilités* louches de commerces douteux de grande ville (*Salomon*, p. 178).

. . . tout au bout de la plage, au bord de l'écume de la première vague, tout seul, un vieux curé s'apercevait tout noir, lisant son bréviaire en *longeant l'immensité* (*ibid.*, p. 341).

From these contrast effects, it is but a step to the *figurative* use of abstract terms. Many of these figures are metaphorical, based on some similarity or analogy between the two ideas. Occasionally, the resemblance is explicitly indicated, in the form of a comparison: 'un torse de jeune fille, encore contenu et comprimé dans sa grâce, à demi-mûr, *serré dans sa jeunesse comme dans l'enveloppe* d'un bouton' (*Salomon*, p. 184). But it is more usual for the similarity to remain implicit, which makes for greater density in the image. Some of these metaphors bring two different senses into play:[1] 'la tête d'un arbre vert, se *colorant* dans ce ciel d'hiver d'une *chaleur olive*' (*Salomon*, p. 4). But even this figure tends to acquire an abstract air in the hands of the Goncourts:

. . . se tenaient dans des poses lassées, avec des *silences affamés* (*Salomon*, p. 239).

. . . comme si elle *caressait du bout des doigts le silence* du piano (*Mauperin*, p. 199).

[1] See Sabatier, *op. cit.*, pp. 416f.

Penchée sur la musique qu'elle faisait, elle semblait battre les notes ou les caresser. . . . Elle *appuyait sur le tapage*; elle *jouait avec la mélodie* (*ibid.*, pp. 40–1).

Far more frequent are those metaphors which translate a moral quality into concrete terms: 'au frottement de ces mains qui *retâtaient* une vieille *amitié*' (*Salomon*, p. 394); 'la souffrance qui nous *enfonce la charité dans la chair*' (*Mauperin*, p. 326); 'elle *préparait* et *travaillait* son *amabilité* pour le château' (*ibid.*, p. 114).

Another group of images are metonymic, based on some relation other than similarity: action and agent, a quality and its bearer, etc. More often than not, they appear as a kind of elliptical *personification*. Instead of saying that the fashionable abbé Blampoix was consulted by mothers and expectant mothers, the Goncourts prefer the somewhat artificial figure: 'La *maternité se recommandait* à ses lumières, la *grossesse écoutait* ses prévisions' (*Mauperin*, p. 71). The whole passage is couched in the same abstract, pseudo-allegorical style:

> Les *désespoirs*, les grands *chagrins* recouraient à lui, et il leur ordonnait un voyage en Italie. . . . Ses conciliations *s'interposaient entre l'amour* des épouses et la *jalousie* des belles-mères. . . . Les *ambitions* sociales *recouraient* à son obligeance.

Elsewhere in the novel, 'des *gloires* d'Europe' meet 'des *réputations* de Paris' in the salon of Madame Bourjot (p. 117). In *Manette Salomon*, the device assumes even bolder forms: 'faisaient *retourner* jusqu'à l'*étonnement* des gens du peuple qui passaient' (p. 315); 'assis par terre et la *curiosité* de deux petites filles *dans le dos*' (p. 234); 'les *faims dévorant* les pains de huit livres' (p. 99); 'le *travail allait* à l'ouvrage' (p. 88); 'dont la *badauderie allait* instinctivement aux quartiers . . . du peuple' (p. 363). Sometimes there is a tendency to elaborate the concrete element in these images:

> . . . il y a des *admirations* stupéfiées, religieuses, et qui semblent *prêtes à se signer.* . . . Il y a des *attentions* qui ont *les mains sur le ventre,* d'autres qui restent en arrêt, *les bras croisés et le livret sous un bras, serré sous l'aisselle* (*Salomon*, pp. 155–6).
> . . . une de ces *siestes* débraillées, *étendues sur la verdure, allongées sous des ombres de branches* (*ibid.*, p. 99).

In another passage, personification develops into caricature: Anatole's histrionic performances are likened 'à l'agonie se regardant dans une cuiller à potage, et au choléra se tirant la langue dans une glace' (*Salomon*, p. 129). At one point in *Manette Salomon*, personification is raised to an almost mythological level: 'La *Nuit*, au fond de cette barque de Bohème, *embrassait au front* et dégrisait l'*ivresse* du vin bleu' (p. 106).

Even inanimate objects can be brought to life and endowed with human characteristics. In the description of two riotous parties in *Manette Salomon*, this 'animistic' vision[1] is heightened to a hallucinatory pitch. There is a nightmarish effect in all the objects suddenly awakening to life, like 'Birnam wood coming to Dunsinane':

> Les tables peu à peu marchaient vers lui, se soudaient l'une à l'autre; et tous les soupers, en se pressant, ne faisaient plus qu'un souper où les folies, débitées par Anatole, couraient à la ronde avec des bouteilles de Champagne passant de mains en mains comme des seaux d'incendie (p. 87).

> Le petit vin moussait dans les verres, les fourchettes piquaient les plats, les assiettes couraient à la ronde, les couteaux frappant sur la table demandaient des suppléments, la porte battait sans cesse, le tablier de la fille qui servait volait sur les convives, les bouteilles vides faisaient la chaîne avec les bouteilles pleines, les serviettes fouettaient les chiens. . . . Et autour de la table égayée tout riait: le grand buffet avec ses soupières à coq et sa grande tête de dix-cors; la salle à manger avec toutes ses peintures dans des baguettes de bois blanc (pp. 239–40).

Caught by the mood of the parties which they are trying to evoke, the authors become intoxicated by their own words and reverse the natural order of things: the objects are seen as the real protagonists, they are in the forefront, and the human element is only incidentally mentioned and merely provides the background of the scene.

'Les Goncourt, pétrisseurs de langage'—this is how a recent critic summed up their attitude to style.[2] The analysis of two of their novels from one particular point of view has shown the

---

[1] On the affinity between impressionism and animism, see E. Richter, *Impresionismo*, pp. 61ff. and 91ff.; cf. also Lombard, *op. cit.*, pp. 92ff. and 143ff.; Bruneau, *op. cit.*, vol. XIII, pt. 1, pp. 322ff. and *passim*.

[2] P. Descaves in *La France au Combat*, 4 July 1946.

boldness and persistence with which they moulded the French language to suit their aesthetic programme. The Goncourts were acutely language-conscious; they had a clear idea of the aims they meant to attain and of the means best suited to attain them. In their novels, prefaces and journal, they made a number of statements on the subject,[1] most trenchantly perhaps in Edmond's novel *La Faustin*:

La langue française me fait l'effet d'une espèce d'instrument dans lequel les inventeurs auraient bonnassement cherché la clarté, la logique, le gros à peu près de la définition, et il se trouve que cet instrument est, à l'heure actuelle, manié par les gens les plus nerveux, les plus sensitifs, les plus chercheurs de la notation des sensations indescriptibles, les moins susceptibles de se satisfaire du gros à peu près de leurs bien-portants devanciers.

Faced with this problem, the Goncourts did not hesitate to enrich the resources of the language, both in grammar and in vocabulary. In the preface to his last novel, *Chérie*, Edmond proudly proclaimed that the novelist would not forgo 'un tour pouvant faire de la peine aux ombres de MM. Noël et Chapsal,[2] mais lui paraissant apporter de la vie à sa phrase', and would even coin new words if no suitable term was available. We have seen how these principles were put into practice in their novels.

This constant struggle to reshape and recast a plastic and yet resistant medium must have placed a great strain on the two writers. There is no reason to doubt Edmond's statement that his brother's health was undermined by his unremitting efforts to 'faire rendre à la langue française tout ce qu'elle pouvait rendre et au delà. . . .'[3] The most curious feature of this experiment was that, on all essential points, it was in line with the basic tendencies of Modern French. The Goncourts' originality in

[1] A number of these are quoted in Loesch, *op. cit.*, pp. 13–17. Cf. also this passage in *Manette Salomon*: 'cette langue qu'ont les peintres, ces mots qui redoublent l'expression, des paroles qui ressemblent à une succession de touches, à de petits coups de pinceau avec lesquels ils semblent vouloir se montrer à eux-mêmes les choses dont ils parlent' (p. 303).

[2] This is a reference to the *Grammaire* of F.-J. Noël and Ch.-P. Chapsal, first published in 1823 and which ran to no less than eighty editions. Cf. Bruneau, *op. cit.*, vol. XII, pp. 519f.

[3] Quoted by Sabatier, *op. cit.*, p. 408. On Jules' illness see Ricatte, *op. cit.*, pp. 40f.

le lay not so much in opening new paths as in pursuing exist-
...g ones far beyond their ordinary limits.[1] All the major tendencies noticed in this chapter exist also in ordinary French,
though in a more discreet and moderate form: abstractness in
vocabulary and in grammar, preference for static rather than
dynamic presentation, frequent use of the 'style substantif', etc.
Even the most daring innovations of the Goncourts have their
prototypes in the common language: constructions like 'une
voix *de nuit*', 'une bête *de graisse*',[2] abstract terms used in a
concrete sense and placed in the plural,[3] and other similar
features.

The success of the experiment can be judged by aesthetic or
by historical criteria.   Aesthetically, the result is somewhat
mixed.   In many respects, the Goncourts were conspicuously
successful in bending the French language to the requirements of
impressionism.   One cannot but admire the virtuosity with
which they manipulated and extended the resources of the
literary idiom.   But their efforts were vitiated by some fundamental weaknesses: a certain air of affectation and preciosity;
a curious lack of sensitivity to the clumsiness of some constructions and the unpleasantness of some sound-sequences;
above all, the ease with which their innovations developed into
ready-made formulas. We have seen various examples of how
they overworked and misused some of their most valuable stylistic discoveries. The frequent recurrence of certain effects
robbed them of all novelty and hardened them into a mannerism. It was also an error of judgement to extend essentially
pictorial methods to abstract ideas which had nothing to gain
from such treatment.

Whatever the intrinsic merits of the Goncourts' style, these
were entirely out of proportion to their influence and their
historical significance. Many greater artists have left a less pro-
found mark on the literary language. The Goncourts were the
pioneers of modern prose. They stand at the starting-point of a

[1] 'Les impressionnistes semblent avoir poussé à l'extrême plutôt que répudié
certaines tendances du français d'aujourd'hui' (Bally, *Linguistique générale et linguistique française*, p. 362).
[2] Cf. 'statue *de marbre*', 'homme *d'importance*' etc.; see Bally, *ibid.*, pp. 247 and
356f., and Lombard, *op. cit.*, pp. 174ff.
[3] Cf. *des bontés, des fatalités*, 'une *des gloires* de la France'; see Bally, *ibid.*, p.
306.

number of stylistic tendencies fundamental to the contemporary novel, and it is astonishing how many of their innovations have survived and matured. Next only to Flaubert and perhaps to Chateaubriand, they were the most decisive influence in nine-teenth-century narrative prose, and it is safe to say that without them, the development of French literary style would have taken a different course.

CHAPTER IV

WORD-ORDER AS A DEVICE OF STYLE

'IL y a souvent', Stendhal once remarked, 'une physionomie dans la position des mots, qu'aucune traduction ne saurait rendre.'[1] This is probably true of most languages, but it is particularly true of French where delicate modulations and discreet nuances play such a vital part. Moreover, the mobility of words in French is severely restricted, so that any change in the pattern will be all the more effective.

Word-order is a complicated problem since the various elements of a sentence can be arranged in a number of different ways. We have already seen the valuable resource which French possesses in the mobility of the adjective (pp. 7ff.). Other parts of the sentence are equally mobile, or can at least be displaced for stylistic reasons. Flaubert, for example, often relegates an adverb to the very end of the sentence, to throw it the more into relief: 'Descendant tout en amphithéâtre et noyée dans le brouillard, elle s'élargissait au-delà des ponts, *confusément*' (*Madame Bovary*, pt. III, ch. 5). Even minor parts of speech may have some mobility: instead of *il veut me donner*, *tout lui dire*, some writers prefer *il me veut donner*, *lui tout dire*, which have an archaic note.[2] These and other refinements of word-order are, however, overshadowed by the central problem: the sequence of the main elements of the sentence, subject, verb and object.

In this respect, French word-order has been considerably impoverished since Classical Latin times. The result of this evolution has often been summed up in the formula that in Latin, word-order was stylistic, in Modern French it is largely syntactical, whereas Old French stands halfway between the two. In a highly inflected language like Classical Latin, words can be moved about freely in the sentence, without any risk of

---

[1] *La Chartreuse de Parme*, p. 293.
[2] Cf. A. Dauzat, 'Un archaïsme prétentieux: *vous le pouvez faire*; *pour se mieux porter*', Le Français Moderne, vol. IX (1941), pp. 101–14, reprinted in *Etudes de linguistique française*, 2nd ed. (1946). Cf. also Harmer, *op. cit.*, pp. 237ff.

ambiguity. The three key-terms, e.g. *miles equum videt*, can be arranged in any of the six possible sequences, and the endings will still make it clear which is the subject and which the object, that it is the soldier who sees the horse and not *vice versa*. Free from any syntactical function, word-order will be purely stylistic; it will be governed by considerations of euphony, emphasis, variety, or even pure caprice, the *mixtura verborum* which Quintilian criticized in Virgil.[1] But in a language like Modern English, *the soldier sees the horse* and *the horse sees the soldier* have different meanings: the roles are reversed while the words themselves remain unaltered. Here the function of word-order is no longer stylistic but syntactical: it is just as vital to the understanding of the sentence as the case-endings in Latin.

It follows that the disappearance of declensions is usually accompanied by the emergence of a more or less rigid word-order. This is what happened in Middle English,[2] and the Romance languages tell much the same story, though the process is not automatic and may be complicated by special circumstances.[3] In Old French, the Latin inflexions, though drastically reduced, still survive: there is a two-case declension distinguishing between nominative and accusative. The distinction is by no means general: it is confined to the masculine, and there are some exceptions even there. Yet even this rudimentary declension made it possible for word-order to retain some of its old mobility. But this mobility was already greatly restricted: of the six possible combinations of subject, verb and object, some were predominant in ordinary speech, others had a literary flavour, others again were only exceptionally used.[4] With the disappearance of declension, a more or less uniform system of word-order began to take shape in Middle French, though there was a relapse in the sixteenth century, due mainly to the

---

[1] J. Marouzeau, *Traité de stylistique latine*, p. 322.

[2] Cf. Jespersen, *A Modern English Grammar on Historical Principles*, vol. VII (1949), pp. 59ff.

[3] Spanish and Italian, for example, have a far more flexible word-order than French. This and other considerations have led E. Lerch to deny any connexion between the disappearance of declension and the standardization of word-order (*Historische französische Syntax*, vol. III, 1934, pp. 269ff.), but in view of similar developments in English and elsewhere, there is little doubt that the two processes are closely related.

[4] Cf. L. Foulet, *Petite syntaxe de l'ancien français*, 3rd ed., Paris (1930), pp. 36–44 and 306–29.

influence of Humanism. It was not till the seventeenth century that the rules still in force were established. At the end of that period, Fénelon painted the following picture—or caricature— of French sentence-structure: 'on voit venir d'abord un nomi- natif substantif, qui mène son adjectif comme par la main; son verbe ne manque pas de marcher derrière, suivi d'un ad- verbe qui ne souffre rien entre deux; et le régime appelle aus- sitôt un accusatif, qui ne peut jamais se déplacer.'[1] In other words, the order Subject-Verb-Object (or Subject-Verb-Com- plement) had become compulsory in the vast majority of French sentences.

This sequence, which has also come to prevail in English, was regarded during the classical period as the natural and logical way of arranging a sentence.[2] There is of course nothing in- trinsically natural about it, and it is only logical in the sense that it starts with the subject, stating straightaway what the sen- tence is about; then it proceeds to predicate something of the subject, adding any further information that may be required. This is in line with a fundamental tendency of French syntax, which Bally has called 'progressive sequence': the tendency so to construct a sentence that each term will be followed by that which qualifies, modifies or determines it.[3] Be that as it may, the standardization of word-order has led to an impoverishment in stylistic resources: a certain rigidity and monotony is the price which had to be paid for the simplification of flexions. This was already noticed by some contemporary writers. In *Le Bourgeois Gentilhomme*, Act II, sc. 6, the *maître de philoso- phie* confronts his bewildered pupil with five different ways of arranging a sentence, but has to admit that the best order is the one instinctively chosen by M. Jourdain. Diderot went even further; at a time when it was customary to extol the logical qualities of French, he declared, with scarcely veiled regret: 'Nous avons gagné, à n'avoir point d'inversions, de la netteté, de la clarté, de la précision, et nous y avons perdu de la chaleur, de l'éloquence et de l'énergie.'[4] Yet the view was still prevalent that inversion was somehow a regrettable lapse from natural

---

[1] *Lettre à l'Académie*, v; quoted by G. and R. Le Bidois, *Syntaxe du français moderne*, vol. II, Paris (1938), p. 4.

[2] See on this point Harmer, *op. cit.*, pp. 52ff.

[3] *Linguistique générale et linguistique française*, pp. 205, 212ff., 224.

[4] *Lettre sur les sourds et muets*, quoted in Le Bidois, *loc. cit.*

word-order—a lapse from which French had remained happily immune. 'Le français, par un privilège unique, est seul resté fidèle à l'ordre direct,' Rivarol claimed in his *Discours sur l'universalité de la langue française*,[1] while Madame de Staël saw in German word-order a sign of inferiority: 'Une construction de phrases à peu près telle qu'elle existe chez les anciens s'y est introduite plus aisément que dans aucun autre dialecte européen; mais les inversions ne conviennent guère aux langues modernes.'[2]

Nevertheless, the ban on inversion left some loopholes which have permitted, in recent times, a spectacular revival of this construction. It has been suggested that the modern vogue of inversion can be traced to the influence of Symbolism, to the disintegration of rational syntax advocated and practised by Mallarmé. Some of Mallarmé's sentences have an unmistakably twentieth-century ring:

> ... le reste mal abjuré d'un labeur linguistique par lequel quotidiennement sanglote de s'interrompre ma noble faculté poétique (*La Pénultième*).[3]

Among later writers, Proust and Gide are said to have played a major part in the rise of inversion. Meanwhile, a curious situation has arisen in contemporary French. The spoken language is strongly opposed to inversion and resorts to all kinds of subterfuges to avoid it, even in interrogative sentences. At the same time, literary usage, including journalism and academic prose, is more than ever wedded to the construction. It is an interesting barometer of modern tendencies that inversion has even found its way into examination papers.[4] These excesses have provoked harsh strictures from some grammarians;[5] even the leading authority on the subject, Professor

---

[1] Quoted by Harmer, *op. cit.*, p. 55, n. 2.

[2] *De l'Allemagne*, in the chapter 'Du style et de la versification', quoted by H. Rabe, *Die Inversion des Subjekts im Französischen des XIX. Jahrhunderts*, Diss. Tübingen (1910), p. 106.

[3] Further examples in J. Schérer, *op. cit.*, pp. 143ff. On the part played by Mallarmé, Proust and Gide, see E. Lerch, 'Die Inversion im modernen Französisch', *Mélanges Bally*, Genève (1939), pp. 347–66.

[4] See L. Foulet, 'L'influence de l'ancienne langue sur la langue moderne', *Romania*, vol. LII (1926), pp. 147–56.

[5] Cf. e.g. this passage in Boulenger and Thérive's *Les Soirées du grammaire-club:* '... nous avons une horreur naturelle pour l'inversion qui met le verbe en tête de sa proposition et lui donne une manière de panache insolent. Nos petits maîtres en

R. Le Bidois, has spoken of 'la manie de l'inversion',[1] echoing
H. W. Fowler's protests against the 'lamentable craze for inversion' in English. Most students of French would agree that
inversion can degenerate into an affectation and a mannerism;
yet they welcome the greater variety and flexibility made
possible by this device.

Inversion in Modern French can have two different forms and
two different functions.[2] From the formal point of view, it may
be either simple or complex. In simple inversion, the subject,
whether noun or pronoun, is placed after the verb instead of preceding it as usual: 'Que sais-*je*?'; 'Quand arriva la *réponse*...'.
All pronominal subjects are inverted in this way. In the case of
nominal subjects, there is also a complex type: the noun itself
stands in its normal place before the verb, but is repeated after
it in the form of a third-person pronoun: 'Votre *ami* est-*il*
déjà arrivé?' This construction represents an ingenious compromise between two conflicting tendencies: the customary
subject-verb sequence is preserved as far as the key-terms are
concerned, whereas the interrogation is expressed by the inversion of the pronoun.[3]

Cutting across this formal distinction, though not quite
independent of it, there is a fundamental duality of function: the
difference between 'grammatical' and 'stylistic' inversion. In
interrogative sentences, inversion has in French, as in many
other languages, an important grammatical role. The same

usent pourtant de façon très ridicule. Si l'on peut dire superbement "Restait cette
redoutable infanterie espagnole", il est en revanche dur et barbare d'écrire "je veux
que soient réalisées des économies dans tous les chapitres du budget". Outre que
ce passif est lourdaud il met le verbe trop en avant.' (Quoted after Müller-Hauser,
op. cit., pp. 97f.)

[1] R. Le Bidois, *L'Inversion du sujet dans la prose contemporaine* (1900–1950) *étudiée
plus spécialement dans l'oeuvre de Marcel Proust*, Paris (1952), pp. 425 ff.

[2] The latest and most comprehensive treatment of the subject is R. Le Bidois's
monograph, cited in the preceding footnote. There are many other detailed studies
on inversion; cf. in particular A. Blinkenberg, *L'Ordre des mots en français moderne*,
vol. I, Copenhagen (1928), bk. II; J. Damourette-E. Pichon, *Des mots à la pensée.
Essai de grammaire de la langue française*, vol. IV, Paris (1934), ch. XX; Lerch,
Hist. fr. Syntax, vol. III, pp. 379–461; Harmer, *op. cit.*, pp. 52–78. Further references will be found in my article, 'Inversion as a Stylistic Device in the Contemporary French Novel', *Modern Language Review*, vol. XLVII (1952), pp. 165–
80.

[3] Another compromise solution is the construction with *est-ce que*: 'Est-ce que
ton ami est déjà arrivé?' Here the inversion is confined to the introductory phrase
'est-ce', whereas the actual question has the normal subject-verb order.

applies to exclamations worded in the form of a question ('Est-ce terrible!') and to intercalated phrases like 'dit-il', 'fit-il'. Inversion is also regularly found in certain hypothetical clauses ('Dût-il en mourir', 'N'eût été la guerre'); after the adverbs *peut-être, aussi, encore, à peine* and one or two others ('Peut-être faut-il ajouter'); in some literary or archaic turns and petrified phrases ('Grande fut sa surprise', 'Advienne que pourra', 'Toujours est-il', 'Béni soit-il!'), etc. Elsewhere, inversion is purely optional, the choice between the two orders being dictated by stylistic considerations alone ('La lettre que mon frère a écrite—La lettre qu'a écrite mon frère', 'Le ministre arrive —Arrive le ministre'). There is not always a sharp demarcation-line between the two classes; in some cases of grammatical inversion, two or even three alternative constructions are possible: ('Quand viendra ton frère?—Quand ton frère viendra-t-il?—Ton frère viendra quand?'). On the whole, however, the two types are quite distinct.

Optional inversion is a happy hunting-ground for the student of style, as it is an exceptionally clear instance of the principle of choice which, as we have seen, is fundamental to modern stylistics. Take for example this sentence in Proust:

Au fur et à mesure que la saison s'avança, changea le tableau que je trouvais à la fenêtre.

As far as grammar is concerned, the sentence could have been phrased in a different way:

Au fur et à mesure que la saison s'avança, le tableau que je trouvais à la fenêtre changea.

But if both sentences are grammatically correct, the one which Proust chose had several advantages. Thanks to inversion, he was able to avoid an unbalanced construction ending on an anticlimax: the short verb *changea*, coming after the clause *que je trouvais à la fenêtre*, leaves the sentence, so to speak, in mid-air; it produces the unpleasant rhythmical effect known as 'cadence mineure'. There is also an undesirable rhyme between the two halves of the sentence: *s'avança—changea*. Syntactically, too, the alternative order is unsatisfactory: the short subject *tableau* and the equally short predicate *changea* are separated by the intrusion of a longer clause. On the positive side, the inverted order has the advantage of a skilfully contrived symmetrical pattern, a *chiasmus* (cf. above, p. 8): in the first clause, we have the order subject—verb, whereas in the second, the sequence is reversed. This is more than a mere rhetorical figure: the juxtaposition of the two verbs serves to emphasize the simultaneity and parallel course of the two processes.

The main purpose of this chapter is to study the role of inversion in the language of contemporary fiction. The problem is so complex and has so many facets that the inquiry must be broadly based: the material will be drawn from half a dozen twentieth-century novels, as different as possible in content and in style. But contemporary experiments can only be understood if set against the background of earlier usage. I shall try therefore to outline first the rise of inversion in the nineteenth century, as reflected in several novels belonging to successive generations.

1. CHATEAUBRIAND

Les Martyrs

It is usually assumed that inversion in French is largely a modern construction. This is hardly borne out by an examination of Chateaubriand's usage. In *Les Martyrs*, published in 1809 and anything but modern in style and subject-matter, optional inversion is quite common: there are nearly 300 examples, a little less than one per page. We have as yet no terms of comparison which would enable us to evaluate this figure, but it is already clear that inversion was a habitual form of sentence-structure in Chateaubriand.

In sharp contrast to the frequency of the construction is its extreme uniformity. The same limited number of patterns, grammatical as well as stylistic, recur all the time, and this monotony deprives inversion of much of its effect. Grammatically, the range of the construction is very restricted. 'Absolute' inversion—a sentence headed by a verb—is very rare: apart from one or two cases with *rester*, which are hardly optional, there is only one example: '*Viennent* ensuite les choeurs des vierges et des veuves . . .' (p. 237). Optional inversion only appears in a few types of subordinate clause: indirect questions, relative and comparative clauses, and the *c'est . . . que* combination. The overwhelming majority of examples occur in two positions: relative clauses introduced by *que* or *où*, and sentences with an initial complement, usually a complement of place.

As an element of style, inversion is fully integrated into the rhetorical manner which dominates *Les Martyrs*. The epic tone, half biblical half classicizing, which Chateaubriand affects throughout the novel, has its own particular syntax in which inversion plays an important part. Indeed some of its uses are so persistent as to become stereotyped. This is particularly true of the numerous inversions introduced by *ainsi* and by *tel*: '*Ainsi* parle la Mère des sept douleurs . . .' (p. 292); '*Ainsi* se repose un lion de Numidie' (p. 95); '*tel* paroissoit dans le sénat le mouvement de tant d'hommes divers' (p. 291). Other constructions, though less frequent, have the same rhetorical tone: sentences headed by an attribute: '*Insensé* est le mortel qui croit sa prospérité constante' (p. 288); optative exclamations: '*nous* préserve le ciel de manquer de reconnoissance!' (p. 28); '*me* préservent les dieux de mépriser les prières' (p. 34).

Chateaubriand makes full use of inversion to achieve various forms of symmetry. Contrast effects, physical or moral, can be underlined by the parallel structure of two sentences:

A l'une des extrémités de cette salle respiroit l'*Apollon*, vainqueur du serpent ennemi de Latone; à l'extrémité opposée s'élevoit le groupe de *Laocoon et de ses fils* (p. 276).
. . . à ceux-ci a été donné tout pouvoir sur *le feu, l'air, la terre et l'eau*; à ceux-là appartient la direction *des saisons, des vents et des tempêtes* (p. 44).

Even where there is no parallel syntax, inversion can help to throw an antithesis into relief:

. . . c'étoit à la *simplicité* du *premier* qu'étoit accordée la *sublimité* du *second* (p. 162).

Chateaubriand is also manifestly fond of the more elaborate symmetry based on a *chiasmus*:

. . . des *encensoirs* d'or qui *s'élèvent et retombent* avec un bruit harmonieux et d'où *s'échappent* en vapeur légère les *parfums* d'amour et d'innocence (p. 47).

Chiasmus can be reinforced by repeating the introductory adverb or phrase:

Partout la lame croissante se brise et jaillit contre les armes: *partout* disparoit le cavalier qui se noie, le fantassin qui n'a plus que son épée hors de l'eau (p. 100).

En lui la religion va triompher du sang des héros païens et des sages de l'idolâtrie; *en lui* seront honorés par un martyre oublié de l'histoire ces pauvres ignorés du monde (p. 50).

A different kind of symmetry appears in a type of descriptive sentence which is very frequent in the novel. These start with a long complement, or a series of complements, which provides, so to speak, the background for the picture. There follows a short and weak predicate, very often *s'élevoit*. In the second half of the sentence, a fully developed subject, or series of subjects, forms a rhythmical counterweight to the initial complement:

A l'extrémité du Champ de Mars, au pied du tombeau d'Octave, *s'élevoit* un tribunal de gazon surmonté d'une colonne qui portoit une statue de Jupiter (p. 248).
. . . et sur le donjon de ses tristes murs, repliés neuf fois sur eux-mêmes, *flotte* l'étendard de l'orgueil à demi consumé par la foudre (p. 122).

If the predicate is more developed, the rhythmic scheme is somewhat different; we shall then have three groups, a short one in the middle, surrounded by two more ample ones:

Sur des coursiers tachetés comme des tigres et prompts comme des aigles // se balançoient avec grâce // les cavaliers de Numance, de Sagonte et des bords enchantés du Bétis (p. 90).

Inversion is also a valuable means of emphasis: it focuses attention on the subject by placing it in an unusual position, at the rhythmic peak of the sentence. Chateaubriand likes to align a series of inverted sentences, usually three, introduced by the adverb *là* which recurs like the tolling of a bell:

Là résonne le génie de la fausse sagesse, *là* rugit l'esprit de la guerre, *là* sourit le démon de la volupté (p. 122).
Là règnent suspendues des galeries de saphirs et de diamants, foiblement imitées par le génie de l'homme dans les jardins de Baby-lone; *là* s'élèvent des arcs de triomphe formés des plus brillantes étoiles; *là* s'enchaînent des portiques de soleils, prolongés sans fin àtravers les espaces du firmament (p. 43).

These few examples will suffice to show how thoroughly inversion is harnessed to the rhetorical aims of Chateaubriand's epic style. Occasionally, he also puts it to different uses. After an adverb of time, for example, inversion can effectively under-line the simultaneity of two processes:

Tandis que, sous la protection d'Hélène, elle se croit à l'abri de tous les dangers, *déjà s'avance* vers Jérusalem le centurion qui poursuit la colombe fugitive (p. 238).

It can also emphasize the suddenness of a process: '*Alors s'élève* entre Eudore et Cymodocée une contestation à jamais mémorable' (p. 331); '*Soudain* de l'extrémité du désert *accourt* un tourbillon' (p. 159). The dramatic effect can be reinforced by onomatopoeia; in the sentence: '*Tout à coup retentit* le bruit des armes' (p. 330), the clangour of arms is directly evoked by the accumulation of five voiceless plosives, four *t*-s with one *k* in the middle. But such cases are rare; in *Les Martyrs*, inversion is still an essentially rhetorical figure.[1]

2. THREE ROMANTIC NOVELS

(La Chartreuse de Parme; Notre-Dame de Paris; Splendeurs et misères des courtisanes)

In these three novels, we find inversion discharging a number of new functions.[2] This does not mean that the frequency of the construction has increased; on the contrary, there seems to be a slight recession, due no doubt to the disappearance of some of the rhetorical effects which had relied on inversion. There are only about 200 examples in the *Chartreuse* and some fifty more in *Notre-Dame*. Balzac, on the other hand, was particularly given to this construction: *Splendeurs et misères* has yielded no less than 400 examples. Balzac even inverts the subject where the

[1] Most of the characteristic types of inversion discussed above are also in evi-dence in *Atala* and *René*. A small sample will be sufficient to show the similarity: '*Ainsi* passe sur la terre tout ce qui fut bon, vertueux, sensible' (*Atala*, p. 70); '*Malheureux* a été le ventre de ta mère, ô Atala!' (*ibid.*, p. 26); 'ces mausolées de fleurs et de verdure *que parfume* l'abeille, *que balance* le zéphyr' (*ibid.*, p. 66); 'D'un côté *s'étendent les vagues étincelantes*, de l'autre *les murs sombres* du monastère *se perdent* confusément dans les cieux' (*René*, p. 94); 'Dans une vallée au nord, à quelque distance du grand village, *s'élevoit* un bois de cyprès et de sapins, appelé le *Bois de sang*' (Atala, p. 32); '*Alors* s'expliquèrent pour moi plusieurs choses que je n'avois pu comprendre' (*René*, p. 92).

[2] Fuller details in my article, 'L'inversion du sujet dans la prose romantique', *Le Français Moderne*, vol. XXIII (1955), pp. 23–38.

normal order would have been preferable on rhythmical grounds: 'je songeais au péril où pouvait se trouver un jour Lucien' (p. 495); 'et sur toutes les figures se peignit le doute' (p. 287). He was not very sensitive to rhythm and euphony, and inversion seems to have been with him an almost mechanical habit.

The grammatical range of inversion is still limited, but it is gaining ground at several points. Absolute inversion remains an anomaly; apart from the petrified *reste*-construction and some archaizing uses in *Notre-Dame*,[1] there is only one genuine example: '*Arriva* le moment où Fabrice dut changer de place au whist' (Stendhal, p. 459). In principal propositions, there is greater variety and boldness in the use of inversion after an initial complement: '*Derrière*, s'élevait la forêt d'aiguilles du palais des Tournelles' (Hugo, vol. I, p. 196); '*à l'instant* disparut toute émotion qui la veille le touchait jusqu'aux larmes' (Stendhal, p. 217); '*Sur ce lac sublime* où je suis née, m'attend enfin une vie heureuse et paisible' (Stendhal, p. 41). The simultaneity of two processes is effectively brought out in these sentences from the *Chartreuse*.

Pendant que la femme *préparait* le déjeuner, *entra* un homme d'une trentaine d'années (p. 199).

En un clin d'oeil, et à mesure que le prince *s'avançait*, *s'établissait* dans ces salons si bruyants et si gais un silence de stupeur (p. 137).

Balzac, in his fondness for the inverted order, uses it in some combinations which are rare even today: 'car *enfin faut-il* savoir à tout moment ce qui se passe chez l'ennemi' (p. 118);[2] '*de même fait la police* pour l'honnêteté des citoyens' (p. 298).[3]

In subordinate clauses, inversion is extremely frequent but still confined to a small number of positions. There are, however, some violent dislocations which foreshadow modern usage: 'des déboires dont eût été sans doute abreuvée toute autre femme qu'elle' (Balzac, p. 316); 'Ils étaient dans la situation singulière où *se retrouva* depuis, au fameux siège de Turin, en 1640, entre le prince Thomas de Savoie qu'il assiégeait et le marquis de Leganez qui le bloquait, *le comte Henri d'Harcourt*' (Hugo,

---

[1] '*Ont été employés* à cette dite cage neuve quatre-vingt-seize solives de couches . . . et *ont été occupés* dix-neuf charpentiers . . .' (vol. II, p. 282).

[2] Cf. Le Bidois, *op. cit.*, pp. 132 and 139.   [3] Cf. *ibid.*, p. 115.

vol. II, p. 317). There is one example of inversion after *voici*: '*Voici que s'ouvre* la période orageuse des Jacqueries, des Pragueries et des Ligues . . .' (Hugo, vol. I, p. 272).[1] Stendhal sometimes inverts the subject in temporal clauses, to emphasize the suddenness of an action or the simultaneity of two processes:

> Fabrice se rapprochait de la porte par une savante manoeuvre, *lorsque vint éclater* à ses dépens un de ces petits riens de cour que la grande maîtresse savait si bien ménager (p. 455).
>
> . . . la sévérité de Clélia *semblait diminuer à mesure qu'augmentaient* les difficultés matérielles qui s'opposaient à toute correspondance (p. 137).

As a *device of style* inversion rendered valuable services to the Romantics in their quest for expressiveness. In inverted sentences, both predicate and subject stand in an unusual position: they come either earlier or later than one would expect them, and this very fact endows them with expressive possibilities. Victor Hugo is particularly skilful at emphasizing a verb by placing it in front of the subject:

> . . . de vieux toits sur lesquels *s'arrondissait* largement le chevet plombé de la Sainte-Chapelle (vol. I, p. 185).
>
> . . . tout cet orchestre . . . sur lequel *bondissait* une gamme gigantesque (vol. II, p. 189).

These constructions could be described as impressionistic in the sense that the word-order conforms to the order of perception: first we notice some shape or movement which, on closer scrutiny, is attached to a definite object (cf. above, p. 123).

Hugo often inverts the verb *s'échapper* to picture the emergence of light or of sound:

> . . . et de ses longs cils noirs baissés *s'échappait* une sorte de lumière ineffable (vol. I, p. 156).
>
> Et de toute cette foule effervescente *s'échappait*, comme la vapeur de la fournaise, une rumeur aigre, aiguë, acérée, sifflante (vol. I, p. 75).

The subject can be thrown into relief even more effectively, by delaying its arrival as long as possible. This suspense and *crescendo* effect, which we shall see in Proust at the height of its development, is already successfully practised by the Romantics:

---

[1] Cf. this sentence in Mérimée: '*Voilà qu'arrive* la voiture du colonel, avec son valet de chambre sur le siège' (*Carmen*, p. 39).

Et sur ce brancard resplendissait, crossé, chapé et mitré, le nouveau pape des fous, le sonneur des cloches de Notre-Dame, *Quasimodo le Bossu* (Hugo, vol. I, p. 107).

Sur la masse des cinq recors vêtus comme des recors, gardant leurs chapeaux affreux sur leurs têtes plus affreuses encore, et offrant des têtes de bois d'acajou veiné où les yeux louchaient, où quelques nez manquaient, où les bouches grimaçaient, se détacha *Louchard*, vêtu plus proprement que ses hommes (Balzac, p. 152).

Hugo likes to tantalize the reader by arousing his curiosity and then refusing to satisfy it:

... la chaise à bras sur laquelle était assis, le corps disgracieusement plié en deux, les genoux chevauchant l'un sur l'autre, le coude sur la table, *un personnage* fort mal accoutré (vol. II, p. 273).

Even when the subject arrives at last, we are not told directly that this undignified personage is the King of France. On the following page, we have a counterpart to this portrait: the hangman Tristan l'Hermite, standing motionless in the background, is presented in the same way.

When there is a discrepancy between the impressive *crescendo* structure and the mediocrity of the subject, the effect is one of ironical anticlimax:

... mais en revanche on a cette colonnade qui circule autour du monument, et sous laquelle, dans les grands jours de solennité religieuse, peut se développer majestueusement *la théorie des agents de change et des courtiers de commerce* (Hugo, vol. I, p. 207).

Here the irony resides mainly in the vocabulary: the contrast between *solennité religieuse*, *majestueusement*, *théorie*,[1] and *agents de change*, *courtiers de commerce*; but the syntax, with its slow and solemn cadence, helps to make the anticlimax even more striking.

In descriptive sentences, the pictorial effect of inversion is fully exploited by Hugo. He often accumulates a series of complements in front of the verb to imitate by the syntax the disorderly multiplicity of the objects described, or of the impression which they produce:

[1] *Théorie* in the sense of 'solemn procession' is an eighteenth-century borrowing from Greek (Bloch-Wartburg; cf. J. M. Gautier, *Archivum Linguisticum*, vol. III, p. 51).

Aux portes, aux fenêtres, aux lucarnes, sur les toits, fourmillaie⸀ milliers de bonnes figures bourgeoises (vol. I, p. 18).

Puis, *à droite, à gauche, à l'orient, à l'occident, dans cette enceinte si étroite pourtant de la Cité* se dressaient les clochers de ses vingt et une églises, de toute date, de toute forme, de toute grandeur (vol. I, p. 186).

Once again, inversion helps to create an impressionist effect. This is seen at its clearest in the description of an old wall in Paris, as seen from the top of *Notre-Dame*:

Derrière ces palais courait *dans toutes les directions, tantôt refendue, palissadée et crénelée, tantôt voilée de grands arbres comme une chartreuse,* l'enceinte immense et multiforme de ce miraculeux hôtel de Saint-Pol (vol. I, p. 193).

Here Hugo adopts the perspective of a contemporary spectator viewing the city from his vantage-point: the reader follows the meanderings of the sentence in the same way as the eye would follow those of the wall half-hidden in the distance.

Even such age-old rhetorical figures as repetition and chiasmus are turned by the Romantics into expressive devices. By repetition, the writer can achieve the same effect of diversity and chaos as by the accumulation of complements in the sentences just quoted:

. . . la vaste halle *où s'amoncellent* toutes les guenilles de Paris, *où grouillent* mille marchands ambulants, *où babillent* deux cents revendeuses (Balzac, p. 307).

Chiasmus is used with good effect as a means of emphasis and of contrast:

Alors apparaissent les spectres, les fantômes, *alors les rêves prennent* du corps (Balzac, p. 366).

. . . période *que l'évêque Théodore ouvre* en 618 et *que ferme* en 1227 *le pape Grégoire* (Hugo, vol. I, p. 221).

Elle était au dehors suave comme une vierge qui ne tient à la terre que par sa forme féminine, *au-dedans s'agitait une impériale Messaline* (Balzac, pp. 40–1).

Even Chateaubriand's favourite constructions suffer a sea-change in the new stylistic climate of Romanticism:

Ainsi font les castors, *ainsi font* les abeilles, *ainsi font* les hommes (Hugo, vol. I, p. 172).

Dans cette chambre sans aucune apparence se tramèrent des plans, se prirent des résolutions qui fourniraient d'étranges annales et des drames curieux, si les murs pouvaient parler. *Là* s'analysèrent, de 1816 à 1826, d'immenses intérêts. *Là* se découvrirent dans leur germe les événements qui devaient peser sur la France (Balzac, p. 109).

One significant development in the stylistic range of inversion is that it is beginning to be used as an *evocative* device. Inversion, as has been noted before, is a literary construction, alien to ordinary speech in all but its simplest forms. It is very common in scientific and legal language; in suitable contexts, it may also acquire an archaic flavour. These associations make it into an effective means of linguistic portrayal and parody. In *Les Martyrs*, where no attempt was made to imitate ordinary speech and to characterize people through their language, these possibilities remained latent. Now, the new technique of realistic portrayal is beginning to exploit them, though still on a rather modest scale. Inversion is found, for example, in legal documents and historical texts:

Je soussigné déclare rétracter entièrement ce que contient l'interrogatoire que m'a fait subir M. Camusot (Balzac, p. 363).
En cette année ont été faits par ordonnance de justice à son de trompe par les carrefours de Paris cinquante-six cris (Hugo, vol. II, p. 278).

In the *Chartreuse*, the epistolary style of the Archbishop of Parma, which the author himself describes as 'Ciceronian', contains some characteristic inversions which occur side by side with pompous verbal forms like *saisîtes* and *employâtes*:

Le curé de la paroisse qu'habite ce pécheur égaré . . . rectifier les fausses impressions qu'avaient pu causer les discours par lui proférés depuis quinze jours (p. 215).[1]

In dialogue, inversion will normally have an affected and pretentious air, except where the pathos of the situation justifies its use, as in Claude Frollo's confession of love:

[1] For a case of 'biblical' inversion in a Romantic novel, cf. this sentence in *Volupté*: 'Vous avez visité coins et recoins de vous-même, comme avant de se coucher fait dans les détours du logis la servante prudente' (Le Hir, *op. cit.*, p. 59; cf. also Bruneau, *op. cit.*, vol. XII, p. 344).

. . . ce supplice que vous font subir, durant les longues nuits, vos artèr es qui bouillonnent (Hugo, vol. ii, p. 125).

Balzac's magistrates are vividly portrayed through their stilted way of speaking:

La justice doit savoir maintenant si vous êtes ou non complice des crimes que peut avoir commis cet individu depuis son évasion (p. 348).

Au roi seul, sur le rapport du garde des sceaux, appartient le droit de faire grâce (p. 499).

Vautrin himself affects this kind of language when he tries to convince the examining magistrate that he is not an ex-convict but a Spanish priest and diplomat. He talks, as Balzac himself puts it, 'avec la dignité d'un évêque'. We have seen in an earlier chapter how carefully he chooses his words in this game of make-believe.[1] His syntax too is calculated to further this end:

Cette force factice est due, Monsieur, à l'excitation nerveuse que me cause mon étrange situation (p. 324).

La justice a commis des erreurs encore plus fortes que celle à laquelle donnerait lieu le témoignage d'une femme qui reconnaît un homme au poil de sa poitrine (p. 329).

We see the progress made by inversion since the days of Chateaubriand. Though still somewhat restricted in scope, it has become a major device of prose style, and most of its modern functions are already there, either fully developed or at least in germ.

3. FLAUBERT

L'Education sentimentale

Flaubert, as we already know, revolutionized literary syntax on a number of vital points. In the matter of inversion, however, he was no innovator. He was not averse to the construction and used it freely in certain contexts, but on the whole he handled it rather discreetly. In the *Education*, there are only 135 cases of optional inversion, an average of one on three pages, which is rather less than what we found in Chateaubriand and later writers. At the same time, a stylist like Flaubert was bound to

---

[1] See above, pp. 85f.

appreciate the value of inversion, and he showed great finesse in manipulating it.[1]

As far as grammar is concerned, Flaubert did not widen the traditional range of inversion. It is perhaps significant that in the unpublished *Première Education sentimentale*—which, it will be remembered, is quite unconnected with the later novel of the same title—there are some rather daring examples of inversion. It even occurs in positions where it has remained rare to this very day: after *de même*, where Balzac had also risked it, and after *vainement* and *comme si*: '*de même* que s'élèvent les montagnes à mesure qu'on veut les gravir' (p. 265); '*Vainement* se retournait-il de tous les côtés' (p. 214);[2] '*comme si* tout à coup fuyait sous nous le sol que l'on allait frapper du pied' (p. 204).[3] It is of course possible that Flaubert would have altered these and other sentences[4] had he decided to publish the novel. Be that as it may, his practice in the later books was far more conservative.

In the *Education sentimentale*, inversion is only used in a limited number of grammatical positions. Absolute inversion only occurs three times. Two of the examples are conventional (pp. 92 and 265), but the third has some points of interest. It appears in a speech reported in free indirect style:

Après l'abolition de l'esclavage, l'abolition du prolétariat. On avait eu l'âge de haine, *allait commencer* l'âge d'amour (p. 335).

Grammatically, this is an analogical extension of the use of inversion after verbs like *suivre*, *venir*, *apparaître*. More interesting are the stylistic implications of the statement: its dogmatic tone and air of finality. This is partly due to the terse and elliptical syntax, which is even more evident in the preceding sentence where the verb is omitted. At the same time, this type of inversion is very common in scientific and legal style ('*Est correct* ce qui correspond à la norme . . .', '*Sont soumis* à

---

[1] Full details in my article, 'Valeurs stylistiques de l'inversion dans *L'Education sentimentale*', *Le Français Moderne*, vol. xx (1952), pp. 175–88. The references in this section are to the Pléiade ed. of the *Education* and the Connard ed. of the other novels.

[2] Cf. also: '*Vainement* voulait-il quelquefois la voir sortir de cet exclusivisme' (p. 219). On inversion after *vainement*, cf. R. Le Bidois, *op. cit.*, p. 122.

[3] Cf. *ibid.*, pp. 322f.

[4] Cf. e.g.: 'De tout cela cependant résultait son état présent' (p. 244); 'Car viendra vite la saison où les feuilles tombent . . .' (p. 43).

l'impôt tous ceux qui . . .'), and these associations will cling to it even when it is used in a different register.

Apart from one solitary example with *ainsi*,[1] all inversions in principal clauses occur after complements of place or of time. In subordinate clauses too, there is great uniformity: a large number of inversions in relative clauses, a few examples in temporal ones, and one or two in other traditional positions: comparative clauses, indirect questions, and the *c'est . . . que* formula. The most striking feature of the device is its uneven distribution: nearly half the examples occur in descriptive sentences and are preceded by *où* or by a complement of place. Indeed, inversion arises almost automatically in such contexts; whenever we have a sentence starting with a complement like 'Aux deux coins de la vitrine . . .', or a clause introduced by a phrase like '. . .jusqu'à la surface des vallées où . . .', it is a safe guess that the subject will be inverted: '*Aux deux coins de la vitrine s'élevaient* deux statues en bois' (p. 425); '*jusqu'à la surface des vallées où s'avançait* la croupe d'autres collines' (p. 356).

This distribution provides a clue to the main function of inversion in Flaubert: the pictorial effect achieved by detaching the subject from its background.[2]   There was nothing essentially new in this method; it did, however, fit particularly well into Flaubert's technique of description and into the architecture of his prose. There are a number of variations on the theme. Several complements may be accumulated in front of the verb, to give an impression of chaos:

Sur des claires-voies, dans des coins, au milieu des corridors, partout s'alignaient des poteries (p. 277).

The verb may be surrounded and almost submerged by descriptive detail:

[1] In the previous novels there are some highly effective uses of inversion with *ainsi*, e.g. the famous sentence in *Madame Bovary*: '*Ainsi* se tenait, devant ces bourgeois épanouis, un demi-siècle de servitude' (p. 209), or the concluding sentence of *Salammbô*: '*Ainsi* mourut la fille d'Hamilcar pour avoir touché au manteau de Tanit.'

[2] 'Dans ces phrases, le complément placé en tête forme une sorte de fond de tableau sur lequel on fait broder le phénomène en le présentant d'abord dans sa nature propre; le soubassement du phénomène apparaît ensuite non pas tellement comme un élément de moins d'importance que comme quelque chose de plus détaché du phénomène que s'il n'y avait point d'inversion' (Damourette-Pichon, *loc. cit.*, p. 601).

face de lui se dressait, *sur une colline ronde,* un petit château à
...elles (p. 224).

. . . *le buffet de marbre, où* se pressaient, *sous des cloches de verre,* les as-
siettes de petits gâteaux . . . (p. 182).

Two pictures with the same basic design are combined in the
following sentence:

En tête et battant du tambour marchait un nègre, un ancien modèle
d'atelier, et l'homme qui portait *la bannière, sur laquelle flottait au vent*
cette inscription: 'Artistes peintres', n'était autre que Pellerin (p.
326).

Rhythmically, this sentence-structure has the great advantage
that the author can, so to speak, get the verb out of the way and
then develop the subject at leisure. This conforms to the ample
cadence of Flaubert's sentences; it is well known how anxious he
was to contrive a balanced and harmonious 'chute de phrase':

. . . sous son balcon, où palpitaient à la brise les rideaux en damas
rouge du boulevard Montmartre (p. 56).

Contre les murs étaient dressés de larges carreaux de pavage pour
salles de bain et cabinets de toilette, avec sujets mythologiques dans
le style de la Renaissance (p. 146).

In a very different context, one of Frédéric's internal monologues, inversion makes it possible to reproduce his thoughts
as they gradually take shape in his mind:

. . . tandis qu'à la porte stationnerait son tilbury, non, un coupé plutôt! un coupé noir, avec un domestique en livrée brune . . . (p. 129).

Occasionally, inversion is used by Flaubert to achieve an
impressionist effect. The best example of this technique in the
Education is found in the account of Frédéric's wanderings at
night amid the barricades:

Au milieu de cette ombre, par endroits, brillaient des blancheurs de
baïonnettes . . . (p. 315).

Here the word-order closely follows the order of impressions
as they reach Frédéric's mind. First he sees something glinting
in the dark, and it is only on further reflection that he realizes
what these white flashes are. The whole effect would be lost if
the word-order were reversed: 'Des blancheurs de baïonnettes
brillaient par endroits au milieu de l'ombre'. That this analysis
is correct is shown by the presence of another typically impres-

sionist device, one which is familiar to us from the Goncourts but which seldom occurs in Flaubert: the use of the abstract quality-noun *blancheurs* instead of the customary 'des baïonnettes blanches'.[1]

Inversion is frequently employed by Flaubert in the expression of time: after adverbs of time and in temporal clauses. Among the adverbs, *alors* is found in half a dozen cases, either with *commencer* or with a verb of movement, to mark the suddenness of an action or a change: '*Alors avait commencé* l'ère des doutes' (p. 246); '*Alors entra* un gaillard de trente ans' (p. 180). Nearly all temporal clauses with inversion are introduced by *quand*. In several cases, *quand* is followed by *tout à coup*, and this combination provides a ready-made onomatopoeic pattern for the expression of suddenness. Particularly interesting is this description of a sudden burst of rifle-fire:

> . . . et ils entraient dans la rue Caumartin, *quand tout à coup éclata* derrière eux un bruit, pareil au *craquement* d'une immense pièce de soie que l'on déchire (p. 315).

The orchestration of this sentence is very subtle. As in a similar combination which we saw in Chateaubriand (see above, p. 155), a sudden noise is evoked by the rapid succession of voiceless stops, in this case three *t*-s and three *c*-s. The vowel scheme contributes to the same effect: the four sonorous *a* sounds, culminating in *éclata*, imitate the noise of the fusillade. The onomatopoeic word *craquement* fits into the same phonetic pattern. The normal order, 'quand un bruit . . . éclata tout à coup derrière eux,' would have had very little acoustic effectiveness.

Among other uses of inversion, there are some interesting delaying effects. When the Dambreuse couple first appear in the novel, their arrival is heralded by an inversion which focuses attention on the newcomers:

> Il regagnait sa place, quand, au balcon, dans la première loge d'avant-scène, entrèrent *une dame et un monsieur* (p. 187).

[1] A similar use of *blancheur* is found in *Salammbô*, p. 159: 'Ils virent alors sur la *blancheur* de son front une longue cicatrice'. Cf. also two examples of 'impressionist' inversion in *Madame Bovary*: 'où se détachent en écorchures blanches, sur un fond d'acier gris, de loin en loin, des cygnes qui nagent' (p. 53); 'La nuit s'épaississait sur les murs, où brillaient encore, à demi perdues dans l'ombre, les grosses couleurs de quatre estampes' (p. 326).

The *chiaroscuro* of conflicting emotions in the human mind is conveyed by the same technique. A sense of guilt is pictured as a mist hovering over the feeling of grief:

. . . et par-dessus son chagrin planait dans sa conscience, comme un brouillard, le sentiment de sa lâcheté envers son ami (p. 216).

Here the syntax helps to reinforce the expressiveness of one of the rare images in the novel.

The *crescendo* structure is used with ironical intent in the description of the room of Dussardier, a pleasant young man, but not very discriminating in his tastes:

En face, contre la muraille tendue d'un papier jaune, une petite bibliothèque en acajou contenait les *Fables de Lachambeaudie*, les *Mystères de Paris*, le *Napoléon* de Norvins—et, au milieu de l'alcôve, souriait, dans un cadre de palissandre, le visage de Béranger! (p. 293).

The exclamation mark is placed there to dispel any possible doubt as to the intention of the passage.

Inversion is seldom used by Flaubert to portray the speech of his characters. Perhaps one might interpret that way the somewhat pedantic tone—note the capital *P* in *Progrès*—of the financier Dambreuse expounding his economic theory:

Donc, le seul moyen possible était de confier, comme le voulaient, du reste, les saint-simoniens, . . . la cause du Progrès à ceux qui peuvent accroître la fortune publique (p. 268),

which is not far removed from the pontifical style affected by Homais.[1]

The note of solemnity which attaches to certain inversions is put to good account in the description of the Dambreuse's arrival at the races:

Alors passa devant eux, avec des miroitements de cuivre et d'acier, un splendide landau attelé de quatre chevaux, conduit à la Daumont par deux jockeys au veste de velours, à crépines d'or (p. 238).

As was only to be expected, Flaubert found in inversion a valuable resource of style and fitted it with great skill into the new forms of sentence-structure which he had evolved. But he did not handle it experimentally and did not initiate any

---

[1] Cf. e.g.: '. . . où se heurteront quotidiennement tous les efforts de votre science' (*Bovary*, p. 111).

major changes in its use. In the history of inversion, he represents the consummation of a phase rather than the beginning of a new era.

4. E. AND J. DE GONCOURT

Manette Salomon

Although *Manette Salomon* appeared a few years before the *Éducation sentimentale*, in the matter of inversion it is much closer to modern usage.

The very first page of the novel gives some idea of the far greater density of the device. The description of the Jardin des Plantes opens with a series of inverted sentences: 'Derrière les Anglais, marchait une famille en deuil. . . . Puis suivait. . . . Venaient ensuite. . . . Un peu plus loin grimpait un interne de la Pitié.' Though this frequency is not maintained throughout the book, it remains consistently high: there are well over 300 cases of optional inversion, an average of rather more than two on three pages.[1] How partial the Goncourts were to this construction is seen from some sentences which, as a result of inversion, become somewhat unbalanced or disjointed: 'Ce qu'avait essayé de remuer Géricault' (p. 15); 'au bavardage que n'entendait même pas Crescent' (p. 277); 'et qu'apprend peut-être là aux femmes légitimes l'exemple de toutes les maîtresses' (p. 276).[2]

The range of inversion in *Manette Salomon* is rather wider than in the *Éducation*. One important difference is the greater frequency of absolute inversion: there are seven examples in the novel, two of them on two consecutive pages (pp. 98–9). All these sentences are introduced by a verb of movement: '*Venaient* ensuite . . .' (p. 1); '*Arrivaient* les jours gris, les temps de pluie' (p. 293). In two cases, they open a new chapter: '*Arrivait* l'Exposition de cette année 1853' (p. 215); '*Venait* l'été' (p. 98), which is interesting in view of a recent suggestion

---

[1] Some examples from other novels by the same authors are given in Loesch, *op. cit.*, pp. 64ff.

[2] Cf. this sentence from *Germinie Lacerteux*: 'Une provision de riz qu'avait eu la bonne idée de faire une de leurs connaissances' (p. 12, quoted by Loesch, *op. cit.*, p. 68).

that absolute inversion can never stand at the beginning of a chapter.[1]

In many cases the subject is inverted after a *complement of time*. Some of the inversions risked by the Goncourts are infrequent even in contemporary prose:[2] 'Et *toujours* revenait le refrain' (p. 190); '*Cependant* arrivait cette année dure à l'art' (p. 117); 'Et *lentement*, ainsi que ces écrans où tournent les tableaux sous les doigts d'enfants, se déroulaient les deux rives' (p. 98). Even after an adverb like *alors*, where inversion had been freely used for a long time, it can have on occasion an artificial ring:

> Et *alors* se fit dans le triste foyer, devant les cendres éteintes de leurs années vécues, l'horrible détachement de mort qui s'établit entre deux êtres vivant, mangeant, dormant ensemble . . . (p. 419).

As in earlier writers, inversion after a complement of time can help to create an impression of suddenness. The following sentence stands at the beginning of a chapter:

> *Au bout de tous ces travaux de raccroc tombait* dans l'atelier la misère que l'artiste appelle de son petit nom la *panne* (p. 109).

The position of the sentence, and the use of the strong verb *tombait*, increase the expressiveness of the construction. The same impression of abrupt change can be produced by inversion in a temporal clause:

> Et d'autres albums faisaient voir à Coriolis une volière pleine de bouquets, des ciseaux d'or becquetant des fruits de carmin,—*quand tombait*, dans ces visions du Japon, la lumière de la réalité, le soleil des hivers de Paris, la lampe qu'on apportait dans l'atelier (p. 174).

Once again the same verb is used to achieve the same effect. This sentence is also characteristic of another favourite device of the Goncourts: the verb is followed by an enumeration of a series of subjects.

In the following example, inversion after *tandis que*, reinforced by the intrusion of an adverbial phrase between predicate and subject, has a very modern air:

---

[1] L. Spitzer, 'De l'inversion "absolue"', *Publications of the Modern Language Association of America*, vol. LVI (1941), pp. 1150–62, esp. p. 1154. Cf. some examples to the contrary in Le Bidois, *op. cit.*, p. 21.

[2] Cf. Le Bidois, *ibid.*, pp. 137f.

Il faisait un de ces jours de printemps de la fin d'avril où souffle dans l'air la dernière aigreur de l'hiver, *tandis que s'essayent* sur les murs de Paris de pâles chaleurs et les premières couleurs de l'été (p. 390).

It has been suggested that Edmond de Goncourt was especially fond of inversion in temporal clauses, as the construction became increasingly frequent in the novels he wrote after his brother's death.[1]

On the whole, however, inversion in subordinate clauses is still confined in *Manette Salomon* to the traditional types. The only point where the Goncourts anticipate later tendencies is the use of inversion after *comme si*, with which Flaubert had experimented in the *Première Education*. Yet even here the shock is mitigated, as *comme si* is followed by an adverbial phrase which would have sufficed by itself to invert the subject:

. . . *c'est comme si dans un talent* crevait le fiel, cette poche, chez certains génies, de certains chefs-d'oeuvre (p. 347).
. . . *comme si, devant les morceaux de la vie de son mari vendus si bon marché*, pleurait et saignait l'orgueil qu'elle avait placé sur son talent (p. 116).

The stylistic effects which the Goncourts derive from inversion are intense and varied rather than subtle. The pictorial element is of course very prominent in a book which deals with painters and painting and abounds in descriptions. At one point in the novel, there is a series of five descriptive sentences built on the same pattern:

Elles avaient été par les boues *où marchent* les petits garçons pieds nus . . . par ces rues *où ne s'aperçoivent*, à travers la baie des portes, que des montagnes de tan. . . . Elles mettaient devant les yeux ces chemins noirs de houille qui vont le long de ces carrés marécageux *où pâturent* des rosses; ces lignes d'horizon et de collines bossues *où éclate* un blanc brutal de maison neuve, ces sentiers à côté de champs de blé blanchissant au soleil, *où finissent* les réverbères à poteaux verts (pp. 287-8).

The pictorial effect can also be heightened by accumulating descriptive details in front of the verb:

Au delà de la balustrade, dans les stalles de bois, au-dessous des peintures, se dessinaient deux spirituelles silhouettes de prêtres (p. 330).

[1] Cf. Loesch, *loc. cit.*

*u milieu de l'atelier, au plus beau jour, sur un chevalet d'acajou à col
'gne,* reposait un portrait de femme entièrement terminé et verni
(52).*

As was only to be expected, the Goncourts often use inversion to obtain *impressionist* effects. These are particularly striking on the opening pages of *Manette Salomon.* We saw in the preceding chapter some of the impressionist techniques used in the description of Paris at a distance, as seen from a high point in the Jardin des Plantes. In this passage, inversion plays a vital part. Take for instance the following sentence whose structure reflects the receding perspectives of the panorama, seen mainly in terms of colour:

> Sur le quai, les carrés de maisons blanches, avec les petites raies noires de leurs milliers de fenêtres, formaient et développaient comme un front de caserne d'une blancheur effacée et jaunâtre, sur laquelle *reculait,* de loin en loin, dans le rouillé de la pierre, *une construction plus vieille* (p. 3).

The subject seems to elude our grasp in the same way as the remote objects elude the eye. The observer is first struck by a contrast of colours; the old buildings on the fringes of the horizon are only picked out later, by focusing the eye on them. The same pattern runs through the entire passage:

> Au delà de la cime des sapins, un peu balancés, sous lesquels *s'apercevait* nue, dépouillée, rougie, presque carminée, *la grande allée du jardin* (p. 4).
>
> . . . où *s'effaçaient, se mêlaient, se fondaient,* en s'opalisant, *une fin de capitale, des extrémités de faubourgs, des bouts de rues perdues* (p. 4).

And, to take an example from another part of the novel, here is the picture of a beach so far away that one can only just see it by straining the eye:

> . . . plus loin encore, au delà de la dernière *nau,* avec cette touche nette et ce piquage de ton que l'horizon de la mer donne aux promeneurs microscopiques qui la côtoyent, se détachait une folle cavalcade d'enfants sur des ânes (p. 341).

Inversion is also used to evoke fleeting or inchoate mental processes:

> A fond de lui *passaient* des crayonnages en idée, des méditations de caricatures, des figurations bouffonnes (p. 47).

. . . et dans l'ancien élève de Langibout *se glissait et commençait à s'établir* un nouvel être (p. 371).

The construction gains in expressive force if placed in a prominent position. The following sentence opens a chapter and forms a paragraph by itself:

Et dans cet intérieur attristé *grandissait* le découragement de Coriolis (p. 353).

Akin to these cases is the use of inversion in presenting the *emergence* of some phenomenon, physical or moral. In the examples which follow, the verb is surrounded by complements so that the key-elements of the sentence emerge gradually, like the process which they express:

Et à la fin, comme sous un long modelage d'une volonté artiste, *se levait* de la forme ondulante et assouplie, *une admirable statue d'un moment* (p. 214).

De l'inconnu auquel ils vont, *commence à se lever* devant eux *la figure redoutable et nouvelle du Lendemain* (pp. 387–8).

Here a *crescendo* leads up to a complex subject culminating in the terrifying *le Lendemain*, significantly spelt with a capital *L*.

The impression of a person or object towering over a crowd can also be tellingly evoked by this type of inversion:

Du milieu de la légèreté des élégances, *se levait*, dans une couleur puissante et magnifique, *un suisse tenant de la main gauche une hallebarde* (p. 330).

One interesting feature of inversion in *Manette Salomon* is that in a number of cases it appears in the opening sentence of a chapter. Most of these sentences also form a separate paragraph. In this particular position, inversion has a strong dramatic quality: it heralds an important development, or even a turning-point in the story. As we have seen, some of the boldest forms of the device, including some cases of absolute inversion, arise in such contexts. Even where the construction is more orthodox, the dramatic effect is undiminished:

A ce triomphe du premier jour *succéda* bien vite une réaction (p. 158).

Alors commençait pour tous les deux le supplice du concubinage (p. 418).

In one such example, the dramatic quality is enchanced by a note of solemnity which is also partly due to the syntax:

A minuit, le 20 juin, *commençait* dans l'atelier de Coriolis ce bal qui devait devenir historique et laisser dans les légendes de l'art une mémoire encore vivante (p. 227).

In some cases, two inversions are combined within the same sentence. This can be done in various ways. There may be two inverted verbs connected by *et*:

Sur le ciel violet et froid, *roulait et moutonnait* le caprice d'un grand nuage (p. 311).
Au fond d'elle *dormaient et revivaient* sourdement les crédulités du passé (p. 290).

Elsewhere, the whole construction is repeated, as in the following sentence whose structure helps to evoke the quiet and drowsy atmosphere of the landscape:

. . . et il avançait dans ce silence de la forêt muette et murmurante, *où tombe* des arbres comme une pluie de petits bruits secs, *où bourdonnent* incessamment, pour le bercement de la rêverie, tous les infiniment petits de la vie (p. 243).

It may even happen that two inverted verbs follow each other without any connecting link:

Au-dessus *pesait* le ciel d'un froid ardoisé, *pendaient* des nuages arrêtés, plombés et lourds d'avance des neiges de l'hiver (pp. 294–5).

Compared to the delicate harmonies and inflexions of Flaubert's prose, some of the Goncourts' methods may appear rather crude. Yet the progress is unmistakable both in the range of inversion and in the uses to which it is put. The Goncourts were more interested in novelty and expressiveness, in the nervous tension of prose, than in harmony or euphony; they did not even shrink from disjointed and dislocated constructions if it suited their purpose.[1] On this point as on many others, they were the direct precursors of twentieth-century

[1] Cf. their acid comments on Flaubert's syntax in the *Journal*: 'Puis une trop belle syntaxe, une syntaxe à l'usage des vieux universitaires flegmatiques, une syntaxe d'oraison funèbre, sans une de ces audaces de tour, de ces sveltes élégances, de ces virevoltes nerveuses dans lesquelles vibre la modernité du style contemporain' (quoted by Moser, *op. cit.*, p. 125). See also L. Priestley, 'Reprise Constructions in French', *Archivum Linguisticum*, vol. vii (1955), pp. 1–28, esp. pp. 25f.

tendencies, though there is still a wide gap between their practice and the experiments of some of our contemporaries.

5. INVERSION IN THE CONTEMPORARY NOVEL

To secure a broad enough basis for the study of the modern position, I have examined the following six novels:[1]

> Gide, *Les Faux-Monnayeurs*
> Giraudoux, *Suzanne et le Pacifique*
> Mauriac, *Thérèse Desqueyroux*
> Proust, *Du Côté de chez Swann*, vol. I.
> Romains, *Les Amours enfantines*
> Sartre, *La Mort dans l'âme*

These six novels are representative of various types and levels of style. Sartre, Romains and Mauriac aim at three very different modes of expression: Sartre is colloquial and often vulgar, Mauriac highly literary, while Romains stands between the two and nearest to ordinary narrative practice. Proust, Gide and Giraudoux have been included because of their original and experimental use of language; the first two are considered, as we have seen, to have played a major part in the rise of modern inversion.

The first question to arise is whether optional inversion has become more frequent in the novel as a result of its modern vogue. At first glance, this question is difficult to answer as there are considerable divergencies in the frequency of the device. The two extremes are Proust and Sartre, with some 275 examples in the former and only fourteen in the latter. In the other novels, the totals range from 100 to 200, with the highest number in Gide and the lowest in Romains. It must of course be remembered that these novels are of unequal length, Mauriac's being rather shorter than the rest, and that, on the whole, they are shorter than the nineteenth-century novels we have examined.

The discrepancy between these results is not difficult to interpret. The rareness of inversion in *La Mort dans l'âme* is

---

[1] Full details in my article, 'Inversion as a Stylistic Device in the Contemporary French Novel', referred to above, p. 150, n. 2.

hardly surprising in a novel of this type. Colloquial language, it will be remembered, is hostile to inversion and tends to avoid it even in its traditional contexts. It would therefore be out of place in Sartre's dialogues, which often have a vulgar and slangy flavour, and even in the narrative passages which are also close to ordinary speech. As will be seen in the last chapter, much of the book is written in a special kind of free indirect style which, but for its looseness, would have delighted Flaubert, and it is easy to see why inversion would have been inappropriate in such a setting.

Nor is it suprising to find a heavy concentration of inversions in Proust, where their frequency is roughly one per page. There were various reasons why Proust should have been addicted to this construction. Some of the stylistic effects of inversion fitted particularly well into his aesthetic. His syntax was remote from ordinary language and would naturally welcome a literary device of this type. The legacy of Symbolism may also have played a certain part.[1] Even more important, the particular form of sentence-structure evolved by Proust made inversion almost inevitable. The intricate interlocking of clauses and parentheses—a recent critic has likened them to concentric circles[2]—found a powerful support in the possibility of inversion. Without this possibility, sentences like the following would never have arisen:

> ... le moment où je l'entendais monter, puis *où passait* dans le couloir à double porte le bruit léger de sa robe de jardin en mousseline bleue, *à laquelle pendaient* de petits cordons de paille tressée, était pour moi un moment douloureux (p. 25).

It is sufficient to rewrite such a sentence in the normal order to realize the vital role of inversion. Without it, the sentence would not only have become clumsy and unbalanced: it would have been reduced to an incomprehensible jumble. And, as every reader of Proust knows, this type of syntax is one of the distinctive features of his style.

Allowing, then, for the anomalous position of Proust and Sartre, we find that, in the four remaining novels, inversion is not much more frequent than it was in the nineteenth century.

[1] Cf. Spitzer, *Stilstudien*, vol. ii, p. 497, n.1.
[2] Devoto, *Studi di stilistica*, pp. 148f.

In some cases, it is actually less frequent. In *Les Amours enfantines*, there are relatively fewer inversions than in *Splendeurs et misères* or in *Manette Salomon*. Even in Gide and in Giraudoux, the device appears in a rather diluted form, however startling and even baffling some of its examples may be. Whatever has changed in inversion since the *fin de siècle*, there has been no significant increase in its frequency.

Nevertheless, the construction has undergone far-reaching changes in the hands of twentieth-century writers. The new vogue of inversion has made itself felt in three main ways: (*a*) the appearance of the device in a number of new positions; (*b*) the daring and even reckless manner in which some writers use it in traditional contexts; (*c*) lastly, a very considerable extension of its stylistic scope.

The new positions which inversion has conquered in recent times are certain types of subordinate clauses to which it was not admitted before. By their unusual and rather provocative appearance, these constructions are apt to attract the reader's attention; yet they are by no means frequent in our texts. They are still something in the nature of an anomaly. A few examples will suffice to illustrate the various new types:

CAUSAL CLAUSES, only three examples: '*Comme n'était jamais survenu* aucun de ce genre' (Proust, p. 170); '*parce qu'avec lui meurt* une découverte' (Giraudoux, p. 116).

FINAL CLAUSES, eleven examples: 'Il n'est pas en mon pouvoir *que soupire* à mes genoux Francis Jammes' (Romains, p. 201); '*jusqu'à ce que fût passé* le troupeau' (Mauriac, p. 114).

SANS QUE, seven examples: '*sans que la délivrât* le sommeil' (Mauriac, p. 186); '*sans que nous puissent jamais séparer* les choses accomplies' (*ibid*., p. 34).

CONDITIONAL CLAUSES, only four examples, all in Giraudoux. Two occur after *si*: 'Tant pis si je devais être un peu fatiguée et *si devait en souffrir* cette bonne forme physique . . .' (p. 119); '*Si n'en jaillissait* aussitôt une grande flamme bleue, suivie d'une flamme rouge, Rimbaud perdait sa femme' (p. 134). The other two are found after *comme si*.[1] We have seen that both Flaubert

---

[1] On Giraudoux's fondness for the phrase *comme si*, cf. G. Høst, *L'Œuvre de Jean Giraudoux*, Oslo (1942), pp. 153f.

and the Goncourts had been tempted to invert the subject after *comme si*, but the construction has remained rare even in modern times: '*comme si allait virer* ce que mademoiselle appelait chaque soir le char de la nuit' (p. 7); '*comme si venait d'avoir lieu*, à cette place, la faute qui vous change en arbre' (p. 81).

CONSECUTIVE CLAUSES, one example: '. . . à la voix si mal assurée, *que devant lui déjà cédait* la crainte à la curiosité' (Gide, p. 190).

SUBSTANTIVAL CLAUSES INTRODUCED BY 'QUE'. In 1887, Ferdinand Brunot declared of this construction that it was once freely used but had completely dropped out of modern usage, even in poetry.[1] This may well have been true at the time of writing, but it is no longer so to-day. Of the twelve examples found in our texts, nine have a complement between *que* and the verb, which makes the construction sound reasonably natural as we are accustomed to find inversion after an initial complement: '*Je savais *que là résidaient* des châtelains' (Proust, p. 246); 'Je soupçonnais *que derrière cet amour se dissimulait* un instinct de vagabondage' (Gide, p. 134). Where *que* is immediately followed by the verb, the sentence has an artificial ring: 'Parfois à un clignement, à un sursaut on devinait *que cheminait* en lui, comme une aiguille dans le corps d'un enfant, une de ses futures légendes, un de ses sarcasmes futurs' (Giraudoux, p. 209); 'en m'avouant à moi-même *qu'était de moins en moins probable* le hasard qui l'eût mise sur mon chemin' (Proust, p. 229).

SUBORDINATE CLAUSES OF THE SECOND DEGREE INTRODUCED BY 'QUE'. Subordinate clauses which are themselves dependent on a subordinate clause are a regular feature of Proust's syntax, and it is not surprising that six out of the eight relevant examples should have been found in that author: 'bien des images différentes sous lesquelles il y a longtemps *qu'est morte* la réalité pressentie' (Proust, p. 258); 'de celles (viz. conséquences) qu'il aurait cru *que pouvaient* produire seules des fautes vraiment douteuses' (*ibid.*, p. 53); 'dont l'accord prouvait *que passait* là-bas un être sur lequel les singes ne sauraient avoir d'avis' (Giraudoux, p. 100).

[1] Quoted by R. Le Bidois, *op. cit.*, p. 288.

In those positions where inversion was always permissible, modern writers can achieve strong effects by using it in unorthodox combinations. These effects can be brought about in two ways: by inverting the subject after complements which do not normally cause inversion, or by drastically dislocating the sentence and placing a heavy strain on it. Again I shall have to confine myself to a few characteristic specimens:

Absolute inversion

Although this type seems to be idiosyncratic with certain writers, such as Saint-Exupéry,[1] it is uncommon in our texts. Most of the examples are on traditional lines: '*Vint* le tour d'Hélène' (Romains, p. 63); '*Suivait* la notation' (Gide, p. 166). Sentences like '*Resta* la calme surface du Néant' (Sartre, p. 69) are usually avoided because of their slightly pedantic appearance. The most interesting example is an inversion after *et* in Giraudoux:

Tous mes sens de France s'engourdissaient,—*et s'agitaient* au contraire en moi, mais tout petits encore, des désirs subits et limités (p. 48).

Inversion in principal clauses after a complement

(*a*) *Complements of place.* This is, as we know, one of the oldest strongholds of inversion, yet even here it is possible to obtain novel effects, as a few examples from Giraudoux will show:

En moi poussaient je ne sais quels germes (p. 130).

De chaque noix de coco qui tombait, dès qu'elle touchait terre, *comme d'un obus partaient* des flammes fulgurantes qui étaient les paradisiers (p. 156).

Sur deux trépieds à mes côtés brûlent des pommes de pin, pour faire deux fumées; *du palmier de gauche au palmier de droite est tendu* derrière moi un rideau de plumes rouges, haut de trois mètres (p. 163).

Giraudoux even uses this construction when there is an object in the sentence, leaving it to the context to clarify the meaning:

Mais, *à l'extrême cime des arbres, reprenait* déjà son vacarme toute une faune ventriloque de rhinocéros et de zèbres (p. 100).

[1] Cf. *ibid.*, pp. 429ff.

(*b*) *Complements of time.* Here too there are some unusual examples: '*Jamais ne s'y trouvait* la paysanne que je n'eusse pas manqué d'y rencontrer' (Proust, p. 228); '*Aujourd'hui me revenait* cette strophe de notre petit cours de morale' (Giraudoux, p. 118); '*Trois jours dura* le printemps' (*ibid.*, p. 95).

(*c*) *Other complements.* The most interesting case is an inversion in Gide after an exclamatory *que*: 'Ah! *que paraît* salubre à tout être l'air qui n'a pas encore été respiré!' (p. 90). Note also this sentence from *Suzanne et le Pacifique*:

Et *d'elle* toujours oisive, égoïste, *nous est resté* le même souvenir que si elle s'était dévouée à une grande cause (pp. 11–12).

Subordinate clauses

(*a*) *Relative clauses.* This is still the most frequent type of all, representing well over one half of the total figure. While most of the examples are conventional, an inordinate expansion of the predicate may place a certain strain on the sentence, as in these examples from Proust:

... le plaisir *que m'avait fait toute à l'heure éprouver* leur vue (pp. 259–60).

... (les relations) ... *qu'avaient honorablement entretenues et engrangées pour leurs enfants* les familles prévoyantes (p. 36).

... *sur lesquelles* (les joues de la grand-mère), amené là par le froid ou quelque triste pensée, *était toujours en train de sécher* un pleur involontaire (pp. 24–5).

At one point, Giraudoux has a string of four parallel inversions, all hinging on the verb *donner*:

... j'éprouvais ce délire intérieur *que donne* l'idée du singe bleu, et l'apitoiement sur le mal humain *que donne* le tatou, et le dévouement pour la patrie *que donne* la petite antilope grise, et cet amour des savants, des poètes *que donne* l'antilope rayée (p. 102).

(*b*) *Temporal and comparative clauses, indirect questions, 'c'est ... que' and allied formulas.*—In these positions, inversion has always been freely used; yet even here there are some unexpected combinations:

...*quand* la nuit, dans un réveil subit, *m'arrivaient* un vers de Musset, de Shakespeare (Giraudoux, p. 130).

... *comme* à un jockey *est soudain révélé* qu'il était né pour la médecine (*ibid.*, p. 175).

. . . pour voir *de quelle nuance me laissait* aujourd'hui l'aurore (*ibid.*, p. 122).

. . . *il y avait* bien longtemps *qu'était dissipée* la brève incertitude de mon réveil (Proust, pp. 267–8).

In indirect questions, inversion is sometimes used when there is an object in the sentence; once again it is left to the context to dispel any ambiguity:

Mais je ne peux dire *quel malaise me causait* pourtant cette intrusion du mystère et de la beauté (Proust, p. 21).

J'ai souvent remarqué, chez des conjoints, *quelle intolérable irritation entretient* chez l'un la plus petite protubérance du caractère de l'autre (Gide, p. 234).

It is clear even from this rapid survey that inversion in modern prose is radically different from what it was in the days of Flaubert and the Goncourts. This impression will be further strengthened by a study of the stylistic uses of the device.

The stylistic role of inversion in contemporary prose is not basically new. Most of its functions have some precedent in nineteenth-century literature. But if the functions are essentially the same, the effects have changed very considerably, sometimes beyond recognition. A modern writer can take all sorts of liberties with syntax, and some of the intricate and ambiguous uses to which he puts inversion are only conceivable in the literary climate of our own time.

Leaving aside some of the more obvious tasks of inversion —balancing the sentence, avoiding unpleasant sound-sequences, introducing enumerations, ensuring cohesion and variety in syntax—we find it frequently and tellingly employed as a means of *emphasis*. Modern writers have their own ways of emphasizing the verb by springing it unexpectedly on the reader. This helps to stress the sudden and dramatic quality of a change:

Mais *soudain a jailli* la lueur du réverbère voisin (Gide, p. 176).

Quand dans la rue de Lima *résonnait* le clairon qui annonçait les listes de morts (Giraudoux, p. 143).

Comme un fruit caché qui serait parvenu à maturité sans qu'on s'en aperçût et se détacherait spontanément, *survint* une nuit la délivrance de la fille de cuisine (Proust, p. 153).

But even continuous processes can be emphasized by inversion:

> . . . demain, au-dessus de la barrière blanche de Tansonville, *onduleraient*, aussi nombreuses, de petites feuilles en forme de coeur (*ibid.*, p. 220).

More elaborate are the methods of emphasizing the *subject*. Even where there is no particular suspense effect, the withholding of the subject till the end of the sentence will give it special prominence. This is well brought out in an example from Proust, where two sentences, the second more ample than the first, are both built on the same ascending pattern:

> . . . le garder (le baiser de maman) pendant tout le temps que je me déshabillais, sans que se brisât *sa douceur*, sans que se répandît et s'évaporât *sa vertu volatile* (p. 39).

The care with which the child treasures his mother's kiss, fragile and evanescent, is delicately rendered by the design of the sentence.

It is characteristic of the ambivalent attitude of modern writers that most devices of style can be turned inside out, made to serve a purpose diametrically opposed to their normal role. Thus, inversion is usually designed to balance the sentence and avoid an anticlimax. On occasion, however, it is used to bring about a deliberate anticlimax which will throw a short subject into full relief:

> . . . ces acteurs de l'art, bien qu'il me fût alors inconnu, était la première forme, entre toutes celles qu'il revêt, sous laquelle se laissait pressentir par moi, l'*Art* (Proust, p. 110).

In another example from Proust, a similar effect is obtained by phonetic rather than rhythmical means:

> Legrandin se rapprochait de la duchesse, s'estimant de céder à cet attrait de l'esprit et de la vertu qu'ignorent les infâmes *snobs* (p. 188).

Attention is effectively focused here on the word *snob* which, by its phonetic structure, is expressive of Legrandin's scorn and contempt. The passage derives added piquancy from our knowledge that Legrandin is really deluding himself: he is not acting from lofty motives but is in actual fact one of the worst snobs among the many who crowd the pages of the *Temps perdu*.

The delaying effect of inversion, which is one of the classic functions of the device,[1] is fully exploited by some modern writers. In the following examples from Giraudoux, the reader is kept in a state of suspense and has to work his way through a maze of subsidiary details before being told what the sentence is about:

Déjà filait à l'avance vers le large, comme dans une petite course à pied entre amis pour contrôler leur arrivée, un gros *nuage* (p. 44).

Là, un cercle de gazon sur lequel finissaient leur vie, après mille ans de voyages de l'un à l'autre pôle, *les tortues* (p. 81).

Proust is particularly given to this type of sentence-structure, which is only one of the various delaying devices he employs:[2]

. . . et de la terre duquel (du jardin) s'élevait par deux degrés, en saillie de la maison et comme une construction indépendante, *l'arrière-cuisine* (p. 107).

Intercalé dans la haie, mais aussi *différent* d'elle qu'une jeune fille en robe de fête au milieu de personnes en négligé qui resteront à la maison, tout *prêt* pour le mois de Marie, dont il semblait faire partie déjà, *tel* brillait en souriant dans sa fraîche toilette rose, *l'arbuste catholique et délicieux* (p. 203).

In the last example, the subject is, to use Professor Spitzer's expression, 'heralded' by a series of adjectives, only to be still further delayed by inversion.

Proust derives quite unexpected effects from this device in a famous passage of *Du côté de chez Swann*. The narrator's aunt, a bedridden old lady, is tormented by entirely unfounded suspicions which centre on her maid Françoise. Unable to leave her room and spy on the maid, she becomes obsessed with the idea:

Peu à peu son esprit n'eut plus d'autre occupation que de chercher à deviner ce qu'à chaque moment pouvait faire, et chercher à lui cacher, *Françoise* (p. 171).

We have here a kind of syntactical hide-and-seek: the reader has to track down the subject in the same way as Madame Octave is trying to track down the maid in her devious and

---

[1] Cf. Bruneau, *op. cit.*, vol. XII, p. 30; Spitzer, *Stilstudien*, vol. II, pp. 465f.; Le Bidois, *op. cit.*, pp. 381ff.

[2] Cf. Spitzer, *loc. cit.*, and J. Mouton, *Le Style de Marcel Proust*, Paris (1948), pp. 116f.

secretive pursuits—which only exist, of course, in her employer's morbid imagination. It is worth pausing here for a moment to see how these implications have been rendered in the English translation. The translator, Mr Scott Moncrieff, was faced with a difficult problem. He realized that the name *Françoise* had to be withheld till the very end of the sentence; but this could not be done in English by inverting the subject. The only alternative was to rephrase the whole sentence and put it in the passive:

> And so on by degrees, until her mind had no other occupation than to attempt, at every hour of the day, to discover what was being done, what was being concealed from her by *Françoise*.

The zigzagging course of the sentence is faithfully preserved, but the impact is weaker than in Proust: the sinister schemer Françoise ought really to be the subject, actively plotting against the passive and defenceless invalid.

Modern novelists, like their predecessors, find inversion particularly useful when describing a process of emergence:

> Du fond de sa mémoire, *surgissaient*, maintenant qu'il était trop tard, des lambeaux de cette confession préparée durant le voyage (Mauriac, p. 175).
> . . . sa conversation n'était qu'un graillonnement indistinct duquel *émergeaient* de temps à autre les vocables dont elle se sentait sûre (Proust, p. 293).
> . . . pendant que par en dessous *commençait à s'enfler* le ballon des doubles jupes (*ibid.*, p. 284).

In the last sentence, the rising movement is underlined by onomatopoeic effects, especially the recurrence of *l* sounds and nasal vowels.

The ancient figure of *chiasmus* can also be successfully adapted to modern needs. There is a very elaborate example in Mauriac:

> . . . et déjà les cigales // s'allumaient // de pin en pin ///   ous le ciel // commençait à ronfler // la fournaise de la lande (p. 45).

Here the sequence Subject-Verb-Complement in the first sentence is reversed in the second. At the same time, the second verb and subject are more ample than their counterparts, and this introduces a *crescendo* rhythm into what would otherwise ᵇᵉ static symmetry.

In Giraudoux's hands, chiasmus can formulate a contrast with epigrammatic terseness:

. . . cette dignité qui soulève à Bellac une bourgeoise de la première caste quand apparaît une de la seconde (p. 124).

It can also have a precious air:

. . . je permis une fois *que la soeur de Rimbaud tombât* d'une échelle, une fois *que se noyât l'amie de Mallarmé* (p. 133).

Impressionist forms of word-order are also practised by modern writers. These may sometimes run counter to the requirements of balance and harmony. Thus, when Giraudoux writes: 'Voici que du plus gros de ces arbres s'échappe *une pie*' (p. 215), he is not trying to emphasize the subject by contriving a deliberate anticlimax; he is simply following the sequence of impressions in the spectator's mind. We see some kind of bird emerging from the tree: looking at it more closely we find that it is a magpie.[1] Elsewhere it will be a question of importance rather than priority. In the drowsy summer scene evoked in the following sentence, the air is filled with the monotonous noise made by hundreds of insects:

. . . et tandis que *bourdonnaient* les mouches, qu'au dehors *grinçaient* les cigales d'un jour de feu (Mauriac, p. 210).

The onomatopoeic overtones of the two verbs are skilfully brought into play thanks to the prominence which the syntax confers on them.

The use of inversion as an *evocative* device shows considerable progress in modern prose. The most interesting problem here is the role of inversion in direct speech. The position is rather more complicated than in the case of a form like the Past Definite, which is never used in ordinary conversation, so that whenever it appears in dialogue in a literary work there must be some special reason for its presence. Although the spoken language tends to avoid inversion, some of its simplest forms are quite current and have no pedantic air at all. A peasant

---

[1] On Giraudoux's impressionism, see Høst, *op. cit.*, pp. 152ff., and Moser, *op. cit.*, pp. 120ff. and 256ff.

girl in Proust can say quite naturally: 'Comme me disait hier encore Mme Sazerin' (p. 105). Even Sartre, normally so averse to inversion, does not hesitate to make a prisoner of war say: 'Tu n'as pas entendu ce qu'a dit Moûlu?' (p. 288). This type of inversion is even found side by side with colloquial forms like the pronoun *ça* and the phrase *un nommé*: 'Ce que m'en disait un collègue, qu'on avait chargé de *ça*, *un nommé* Leclerc' (Romains, p. 280).

There are also cases where a writer is obviously not trying to give a faithful transcription of ordinary speech. Some of Gide's characters, for instance, do not talk as people would in real life. When, combining inversion with a Pluperfect Subjunctive, a Polish lady doctor says: 'Le changement de vie, qu'entraînait la mort de son père, eût suffi' (p. 301), this might be due to professional habit or even to imperfect command of the finer nuances of French. But when the same combination occurs in the speech of Edouard's sister Pauline, who is neither a foreigner nor an intellectual (p. 397), this explanation breaks down and we simply have to accept that the author did not wish to imitate the style of ordinary conversation.

Elsewhere the writer may have felt that inversion was not out of place in the speech of cultured people, especially when discussing abstract subjects. This may account for the many examples found in Gide most of whose characters are intellectuals: writers, students, clergymen, professional people. In *Les Amours enfantines*, a conversation between Jaurès and another left-wing politician contains several turns of phrase more like a speech or a leading article than informal talk: 'C'est là où reparaît ma tare philosophique' (p. 297); 'Convaincu comme vous que d'une guerre générale sortirait la Révolution' (p. 299). Inversion is here a discreet means of portrayal through style.

When the effect is intensified, portrayal changes into *parody*. The parody may be explicit or implicit: it may be deliberately aimed at by the speaker, adopting a mockingly grandiloquent tone, or it may be a kind of pastiche where the author is laughing at the mannerisms of his characters. In *Les Faux-Monnayeurs*, there are several examples of explicit parody. Take for instance the harangue of the young cynic Strouvilhou, outlining his 'editorial policy':

Tout ce que supprimerait de délicatesses et de subtilités sentimen-
tales la production de cette humanité robuste (p. 466).

Seront considérés comme antipoétiques, tout sens, toute signification
(p. 468).

The general effect is considerably enhanced by the word-
order, especially in the second sentence, with its air of pseudo-
legal, or pseudo-scientific, finality.

The most interesting case of inversion as an element of
pastiche is its repeated use by Proust in the linguistic portrait
of Legrandin. We have already met Legrandin, the engineer
with intellectual leanings disfigured by crude snobbery. He is
one of those Proustian characters who would be quite inconceivable without their highly personal way of speaking.[1] His
style has a curious quality, engaging in some ways and not
without artistic merits, but too high-flown for ordinary conversation. His images and choice of words are matched by the
literary turns of phrase which he affects. Inversion is a recurrent feature of his speech:

. . . les oreilles ne peuvent plus écouter de musique que celle que
joue le clair de lune sur la flûte du silence (p. 184).

Quand ne sont pas encore fondues les dernières boules de neige des
giboulées de Pâques (p. 183).

Mais dans cette atmosphère humide et douce s'épanouissent le soir
en quelques instants de ces bouquets célestes, bleus et roses, qui sont
incomparables et qui mettent souvent des heures à se faner (p. 189).

Aux coeurs blessés comme l'est le mien, un romancier que vous
lirez plus tard prétend que conviennent seulement l'ombre et le silence
(p. 184).

Some of these inversions are not only very remote from
everyday speech: they are rare even in literature and have an
unmistakably Proustian stamp. Was Proust parodying his
own style through that of Legrandin, and laughing gently at

---

[1] 'Et que dire de ceux qui ne sont que langage, qui n'existent que par une
manière plus ou moins recherchée de s'exprimer. Que restera-t-il de la personnalité
de Legrandin si on supprime de son vocabulaire toute cette flore abondante qui
englobe les primevères, les barbes de chanoine, "la glorieuse vêture de soie des lis"
aussi bien que les oeillets et les hydrangeas formant un petit nuage rose au-dessus
de la mer? Que deviendrait cet homme raffiné, à mi-chemin entre une poésie
assez subtile et un touchant ridicule, s'il ne pouvait plus placer la mention de cette
musique que "joue le clair de lune sur la flûte du silence"?' (Mouton, *op. cit.*,
p. 192). Cf. also R. Le Bidois, 'Le langage parlé des personnages de Proust', *Le
Français Moderne*, vol. VII (1939), pp. 197–218.

one of his own linguistic idiosyncrasies? If so, the procedure was not isolated; it would be a case of what Professor F. C. Green has called 'a Proustian pastiche of Proust' himself.[1]

Thanks to its literary associations, inversion can acquire, in appropriate contexts, a *solemn* and slightly archaic note. This will be particularly marked when the construction is introduced by *ainsi* and when the verb stands in the Past Definite which has similar associations:

. . . aux tapis rouges qu'on y avait étendus pour la solennité et sur lesquels *s'avançait* en souriant *Mme de Guermantes* (Proust, p. 256).

Ainsi passa près de moi *ce nom de Gilberte*, donné comme un talisman . . . *Ainsi passa-t-il*, proféré au-dessus des jasmins et des giroflées, aigre et frais comme les gouttes de l'arrosoir vert (*ibid.*, p. 205).

The magic of proper names—a favourite theme of Proust's, as we shall see in the next chapter—finds here its congenial expression in the solemn and archaizing syntax.

That some writers are fully aware of these nuances can be seen from an occasional parody of the grand manner, as in this passage from Giraudoux:

Ainsi arriva à midi, un paon blanc grattant du bec sa queue . . . *l'académicien Henri de Régnier* . . . *Ainsi vint*, le soir même du jour . . . *l'académicien René Boylesve* (p. 128).

Elsewhere, inversion will have a note of *finality* which it derives partly from its solemn and archaic overtones, partly from its scientific and legal associations.[2] Once again, this nuance of inversion may be reinforced by the presence of a Past Definite, though it can also arise with other tenses:

. . . tandis qu'alentour les chemins se sont effacés et que *sont morts ceux qui les foulèrent* et le souvenir de ceux qui les foulèrent (Proust, p. 264).

---

[1] *The Mind of Proust*, Cambridge (1949), p. 40.

[2] Cf. Spitzer, *Stilstudien*, vol. II, pp. 466f. There are some parallels in the classical epic:

> *Venit* summa dies et ineluctabile tempus
> Dardaniae. *Fuimus* Troes, fuit Ilium et ingens
> gloria Teucrorum   (*Aen.* II, 324–6);

> Ἔσσεται ἦμαρ ,ὅτ' ἄν ποτ' ὀλώλῃ Ἴλιος ἱρὴ
> καὶ Πρίαμος καὶ λαὸς ἐϋμμελίω Πριάμοιο.
>   (*Il.* VI, 448–9).

... et de nouveau *régnera le silence solennel,* comme devant les nuits (Mauriac, p. 22).

Car je sens, à trop de plumes qui tombent, à trop de poil qui pousse, *qu'arrive l'année* où mes perroquets auront cent ans, mes gazelles douze ans, et commenceront à mourir (Giraudoux, p. 172).

As usual, Giraudoux likes to give the device an ironical twist. He has at one point a majestic period of seven clauses all introduced by *quand,* which lead up to the anticlimax: 'alors mourut la guenon' (p. 106).

It also happens once or twice that an entire novel, or a major section of it, ends on a sentence with inverted order. Inversion is used here not so much to mark any finality as to conclude the work on a suggestive detail which will linger on in the reader's mind. Flaubert, it will be remembered, had ended *Salammbô* in this way, and Romain Rolland concluded the tenth and last part of *Jean-Christophe* with the sentence: 'Et l'ont suivi longtemps leurs railleries et leurs rires'.[1] 'Combray', the first part of *Du Côté de chez Swann,* ends on a similar note:

... la demeure que j'avais rebâtie dans les ténèbres était allée rejoindre les demeures entrevues dans le tourbillon du réveil, mise en fuite par ce pâle signe qu'avait tracé au-dessus des rideaux le doigt levé du jour.

It is perhaps significant that one of the very few inversions in *La Mort dans l'âme,* and certainly the most daring one, appears in the final sentence of the book: 'Demain viendront les oiseaux noirs.' Inversion is barely possible after an adverb like *demain*;[2] thanks to this possibility, Sartre is able to end his novel by leading up to a sombre and mysterious image.

Looking back on the history of inversion in the last hundred and fifty years, one is struck by a series of paradoxes. There is first of all the contrast between literary style and ordinary speech. These two forms of language have evolved along diverging paths: while there has been a spectacular resurgence of inversion in literature, French conversation has become more and more inhospitable to it. But this very contrast has en-

---

[1] Quoted by R. Le Bidois, *Le Français Moderne,* vol. IX, p. 126. Cf. also Mallarmé's last instructions to his family, written the day before his death: 'pour quand le liront mes chéries' (quoted by Schérer, *op. cit.,* p. 145).

[2] Cf. R. Le Bidois, *op. cit.,* pp. 138f.

riched the construction with fresh overtones, so that its evocative power has become almost as effective as its expressive force.

In literary usage, too, there is a paradoxical situation. The French sentence is so rigidly organized that any unusual arrangement, any deviation from the norm will become all the more effective. There is therefore a natural temptation for the writer, especially the modern writer, to exploit these possibilities and even to extend their scope. But there is a real danger that the technique will defeat its own ends: the more frequent inversion becomes, the less expressive will it be. Moreover, the licences and affectations of some writers are bound to bring discredit on the whole device, though few students will accept Thérive's wholesale condemnation: 'C'est du français de version latine. C'est grotesque.'[1] Clearly there is need for moderation and self-discipline if the language is to retain one of its most subtle and most versatile resources. To become fully effective, French word-order needs a set of restrictions regulating its use: only then can it contribute to that skilful and discreet manipulation of nuances which is the supreme quality of French style.[2]

[1] Quoted by Le Bidois, *Syntaxe*, vol. II, p. 44.
[2] The following words of Bréal, written on the eve of the modern vogue of inversion, contain a timely warning: 'On a vanté la liberté du latin et du grec, qui permet soit de jeter en avant soit de réserver pour la fin le mot sur lequel on veut attirer l'attention, diriger la lumière. Mais, pour être juste, il faut reconnaître que les langues modernes, quoique habituellement restreintes à un certain ordre, n'y sont pas absolument enchaînées. Peut-être même l'inversion fait-elle d'autant plus d'effet qu'elle rompt davantage avec les habitudes de tous les jours' (*Essai de sémantique*, 6th ed., p. 219).

CHAPTER V

TRANSPOSITION OF SENSATIONS IN PROUST'S IMAGERY

1

EVERY attentive reader of Proust must have been struck by the frequency and the strange quality of images which bring two or more senses into play. A number of critics have remarked on this peculiarity, but only few of them have examined it in detail.[1] It has been suggested that Proust's fondness for this type of image was due to Symbolist influence,[2] but there is no evidence of any specific connection. Both as an aesthetic principle and as a stylistic device, transpositions had been in vogue for some time, and Proust merely developed them, with characteristic intensity, to suit his own conception of art and of style.

Transposition of sensations is a special aspect of a wider phenomenon known to psychologists as *synaesthesia*: the perception of analogies between the various senses.[3] Such analogies underlie a number of petrified metaphors in ordinary language, such as *warm voice, sweet sound, bruit aigu, teinte chaude* and many more. As a figure of speech, they are already found in Greek literature: one of the earliest modern images of this type, the red colour of the sound of a trumpet, which is mentioned by Locke and other English writers, has close parallels in Aeschylus and Euripides. In French literature, the first synaesthetic passage on a major scale is the episode of 'frozen words' in Rabelais's *Quart Livre*:

[1] See esp. J. Pommier, *La Mystique de Marcel Proust*, Paris (1939), pp. 47–55; M. E. Chernowitz, *Proust and Painting*, New York (1945), pp. 35f., 61f. and 176f.; J. Mouton, *op. cit.*, pp. 81f. and 87; J. Monnin-Hornung, *Proust et la peinture*, Genève-Lille (1951), pp. 192ff.; H. C. R. Stockwell, 'L'image dans l'oeuvre de Marcel Proust', *Modern Languages*, vol. xxv (1944), pp. 10–15; Id., 'An Analysis of a Passage in Proust', *The Cambridge Journal*, vol. v (1952), pp. 236–46; M. Hindus, *The Proustian Vision*, New York, 1954, pp. 47ff.

[2] Cf. E. Fiser, *Le Symbole littéraire*, Paris (1941), pp. 197–208; see also Professor Bisson's comments in *French Studies*, vol. i (1947), pp. 211ff.

[3] Further details and bibliographical references will be found in my *Principles of Semantics*, pp. 266–89.

Lors nous jecta sus le tillac pleines mains de paroles gelées, et sembloient dragée perlée de diverses couleurs. Nous y vismes des mots de gueule, des mots de sinople, des mots d'azur, des mots dorés. Lesquels estre quelque peu eschauffés entre nos mains fondoient comme neiges, et les oyons réalement.

Transpositions occur sporadically in Shakespeare—as for instance in the opening lines of *Twelfth Night*—and are conspicuous among the conceits of Donne and other metaphysical poets. In the eighteenth century, interest in the subject was stimulated by Castel's *clavecin oculaire* and, on a higher plane, by the debate on the delimitation of the arts, in which Lessing played a leading role. But it was not till the advent of Romanticism that the theory and practice of modern synaesthesia took shape. In France, Hugo and Gautier were the chief exponents of the new technique.[1] In his poetry, Hugo used transpositions with a concentration and virtuosity which sometimes degenerated into a mannerism. Gautier was more discreet, but focused attention on the problem in *Symphonie en blanc majeur* and other poems and in an often-quoted passage of the *Club des Hachichins*:

Les notes vibraient avec tant de puissance qu'elles m'entraient dans la poitrine comme des flèches lumineuses; bientôt l'air joué me parut sortir de moi-même; mes doigts s'agitaient sur un clavier absent; les sons en jaillissaient bleus et rouges, en étincelles électriques.

The second great wave of synaesthesia in literature came with the Symbolist movement, and was ushered in by Baudelaire's *Correspondances*:

Les parfums, les couleurs et les sons se répondent.
Il est des parfums frais comme des chairs d'enfants,
Doux comme les hautbois, verts comme les prairies.

Elaborate systems of correspondences between sounds and colours were constructed, most famous among them the scale of vowels in Rimbaud's sonnet *Voyelles*, which, as we have seen, was probably a residue of childhood experiences (cf. above, pp. 34f.). Transpositions soon became a common device in poetry and prose. Huysmans' novel *A Rebours* played a notable part in their spread, and the Wagnerian conception of the

[1] On transpositions in these two writers, see my articles in *Le Français Moderne*, 1947 and 1951. On Gautier, cf. also Matoré, *Le Vocabulaire et la société sous Louis-Philippe*, pp. 207ff.

Gesamtkunstwerk was another contributory factor.[1] On the stage the most spectacular synaesthetic experiment was the performance in 1891 of Roinard's *Cantique des cantiques*, where the various sense-impressions, including perfumes, were so coordinated as to produce a unified and harmonious effect on the audience.[2] Since the turn of the century, synaesthetic images have, if anything, gained further ground in literature. They are common in poetry; to take but one example, in Paul Eluard we find images like 'le parfum noir rayonne', 'les feuilles à l'ombre des parfums', 'mes images sont sourdes', 'cris de neige', 'la neige de ses rires'.[3] In prose they are equally prominent; we shall often meet with them when we come to discuss the imagery of some contemporary novels in the next chapter.

It was almost inevitable that Proust should realize and exploit the potentialities of synaesthetic images. The crucial part played by metaphor in his conception of art is well known: he himself stated it explicitly in his article on Flaubert, which has already been mentioned, in his analysis of Elstir's paintings and elsewhere, most strikingly perhaps in this passage of *Le Temps retrouvé*:

> La vérité ne commencera qu'au moment où l'écrivain prendra deux objets différents, posera leur rapport analogue dans le monde de l'art à celui qu'est le rapport unique de la loi causale, dans le monde de la science, et les enfermera dans les anneaux d'un beau style, ou même, ainsi que la vie, quand en rapprochant une qualité commune à deux sensations, il dégagera leur essence en les réunissant l'une et l'autre pour les soustraire aux contingences du temps, et les enchaînera par les liens indescriptibles d'une alliance de mots.

The reason why, among the various types of metaphor, Proust should have been particularly given to synaesthetic

[1] See A. G. Lehmann, *The Symbolist Aesthetic in France*, Oxford (1950), pp. 207–215. Professor Lehmann is right in pointing out that the doctrine of correspondences and the Wagnerian conception are not only distinct but incompatible: the former is based on the similarity of the sensations involved, the latter on their co-existence within the same complex experience. But, as we shall see later, both kinds of relation may lead to synaesthetic transpositions. On Wagner's influence see also Monnin-Hornung, *op. cit.*, pp. 199ff.

[2] See G. Maurevert, 'Des sons, des goûts et des couleurs. Essai sur les correspondances sensorielles', *Mercure de France*, vol. ccxcii (1939), pp. 541–85, esp. pp. 561ff. Cf. Gide's remarks in *Journal des Faux-Monnayeurs*, Paris (1927), p. 72.

[3] The first of these examples is from the volume *L'Amour la poésie*, the others from *La Vie immédiate*.

transpositions, is not far to seek. His interest in sensations for their own sake and because of their evocative power was fundamental to his whole psychological system.[1] In his efforts to transcribe sense-impressions with the maximum of accuracy, analogies drawn from other senses were an invaluable resource; they added, so to speak, a new dimension to the original experience. At a different level, the analysis of works of art and of their impact on the mind could be greatly broadened and deepened by adducing parallels from other arts. There were also specifically stylistic reasons. Proust was fascinated by language; he was for ever experimenting with new forms of expression and exploring their possibilities, and his imagination was fired by the rich and bold effects which could be obtained from the intermingling of the senses.

His interest in the problem can also be gauged from some explicit references. He makes some extravagant claims about the possibilities of transposition: '. . . tout peut se transposer, et . . . un univers seulement audible pourrait être aussi varié que l'autre'.[2] Noting that there is a subtle correspondence between Albertine's voice and her features, he adds: 'sa voix était comme celle que réalisera dit-on le photo-téléphone de l'avenir, dans le son se découpait nettement l'image visuelle' (*Jeunes filles*, vol. II, p. 206).[3] When watching Albertine and her companions at Balbec, he feels as though his eyes were acting for all his senses: 'comme déléguée des autres sens . . . capables, grâce aux arts de la transposition, au génie de synthèse où excelle le désir, de restituer sous la couleur des joues ou de la poitrine, l'attouchement, la dégustation, les contacts interdits' (*ibid.*, pp. 173–4). There is also a reference to Gautier's synaesthetic poem: 'les boules de neige qui n'avaient peut-être dans la pensée de la maîtresse de la maison d'autre but que de faire "symphonie en blanc majeur" avec son ameublement et sa toilette' (*ibid.*, vol. I, p. 189), and a significant mention of Baudelaire in a complex image which posits analogies between different arts:

---

[1] Cf. G. Poulet, *Etudes sur le temps humain*, Edinburgh (1949), pp. 387ff.

[2] Cf. Pommier, *op. cit.*, p. 49.

[3] Cf. R. Virtanen, 'Proust's Metaphors from the Natural and the Exact Sciences', *Publications of the Modern Language Association of America*, vol. LXIX (1954), pp. 1038–59, esp. p. 1042.

. . . le soleil . . . ajoutait à leur lainage (viz. of the red carpets) un velouté rose, un épiderme de lumière, cette sorte de tendresse, de sérieuse douceur dans la pompe et dans la joie qui caractérisent certaines pages de Lohengrin, certaines peintures de Carpaccio, et qui font comprendre que Baudelaire ait pu appliquer au son de la trompette l'épithète de délicieux (*Swann*, vol. I, p. 256).[1]

These and other passages give the impression of a high degree of consciousness and deliberateness in the use of transpositions; and this impression is fully confirmed by an analysis of the synaesthetic images themselves.

2

In order to study Proust's synaesthesias in all their complexity and ramifications, it will be necessary to go beyond the limits of a single novel. I have therefore examined the imagery of three books: *Du Côté de chez Swann*, *A l'ombre des jeunes filles en fleurs*, and the first volume of *Le Côté de Guermantes*. This does not mean a departure from the method which has been followed so far in these essays. The three books are three consecutive and closely connected parts of *A la recherche du temps perdu* and represent therefore an extensive sample from a work which it would have been impracticable to examine in its entirety from this particular point of view.[2]

The first impression which emerges from our material is the extraordinary richness and density of synaesthetic associations. It is impossible to state the exact number of transpositions since many of them are too intricate to be resolved into their components. But one can form a rough idea of their frequency: if complex images and series of images with the same synaesthetic background are counted as one example, there is an approximate total of over three hundred transpositions. This total, which does not include clichés like *voix perçante*, would of course be considerably higher if the complex synaesthetic structures could be disentangled. Even so, the figure is impres-

[1] On affinities between Baudelaire and Proust, see R. Galand, 'Proust et Baudelaire', *Publications of the Modern Language Association of America*, vol. LXV (1950), pp. 1011–34, esp. pp. 1032f.

[2] A number of examples from the later volumes of the *Temps perdu* are given by Monnin-Hornung, *loc. cit.*; the same critic suggests (p. 192) that correspondences between sight and sound are more numerous in the early parts of the work.

sive, especially if it is remembered that most transpositions occur in descriptive or analytical passages and that there are hardly any in the dialogues which abound in these novels.

The frequency of synaesthetic images is matched by their variety. They range from simple adjectival phrases to elaborate patterns running into several pages. In some cases, the analogy between the two sensations is stated explicitly, in the form of a comparison: 'Et le plaisir que lui donnait la musique . . . *ressemblait* . . . au plaisir qu'il aurait eu à expérimenter des parfums' (*Swann*, vol. ii, p. 34); 'nuancer la sonorité de la voix *comme si* celle-ci n'était qu'une transparente enveloppe' (*Swann*, vol. i, p. 33). A more intimate fusion of the two senses is achieved when the similarity is left implicit. There are many examples of a noun and an adjective belonging to two different spheres of sensation: *odeur obscure* (*ibid.*, p. 108); 'la *sonorité mordorée* du nom de Brabant' (*ibid.*, p. 20). Often the similarity is apparent rather than real: what happens is simply that the adjective is transferred from its own noun to another.[1] Proust speaks, for example, of the 'brown dryness' of Albertine's hair (*Jeunes filles*, vol. ii, p. 198): the adjective *brown*, which logically qualifies *hair*, is grammatically attached to *dryness* and thus gives rise to a synaesthetic image. Combinations like 'donner une *douceur mauve* au ciel pur' (*Guermantes*, vol. i, p. 95), and 'la *fraîcheur* ombreuse et *dorée* des bois' (*ibid.*, p. 183) have the same grammatical structure.

Simple transpositions involving only two terms may also arise in other types of phrase: possessive constructions: 'je pensai aux *couleurs* . . . desquelles j'allais enfin savoir le *goût*' (*Jeunes filles, vol.* ii, p. 208); adjective and complement: *savoureux à regarder* (*Guermantes*, vol. i, p. 171); subject and predicate: 'par sa blancheur il (viz. le *front* d'Albertine) *mordait* fortement dans mes regards' (*Jeunes filles*, vol. ii, p. 206).

These simple images may be complicated in various ways. Three sensations may be combined instead of two. Of the three, two may belong to the same sphere; in 'le double *tintement* timide, *ovale* et *doré* de la clochette' (*Swann*, vol. i, p. 26), an acoustic term is qualified by two visual adjectives. Elsewhere, three different sensations are packed into a terse phrase; thus,

---

[1] These are cases of 'hypallage' not unlike the transferred adjectives which we saw in the Goncourts; cf. above, p. 124.

the transposition 'savoureux à regarder', which was noted above, is expanded elsewhere into 'savoureuses au toucher du regard' (*Jeunes filles*, vol. ii, p. 135), interlinking three different senses: taste, touch and sight. By further enriching the basic design, Proust arrives at elaborate structures of interlocking imagery, cast into the characteristic moulds of his involved syntax.[1] Here is a typical example of such a complex transposition:

Et ç'avait déjà été un grand plaisir quand au-dessus de la petite ligne du violon mince, résistante, dense et directrice, il avait vu tout d'un coup chercher à s'élever un clapotement liquide, la masse de la partie de piano, multiforme, indivise, plane et entrechoquée comme la mauve agitation des flots que charme et bémolise le clair de lune . . il avait cherché à recueillir la phrase ou l'harmonie . . . qui lui avait ouvert plus largement l'âme, comme certaines odeurs de roses circulant dans l'air humide du soir ont la propriété de dilater nos narines (*Swann*, vol. i, p. 300).

The final stage in the development of synaesthetic images is reached when the initial metaphor becomes the starting-point of a long series of variations on the same theme. Proust, like Hugo, is apt to be carried away by the rhythm of his own imagery and to abandon himself to what might be called a 'chain-reaction' of images, one transposition setting off another. There is such a chain-reaction in the crucial passage when Swann is listening to the *petite phrase de Vinteuil* at Mme de Saint-Euverte's party (*Swann*, vol. ii, pp. 186–94). The images evoked by the music are predominantly visual, but other senses are also involved:

Murmurée comme un parfum . . . cours sinueux et rapide . . . douceur rétractée et frileuse . . . bulle irisée . . . Tel un arc-en-ciel . . . aux deux couleurs qu'elle avait jusque là laissé paraître, elle ajouta d'autres cordes diaprées, toutes celles du prisme, et les fit chanter.

Somewhat different are the images which punctuate the

[1] Some critics suggest that Proust was thinking of his own style when describing Chopin's music in synaesthetic terms: 'les phrases, au long col sinueux et démesuré, de Chopin, si libres, si flexibles, si tactiles, qui commencent par chercher et essayer leur place en dehors et bien loin de la direction de leur départ, bien loin du point où on avait pu espérer qu'atteindrait leur attouchement, et qui ne se jouent dans cet écart de fantaisie que pour revenir plus délibérément—d'un retour plus prémédité, avec plus de précision, comme sur un cristal qui résonnerait jusqu'à faire crier—vous frapper au coeur' (*Swann*, vol. ii, pp. 164–5; cf. A. Feuillerat, *Comment Marcel Proust a composé son roman*, New Haven (1934), p. 130, and R. Le Bidois, *op. cit.*, pp. Xf.).

narrator's reverie about a journey to Italy and about the famous 1.22 train to Balbec, 'magnifiquement surchargé de noms' (*ibid.*, pp. 243 ff.). This series has a simpler, essentially linear structure: it aligns the pictures and colours which the names of towns call up in the narrator's mind: 'Parme . . . compact, lisse, mauve et doux'; 'Bayeux si haute dans sa noble dentelle rougeâtre et dont le faîte était illuminé par le vieil or de sa dernière syllabe'; 'le doux Lamballe qui, dans son blanc, va du jaune coquille d'oeuf au gris perle'; 'Coutances, cathédrale normande, que sa diphtongue finale, grasse et jaunissante, couronne par une tour de beurre.'

It is not surprising that some of Proust's most daring and most sustained synaesthetic images should have been inspired by music and by the magic of proper names. These two themes were among those which most frequently called forth a synaesthetic response in his mind.

3

There are, as we shall see in the next chapter, two basic forms of imagery: metaphor and metonymy. Metaphor is grounded in some kind of *similarity* or analogy between the two terms, whereas metonymy is based on association by '*contiguity*': the two terms, though dissimilar, are part of the same experience or are connected in some other way. Synaesthesia lies astride the boundary between the two types: some transpositions are metaphorical, others metonymic.

The great majority of Proust's transpositions are of the *metaphorical* variety. The analogy may be intellectual or emotive, transparent or recondite, or even entirely subjective; it may be no more than a vague equivalence or parallelism in structure, as in the scales of colours, tastes and scents which he posits, echoing Huysmans (*Guermantes*, vol. I, p. 74); but there is usually some kind of correspondence underlying the association between two senses. Whether the analogy seems far-fetched or not, there can be no doubt that the image is metaphorical, not metonymic, when he speaks of 'le couloir, le filtre obscur du son' (*Swann*, vol. II, p 34), when he likens the peals of the bell at Combray to 'quelques gouttes d'or que la chaleur y avait lentement et naturellement amassées' (*Swann*, vol. I, pp. 239–40), or when he materializes the light shining in Odette's window 'entre les volets qui en pressaient la pulpe mystérieuse et dorée' (*Swann*, vol. ii, p. 83).

But Proust was also attracted to the second type of transpositions: those based on the contiguity of the two sensations, their occurrence in the same mental context.[1] His interest in sense-impressions was not confined to their intrinsic quality and to the analogies which they suggested; he was equally intrigued by their power to call up other sensations and the entire context of experience with which they were associated. Hence the importance of sensations in that process of 'involuntary memory' which is fundamental to Proust's conception of time.[2] Here I am only concerned with the synaesthetic aspect of the problem: the calling up of sensations by an associated but dissimilar sense-impression. Proust himself has repeatedly analyzed this process. When relating his first great revelation, the psychological shock which he received from a piece of *madeleine* dipped in tea, he calls taste 'la contemporaine, l'inséparable compagne' of visual form (*Swann*, vol. i, p. 71). He pictures sight as a kind of window: 'le regard à la fenêtre duquel se penchent tous les sens, anxieux et pétrifiés' (*ibid.*, p. 204). The coolness of his room at Combray gives him a vicarious experience of the summer in all its aspects: '. . . offrait à mon imagination le spectacle total de l'été dont mes sens, si j'avais été en promenade, n'auraient pu jouir que par morceaux' (*ibid.*, p. 123). Sound can act in the same way: 'l'ouïe, ce sens délicieux, nous apporte la compagnie de la rue dont elle nous retrace toutes les lignes, dessine toutes les formes qui y passent, nous en montrant la couleur'.[3] This constant preoccupation with the unity of experience and the evocative power of sensations explains Proust's fondness for *metonymic* transpositions.

The simplest form of these images is the transferred epithet which has already been noted: 'the brown dryness of her hair' instead of 'the dryness of her brown hair'. Elsewhere, the connection is less obvious and the clue is hidden in the context; for example, the somewhat baffling expression, 'la surface azurée du silence' (*Swann*, vol. i, p. 129), becomes at once intelligible if related to the passage which precedes it: the description of a

---

[1] Cf. Pommier, *op. cit.*, p. 54.   [2] Cf. Poulet, *op. cit.*, pp. 373ff.
[3] *La Prisonnière*, vol. i, p. 158, quoted after Monnin-Hornung, *op. cit.*, p. 196.

quiet and sunny afternoon with a blue sky. Even more intricate are those cases where some sort of recondite similarity is implied, whereas on closer inspection it turns out to be a purely external, accidental relationship. Thus, the 'couleur vive, *empourprée* et charmante' of the name *Champi*, in George Sand's novel *François le Champi* (*ibid.*, p. 66), is not just another instance of Proust's habit of attaching colours to proper names: it was doubtless suggested by the red binding of the book, casually mentioned on the preceding page.[1]

Not all such images are based on the coexistence of two sensations in one experience; they may derive from more remote connections. The yellow colour and the tower of butter evoked by *Coutances* is no doubt connected with the butter trade for which that town is famous.[2] It may also happen that the transposition is suggested, not by an association of ideas, but by a chance assonance of the two words. The name *Guermantes*, for example, appears to the narrator as a 'nom amarante et légendaire' (*Guermantes*, vol. I, p. 13); later on he speaks more specifically of the 'couleur amarante de la dernière syllabe' (*ibid.*, p. 188). There can be little doubt that the phonetic similarity between *Guermantes* and *amarante* was the ultimate source of this image.

4

The part played by transpositions in the texture of the *Temps perdu* can best be appreciated by studying the main contexts in which they arise, the types of experience which tend to invite such associations. In Proust as in other writers, the majority of synaesthetic images centre on impressions of sound and, to a lesser extent, those of sight; but other sensations can also be described in terms of a different sense. The wealth of material is such that a few illustrations will have to suffice for each of the major groups.

Sound-impressions. The subject which lends itself most readily to synaesthetic treatment is the recording of musical experi-

---

[1] A far more complicated case has been analysed by Dr. Stockwell (*Cambridge Journal*, vol. v, pp. 238ff.), who has shown that an elaborate synaesthetic description in *La Prisonnière* is an echo of various passages in the earlier volumes.

[2] Cf. Pommier, *op. cit.*, p. 50.

ences.[1] Every detailed analysis of music in the volumes examined contains transpositions on a lavish scale, in particular those passages which deal with the *petite phrase* of Vinteuil and with its effects on Swann. As we have seen, all senses may participate in the description of music. Even taste and touch can furnish some unexpected analogues: the *petite phrase* recedes 'parmi les ramifications de son parfum' (*Swann*, vol. i, p. 304); emerging from sleep, the narrator's consciousness 'n'était touchée qu'avec douceur par les pointes aiguës des fifres qui la caressaient comme un vague et frais gazouillis matinal' (*Guermantes*, vol. i, p. 77). But most of the images are drawn from the visual sphere. Occasionally, effects of colour and of light are introduced, as in the description of the *petite phrase* which was quoted above (p. 195); elsewhere, the transcription is rather in terms of lines, shapes, surfaces or more complex configurations. Some of the analogies are kept fairly general:

Sans doute les notes que nous entendons alors, tendent déjà, selon leur hauteur et leur quantité, à couvrir devant nos yeux des surfaces de dimensions variées, à tracer des arabesques, à nous donner des sensations de largeur, de ténuité, de stabilité, de caprice (*Swann*, vol. i, p. 300).

But music can also conjure up full and detailed pictures. The sound of fanfares reminds the narrator of 'les gerbes épanouies d'un bouquet jaillissant et sonore' (*Guermantes*, vol. i, p. 77); the high notes of the violin preparing the arrival of the *petite phrase* are likened to a door held open (*Swann*, vol. ii, p. 183), to a waterfall, with the small figure of a passer-by silhouetted against it (*ibid.*, p. 71), and, on two occasions, to a 'rideau sonore' (*Swann*, vol. i, p. 304; vol. ii, p. 71). These transpositions have a pictorial quality[2] which comes even more forcefully to the fore when music is compared to painting. We have already seen that Proust perceives a certain affinity between *Lohengrin* and some of Carpaccio's pictures. He also establishes a parallel between the Vinteuil sonata and the paintings of Pieter de Hooch:

. . . la tenue des trémolos de violon que pendant quelques mesures

[1] See F. Hier, *La Musique dans l'oeuvre de Marcel Proust*, New York (1933), pp. 71ff.
[2] Cf. Chernowitz, *op. cit.*, pp. 61ff., and Monnin-Hornung, *op. cit.*, pp. 133ff.

on entend seuls, occupant tout le premier plan, puis tout d'un coup ils semblaient s'écarter et comme dans ces tableaux de Pieter de Hooch qu'approfondit le cadre étroit d'une porte entr'ouverte, tout au loin, d'une couleur autre, dans le velouté d'une lumière interposée, la petite phrase apparaissait (*Swann*, vol. I, p. 313).

In some cases, music is even personified: the various motifs of the music played in the restaurant at Rivebelle are pictured as women ogling, accosting and caressing the guests (*Jeunes filles*, vol. I, p. 103).

Another acoustic theme rich in synaesthetic associations is the sound of proper names.[1] The third chapter of *Du Côté de chez Swann* is entitled 'Noms du pays: le nom'. Here and elsewhere, Proust developed a full theory of proper names. He saw in them an important factor in the fundamental discrepancy between imagination and reality, a problem which often exercised him in the *Temps perdu*. 'Sans doute', he wrote, 'les noms sont des dessinateurs fantaisistes, nous donnant des gens et des pays des croquis si peu ressemblants que nous éprouvons souvent une sorte de stupeur quand nous avons devant nous au lieu du monde imaginé, le monde visible' (*Jeunes filles*, vol. I, p. 112). Our imagination is stirred by the sound of names; we paint them in different colours in the successive periods of our life, until the moment comes when they lose their lustre: 'les noms ont perdu toute couleur comme une toupie prismatique qui tourne trop vite et semble grise' (*Guermantes*, vol. I, p. 12).[2]

Colours have a prominent place in the associative aura of proper names. The most persistent of these associations is the colour of the name *Guermantes*, which recurs almost like a leitmotiv, symbolizing the narrator's youthful enthusiasm for that aristocratic family. He likes to imagine the name 'baignant comme dans un coucher de soleil dans la lumière *orangée* qui émane de cette syllabe: "antes"' (*Swann*, vol. I, p. 247; cf. *ibid.*, p. 252, and *Guermantes*, vol. I, p. 27). There are also minor variations: *amarante*, which we have already seen, and the more explicit image: 'sentir dans ce nom, des aspects de bois *jaunissants* et tout un mystérieux coin de province' (*ibid.*, p. 188).

The associations induced by proper names are not necessarily

---

[1] See esp. J. Vendryes, 'Marcel Proust et les noms propres', in *Choix d'études linguistiques et celtiques*, Paris(1953), pp. 80–8.

[2] On optical imagery in Proust, cf. Virtanen, *loc. cit.*, pp. 1048f.

visual. Like a bubble or a pricked balloon, they may emit the scent stored in them (*Jeunes filles*, vol. i, p. 212; *Guermantes*, vol. i, pp. 11–12). They may be moulded and chiselled into a monument (*Jeunes filles*, vol. i, p. 209). They may even have a taste of their own and may be savoured 'comme un vin de derrière les fagots' (*Jeunes filles*, vol. ii, p. 44). There are also more fully developed images. The name *Faffenheim* 'gardait . . . les lourdes "délicatesses" germaniques projetées comme des branchages verdâtres sur le "Heim" d'émail bleu sombre qui déployait la mysticité d'un vitrail rhénan, derrière les dorures pâles et finement ciselées du XVIIIe siècle allemand' (*Guermantes*, vol. i, p. 230). When Gilberte calls the narrator by his Christian name, her words 'eurent l'air de me dépouiller, de me dévêtir, comme de sa peau un fruit dont on ne peut avaler que la pulpe' (*Swann*, vol. ii, p. 268), whereas her own name, when he hears it in Combray and later on in the Champs-Elysées, prompts his imagination to synaesthetic fantasies as it passes him, 'aigre et frais comme les gouttes de l'arrosoir vert; imprégnant, irisant la zone d'air pur qu'il avait traversée . . . jetant une petite bande merveilleuse et couleur d'héliotrope impalpable comme un reflet' (*Swann*, vol. i, p. 205; vol. ii, p. 255).

Other acoustic phenomena may also invite synaesthetic images. The human voice, its inflections and intonations, interest Proust chiefly as symptoms of character and indications of origin. He detects in the voice of Mme de Guermantes 'l'or paresseux et gras d'un soleil de province' (*Guermantes*, vol. i, p. 184), and in that of Albertine and her playmates 'un tableau vivement coloré . . . le tableau original, unique de son individualité' (*Jeunes filles*, vol. ii, p. 186), 'la savoureuse matière imposée par la province originelle d'où elles tiraient leur voix et à même laquelle mordaient leurs intonations' (*ibid.*, p. 189). The voice of the hotel manager at Balbec is full of the scars of earlier accents forcefully removed (*Jeunes filles*, vol. i, p. 213). The actress Mme Berma exercizes a distant fascination on the narrator's mind; his imagination dwells with delight on the magic voice lending fresh enchantment to the lines of *Phèdre* which he pictures as bathing 'dans l'atmosphère et l'ensoleillement de la voix dorée' (*ibid.*, p. 15). When, later on, he actually sees her on the stage, the image becomes more precise; her voice, attitudes, gestures and costume appear to him as so many superimposed layers: 'des coulées de substances diverses, devenues translucides, dont la superposition ne fait que réfracter plus richement le rayon central et prisonnier' (*Guermantes*, vol. I, p. 44)—one of Proust's numerous images from crystallography.[1] In comparison, the voice of other actresses seems impenetrable like marble (*ibid.*, p. 43). The narrator is also profoundly shaken by his telephone conversation with his grandmother, a premonition of her impending death. Her disembodied voice, 'vue, sans le masque du visage', surprises him by its 'douceur presque décantée de toute dureté', and he is also intrigued by the unseen presence of the telephone operators, 'les Danaïdes de l'invisible qui sans cesse vident, remplissent, se transmettent les urnes des sons' (*ibid.*, pp. 120 f.).[2]

The spoken word is repeatedly presented as a chemical agent capable of solidifying and forming into a crust, thus blocking the channels of our inner life (*Swann*, vol. II, pp. 116 and 198). In Swann's mind, during his infatuation with Odette, certain words 'passaient à l'état solide, s'y durcissaient comme une incrustation, le déchiraient, n'en bougeaient plus', while others 'circulaient aisément en lui, . . . étaient fluides, faciles, respirables' (*ibid.*, p. 143). A mineral analogy of the same kind underlies a striking simile about the ambiguity of the word *grand*, which may denote both physical and moral greatness. The maid Françoise falls into the trap laid by her mother-tongue; she imagines that the two kinds of greatness are somehow inseparable:

. . . n'ayant que ce seul mot de 'grand' pour les deux choses, il lui semblait qu'elles n'en formaient qu'une seule, son vocabulaire, comme certaines pierres, présentant ainsi par endroit un défaut et qui projetait de l'obscurité jusque dans la pensée de Françoise (*Guermantes*, vol. I, p. 21).

Occasionally, synaesthetic associations may develop around non-human noises. The cooing of pigeons appears to Proust as 'irisé, imprévu, comme une première jacinthe, déchirant doucement son coeur nourricier pour qu'en jaillît, mauve et satinée, sa fleur sonore' (*Guermantes*, vol. I, p. 128; cf. *Swann*, vol. I, p. 107). The sudden irruption of outside noises on our ears is registered as 'la lumière, le plein soleil du son . . aveuglant'

---

[1] Cf. Virtanen, *loc. cit.*, pp. 1041f.   [2] Cf. *ibid.*, p. 1042.

(*ibid.*, p. 68). Curiously enough, even silence can be transposed: it can be visualized as a surface (*Swann*, vol. i, p. 129; *Jeunes filles*, vol. i, p. 21; *Guermantes*, vol. i, p. 68), materialized as 'une clôture immatérielle, sans doute, mais impénétrable, . . . tranche interposée d'atmosphère vide' (*ibid.*, p. 110), and even conceived of in terms of taste: 'L'air y était saturé de la fine fleur d'un silence si nourricier, si succulent que je ne m'y avançais qu'avec une sorte de gourmandise' (*Swann*, vol. i, p. 76). Some of these images have a hallucinatory quality. After the passage of a tram-car, 'le silence . . . me semblait parcouru et strié par une vague palpitation musicale' (*Guermantes*, vol. i, p. 125; cf. *ibid.*, p. 63). The peals of distant bells are visualized with an intensity reminiscent of Gautier's experience in the *Club des Hachichins*:

. . . où parvenaient jusqu'à nous, horizontaux, affaiblis, mais denses et métalliques encore, les sons de la cloche de Saint-Hilaire qui ne s'étaient pas mélangés à l'air qu'ils traversaient depuis longtemps, et côtelés par la palpitation successive de toutes leurs lignes sonores, vibraient en rasant les fleurs, à mes pieds (*Swann*, vol. i, p. 245).

Visual impressions. Synaesthetic transcriptions of light and colour are fairly frequent in Proust, but they are inferior in quality and in range to the acoustic group. Three characteristic motifs recur with some persistence. A number of images evoke visual impressions in musical terms, thus inverting the more usual process of translating music into visual imagery.[1] A sunset in Venice is likened to 'l'écho invisible pourtant d'une dernière note de lumière indéfiniment tenue sur les canaux comme par l'effet de quelque pédale optique' (*Guermantes*, vol. i, p. 131). When the setting sun illumines the top of the old stones in the church at Combray, these, 'adoucies par la lumière, paraissaient tout d'un coup montés bien plus haut, lointaines, comme un chant repris "en voix de tête", une octave au-dessus' (*Swann*, vol. i, p. 97). Elsewhere, the growing intensity of light on a stone building is compared to a *crescendo* in music (*Swann*, vol. ii, pp. 257–8).

Rather more interesting are those images which present light and shade as solid substances. Among the fairly numerous metaphors developing this analogy, there are a number of bold and highly expressive transpositions. We have seen that the light

[1] Cf. Hier, *op. cit.*, pp. 60ff.

in a window is pictured as a pulp squeezed by the shutters. Light is also compared to a curtain (*Guermantes*, vol. I, p. 141) and, on two occasions, to the epidermis (*Swann*, vol. I, p. 256; *Guermantes*, vol. I, p. 275). Two young men in a salon give the impression of 'une condensation de la lumière printanière et vespérale' (*ibid.*, pp. 190–1); similarly, the wine left at the bottom of a glass seems like 'une condensation du jour' (*Jeunes filles*, vol. II, p. 153). There are also more elaborate effects. In the Bois de Boulogne, 'la lumière épaississait comme des briques et . . . cimentait grossièrement contre le ciel les feuilles des marronniers' (*Swann*, vol. II, p. 294). In one of Elstir's pictures, the morning sun, 'inventant comme de nouveaux solides', builds a crystal staircase in the sea (*Jeunes filles*, vol. II, p. 127). Colours too can be materialized: Mme de Guermantes's red velvet dress seems to isolate her by 'l'espèce de claustration que la violence de la couleur mettait autour d'elle'; it is like a 'matérialisation des rayons écarlates d'un coeur que je ne lui connaissais pas' (*Guermantes*, vol. I, p. 130).

Akin to the motif of the solidification of light is that of its liquefaction. The lamps in a restaurant 'faisaient sourdre à flots la lumière' (*Jeunes filles*, p. 229); a stained glass window in the old church at Combray 'tremblait et ondulait en une pluie flamboyante et fantastique qui dégouttait du haut de la voûte' (*Swann*, vol. I, p. 91). Associations of taste may also intrude into the image: 'la grasse liqueur qui, à la tombée de la nuit, sourd incessamment du réservoir des lampes pour remplir les chambres jusqu'au bord de leurs parois' (*Guermantes*, vol. I, p. 87).

Taste and smell. These sensations play an important part in Proust's sensuous experiences and in the process of 'involuntary memory'; they furnish many analogies for the description of other sense-impressions,[1] but are themselves rarely transcribed in synaesthetic terms. *Douceur* is sometimes found in unusual combinations, such as the 'ample douceur' of George Sand's sentences (*Swann*, vol. I, p. 66), or 'sans que se brisât sa douceur (viz. of his mother's kiss)' (*ibid.*, p. 39); but the word is used here in a figurative sense. Its primary meaning may, however, be brought to the fore by a development of the image:

[1] Cf. Pommier, *op. cit.*, pp. 52ff.; Mouton, *op. cit.*, pp. 86ff.; A. Maurois, *A la recherche de Marcel Proust*, Paris (1949), p. 187.

Pour un convalescent . . une odeur de fleurs et de fruits n'imprègne pas plus profondément les mille riens dont se compose son farniente que pour moi cette couleur, cet arome que mes regards allaient chercher sur ces jeunes filles et dont la *douceur* finissait par s'incorporer en moi. Ainsi les raisins se sucrent-ils au soleil (*Jeunes filles*, vol. II, p. 189).

On several occasions, taste is associated with other senses in the description of a woman's face: 'la douceur purement carnée qu'il supposait devoir leur (viz. Odette's cheeks) trouver en les touchant avec les lèvres' (*Swann*, vol. II, p. 15; cf. *Jeunes filles*, vol. II, pp. 170 and 174, etc.). Taste can even be made visible:

. . . cette chambre . . . avait l'air d'un prisme où se décomposaient les couleurs de la lumière du dehors, d'une ruche où les sucs de la journée que j'allais goûter étaient dissociés, épars, enivrants et visibles (*ibid.*, pp. 7–8).

Tastes and smells are closely linked in our minds; together they carry, when all other memories are gone, 'sur leur gouttelette impalpable, l'édifice immense du souvenir' (*Swann*, vol. I, p. 73). It is therefore mainly in terms of taste that odours are transcribed in a famous passage of *Du Côté de chez Swann*, the description of Mme Octave's room at Combray:[1]

. . . le feu cuisant comme une pâte les appétissantes odeurs . . . les feuilletait, les dorait, les godait, les boursouflait, en faisant un invisible et palpable gâteau provincial, un immense 'chausson' où, à peine goûtés les aromes plus croustillants, plus fins, plus réputés, mais plus secs aussi du placard, de la commode, du papier à ramages, je revenais toujours avec une convoitise inavouée m'engluer dans l'odeur médiane, poisseuse, fade, indigeste et fruitée du couvre-lit à fleurs (*ibid.*, p. 77).

Visual associations are also present in the same passage: 'odeurs . . . couleur du temps'; 'le feu . . . badigeonnait toute la chambre d'une odeur de suie'. Elsewhere, scent is alleged to have a definite shape: 'leur parfum (viz. that of hawthorns) s'étendait aussi onctueux, aussi délimité en sa forme que si j'eusse été devant l'autel de la Vierge' (*ibid.*, p. 200)—a prefiguration of a passage in *La Prisonnière* where 'les odeurs, . . .

[1] A stylistic analysis of this passage was given recently by Ch. Bruneau in his Taylorian Lecture, *La Prose littéraire de Proust à Camus*, Oxford (1953), pp. 4ff.

verticales et debout, . . . se tenaient en tranches juxtaposées et distinctes'. The scent of hawthorns—the flowers which play such an important role in Proust's journey into past time[1]— has also an acoustic equivalent: a path is described as 'tout bour- donnant de l'odeur des aubépines' (*ibid.*, pp. 199–200).

Touch, mass, heat. The sense of touch was also included in Proust's theory of correspondences. He went so far as to suggest that there is a hidden harmony between impressions of touch, sound and colour emanating from the same person:

> La pression de la main d'Albertine avait une douceur sensuelle qui était comme en harmonie avec la coloration rose, légèrement mauve de sa peau. Cette pression semblait vous faire pénétrer dans la jeune fille, dans la profondeur de ses sens, comme la sonorité de son rire (*Jeunes filles*, vol. II, p. 197).

But his practice was not in line with his theory, and he seldom transcribed sensations of touch in synaesthetic terms. The most interesting images of this type are those which intermingle the various states of matter, presenting fluids as solids, air as liquid, etc. Perhaps the most curious motif here is the solidi- fication of air. The same alchemy which had transmuted light into solid substances is at work in transpositions like the fol- lowing: 'les appétissantes odeurs dont l'air de la chambre était tout grumeleux' (*Swann*, vol. I, p. 77); 'aux chambres de Combray, saupoudrées d'une atmosphère grenue, pollinisée, comestible et dévote' (*Swann*, vol. II, p. 239) ; 'le vent . . . était tout hérissé et grenu d'une approche de neige' (*Guer- mantes*, vol. I, p. 88). The air in a room is likened to a 'cara- pace' (*Swann*, vol. II, p. 253) and to 'un grand manteau, . . . zone ardente et mobile en ses contours thermiques' (*Swann*, vol. I, p. 17). Once again, crystallographical similes are intro- duced to elaborate the image:

> . . . l'atmosphère de la plus grande partie de l'atelier était sombre, transparente et compacte dans sa masse, mais humide et brillante aux cassures où la sertissait la lumière, comme un bloc de cristal, de roche dont une face déjà taillée et polie, çà et là, luit comme un miroir et s'irise (*Jeunes filles*, vol. II, p. 123).

Heat is visualized in the same way:

> . . la chaleur du jour tombait, se déposait, comme au fond d'un

---

[1] Cf. Poulet, *op. cit.*, pp. 385ff.

vase le long des parois duquel la gelée transparente et sombre de l'air semblait si consistante qu'un grand rosier appliqué au mur obscurci qu'il veinait de rose, avait l'air de l'arborisation qu'on voit au fond d'une pierre d'onyx (*ibid.*, vol. ii, p. 100).

The solidification of fluids follows a similar pattern. Glass bottles immersed in water are depicted as 'à la fois "contenant" aux flancs transparents comme une eau durcie, et "contenu" plongé dans un plus grand contenant de cristal liquide et courant', while around the pieces of bread thrown into the water, 'l'eau se solidifiait aussitôt . . . en grappes ovoïdes de têtards inanitiés' (*Swann*, vol. i, p. 242). Culinary associations may enliven the image, as in this terse description of the density of sea-water: 'la mer compacte et coupante comme de la gelée de viande' (*Jeunes filles*, vol. ii, p. 96).

5

By the very nature of things, synaesthetic images are hardly ever used in the spoken language. Occasionally, however, they are found in the speech of certain characters, as a means of parody or portrayal. They take their place among the clichés characteristic of Mme de Verdurin, M. de Norpois and Dr Cottard, as in the latter's naive inquiry: 'Sarah Bernhardt, c'est bien la Voix d'Or, n'est-ce pas?' (*Swann*, vol. i, pp. 289–90) This is a good example of the importance of context and collocation in matters of style. When, in a passage already quoted, the narrator speaks of the 'golden voice' of another actress, Mme Berma, there is nothing platitudinous about the phrase: it is motivated by the mood of youthful enthusiasm which pervades the whole passage, and revitalized by contact with allied images: 'baigner effectivement dans l'atmosphère et l'ensoleillement de la voix dorée'. Here, however, the context and the speaker's personality brand it quite unmistakably as a cliché; and, as if to dispel any doubts, capital letters are used to underline the parody.

Transpositions are also indulged in, as a kind of artists' slang, by the painter Biche—the later Elstir—when speaking about works of art. 'Ça sent bon', he says of a picture, 'ça vous prend à la tête, ça vous coupe la respiration, ça vous fait des chatouilles' (*Swann*, vol. ii, p. 58). More complicated is the

case of Legrandin talking of 'la musique . . . que joue le clair
de lune sur la flûte du silence' (*Swann*, vol. I, p. 184). We
saw in the previous chapter that, by a kind of inverted irony,
Proust had portrayed his own idiosyncrasies of style in the high-
flown yet engaging language used by Legrandin. Quite probably, the poetic transposition with which he is credited here is
yet another case of a 'Proustian pastiche of Proust' himself.[1]

It also happens that, in a moment of relaxed control, the
author makes one of his characters use images which bear the
stamp of Proust's own style but are out of tune with the speaker's
personality. Thus it is somewhat incongruous for the grandmother to say of the bell-tower at Combray: 'Je suis sûre que
s'il jouait au piano, il ne jouerait pas sec' (*Swann*, vol. I, p. 96;
cf. Mouton, *op. cit.*, pp. 192ff.). There is no stylistic intention
here which could justify this typically Proustian image.

Some of Proust's transpositions have been criticized as precious and artificial,[2] and a recent student has this to say about
his more recondite art similes:

> It is passages like this one, characterized by what is almost too
> much of a muchness, a kind of overripe aestheticism, a little ornate in
> its loveliness, that made certain early readers of Proust's work ridi-
> cule what seemed to them a transplantation of euphuistic exaggeration
> into the sober garden of French prose.[3]

It must be conceded that certain transpositions in Proust are
open to criticism, but the technique as a whole is fully vindi-
cated by the use to which these images are put, as well as by
their intrinsic qualities: their exuberant richness and variety,
and the highly original vision and almost uncannily refined
sensitivity which they reflect. The question arises whether
this habit of positing correspondences and intermingling sensations had any organic basis; whether Proust spontaneously
associated one sense with another, as did for example Liszt who
once asked an orchestra to make a sound more 'blue', or the

---

[1] Cf. above, pp. 185f. For a somewhat similar case in *La Prisonniere*, where
Albertine parodies the narrator's fondness for art similes, including synaesthetic
ones, see Hindus, *op. cit.*, p. 55.

[2] Cf. Stockwell, *Cambridge Journal*, *loc. cit.*, and G. Brée, *Du Temps perdu au
temps retrouvé*, Paris (1950), p. 223.

[3] Hindus, *op. cit.*, p. 49.

singer Titta Ruffo who, when singing, mentally 'saw' the brown, red and blue colour of the sounds. However tempting such an interpretation might be, there is no evidence of such an idiosyncrasy in the case of Proust; in fact, the transpositions are so diverse that it would be impossible to ascribe them to a single factor such as coloured hearing. It was rather a case of a general condition of hyperaesthesia, of abnormally heightened sensitivity. Two conclusions emerge from the images themselves. Their frequency, their recurrence in certain contexts, the persistence of some of their themes and motifs, all point to a habitual mode of synaesthetic vision and expression. At the same time, their astonishing variety, originality and expressive force show that this habit was not allowed to grow into a mannerism. The use of transpositions as a means of parody and self-parody is symptomatic in this respect. As a psychological and artistic principle, transpositions fitted admirably into the framework of the Proustian novel. As a device of style, they were invaluable to him in his quest for a new language, metaphorical in its very essence: they provided him with a virtually inexhaustible fund of analogies through which his vision of the universe could be expressed.

CHAPTER VI

THE IMAGE IN THE MODERN NOVEL

THE importance of the image in the texture of poetry was fully recognized by classical rhetoric. Although metaphor was included among other figures of speech, its primacy was emphasized by Aristotle himself when he declared in *The Poetics*: 'The greatest thing by far is to have a command of metaphor. This alone cannot be imparted to another: it is the mark of genius.' This statement has been echoed down the centuries, even though each period had its own views about the function of the image in poetic style. Even a Classicist like Dryden was alive to its supreme importance. 'Imaging', he proclaimed, 'is, in itself, the very height and life of Poetry.' With the Romantic Movement, such claims changed in tone and became more insistent. Coleridge observed with his usual perspicacity: 'In the present age the poet . . . seems to propose to himself as his main object, and as that which is the most characteristic of his art, new and striking images.' Wordsworth gave a precise and pregnant account of the metaphorical process itself:

> . . . The song would speak
> Of that interminable building reared
> By observation of affinities
> In objects where no brotherhood exists
> To passive minds.

In our own time, Ezra Pound went so far as to assert: 'It is better to present one Image in a lifetime than to produce voluminous works.'[1] It will be remembered that Mr Pound was the leader of the so-called Imagist Movement in poetry. The French Surrealists were no less emphatic; according to André Breton, 'to compare two objects, as remote from one another as possible, or by any other method put them together in a

---

[1] These and other views on the role of the image in poetry are discussed in C. Day Lewis, *The Poetic Image*, London (1947), ch. I: 'The Nature of the Image'.

sudden and striking fashion, this remains the highest task to which poetry can aspire'.[1]

Even if one dissents from these extreme views, the paramount importance of the image in poetry is beyond dispute. But what is its function in prose? In his article on Flaubert, from which I have already quoted, Proust categorically declared: 'Je crois que la métaphore seule peut donner une sorte d'éternité au style.'[2] This view is symptomatic of a revolutionary change which has occurred in the style of fiction since the end of the last century. An examination of three contemporary works will, I hope, throw some light on the vital part which the image has come to play in the economy of the modern novel.

This is not the place to discuss the various psychological and aesthetic problems connected with imagery.[3] It might, however, be useful to clarify the terminology and to outline a classification of images on linguistic grounds, so as to provide some tools of analysis for the empirical inquiry.

Image, metaphor, metonymy. It is generally assumed that metaphor is the prototype of all imagery. Metaphor in the wider sense includes a number of allied figures, all of them based on some kind of analogy between two ideas: allegory, hyperbole, irony etc. These tropes, analysed and classified by ancient rhetoric, still have some usefulness in stylistics, but they are mere species of the genus metaphor. It is of metaphor in this wider sense that Mr Day Lewis was thinking when he wrote:

Every poetic image . . . is to some degree metaphorical. It looks out from a mirror in which life perceives not so much its face as some truth about its face (*op. cit.*, p. 18).

The author himself had some qualms about this formula, and on closer examination it turns out to be too narrow since it would exclude a whole range of images which do not derive from metaphorical experiences. Every image is ultimately based on some kind of association between two terms. Such associations

[1] Quoted by I. A. Richards, *The Philosophy of Rhetoric*, New York-London (1936), p. 123.
[2] See above, p. 94.
[3] For the wider background, see Wellek and Warren, *op. cit.*, ch. xv. See also H. Konrad, *Etude sur la métaphore*, Paris (1939), and H. Adank, *Essai sur les fondements psychologiques et linguistiques de la métaphore affective*, Genève (1939). Cf. my *Principles of Semantics*, pp. 222ff., and *Précis de sémantique française*, pp. 277ff.

may, as we already know, work either by similarity or by contiguity.[1] We speak of the *bonnet* of a car because we perceive some resemblance between the two objects. But when we talk of '*the cloth*' in the sense of 'clergy', or of 'town and *gown*' in the sense of 'town and university', there is no resemblance between the two ideas: they are part of the same complex experience, and the association works by contiguity.

It is ultimately a matter of nomenclature whether the term 'image' is so defined as to include metonymic associations. Metonymy certainly lacks the creative inspiration of metaphor; it does not discover hidden analogies and does not establish a link between disparate ideas. As a French student of metaphor has put it, 'la métonymie n'ouvre pas de chemins comme l'intuition métaphorique; mais brûlant les étapes de chemins trop connus elle raccourcit des distances pour faciliter la rapide intuition de choses déjà connues'.[2] But is this a sufficient reason for excluding such figures from the field of imagery? Many of Proust's transpositions discussed in the last chapter are metonymic; yet who would dispute that expressions like 'la surface azurée du silence' are both graphic and striking? They certainly possess the novelty, vividness and sensuous quality which is the hall-mark of the true image. In the title *Le Rouge et le Noir*, the two colours stand metonymically for army and priesthood; at the same time they form a violent contrast which is symbolical of the inner tension pervading the whole novel.[3]

There are also cases where no sharp demarcation-line exists between the two figures. A metonymy may masquerade as a metaphor when the external connection is so remote or so obscure that one is tempted to look for some sort of recondite similarity. We have seen an example of this in Proust: the purple colour of the name *Champi*, which derives not from some intrinsic analogy between sound and colour, but from the mere accident that the book had a red binding. Metonymy may also be transmuted into metaphor when the external relation is strengthened by some inner affinity which makes the name particularly appropriate. In a passage of his correspondence which I

---

[1] See above, p. 196.

[2] G. Esnault, *Imagination populaire, métaphores occidentales*, Paris (1925), p. 31.

[3] Cf. Wandruszka, *loc. cit.*, p. 435.

have already quoted, Flaubert likens style to a *stiletto*: 'Je conçois un style qui nous entrerait dans l'idée comme un coup de
stylet.' But *style* itself derives by metonymy from *stilus*, the
name of the writing implement, of which *stylet* is a regular
diminutive.

It would therefore be wrong to exclude metonymy—and
the allied figure of synecdoche or 'part for the whole'—from
the field of imagery. But how is one to determine what metaphors and metonymies are to be regarded as images? Obviously,
many of them lack the distinctive qualities of an image. The
criterion usually applied is that of 'aesthetic intention'. Some
writers distinguish between 'linguistic' or 'grammatical', and
'aesthetic' or 'rhetorical' figures.[1] But this criterion is too
subjective to provide an absolute test. In practice, one can
usually recognize an image by the presence of certain distinctive
traits: novelty, expressive force, a certain sensuous and graphic
quality; but there is no sharp demarcation-line between images
and other figures, and we must allow for a margin of subjective
reactions and for the existence of borderline cases.

The form of the image. While metonymic imagery has only
one form, metaphorical imagery has two. The metaphor may
be either *explicit* or *implicit*; the resemblance may be either
clearly stated or merely implied. In the former case we have a
simile or comparison, in the latter a metaphor in the strict sense
of the term. The psychological background is the same in both
cases: we perceive and enunciate a certain similarity between
two objects or ideas. But the result differs greatly in density
and expressive power. By suppressing all explicit indication
of similarity, we adopt a form of verbal shorthand which is
tantamount to identifying the two terms. We disregard differences and narrow our attention to the common feature. Instead of explaining that the cover of a motor is *like* a bonnet,
we simply call it a bonnet, thus classing and to some extent
identifying it with that object. Metaphor proper is thus more
terse and more arresting than simile. 'La métaphore est une
comparaison condensée par laquelle l'esprit affirme une identité
intuitive et concrète.'[2]

---

[1] Cf. Konrad, *op. cit.*, pp. 100ff.; Wellek and Warren, *op. cit.*, pp. 210f.; G. Stern,
Meaning and Change of Meaning, Gothenburg (1931), pp. 296ff.

[2] Esnault, *op. cit.*, p. 30.

In view of these differences in expressive quality, it will be important to determine the preference of a writer for the explicit or implicit type. Frequent use of comparisons will not necessarily imply clumsiness or timidity; the author may deliberately choose a naive and unsophisticated or pseudo-epic manner. Conversely, writers aiming at shock-tactics, surprise effects and tenseness in style will prefer the elliptical mode.

The form of the image can have varying degrees of complexity. Once the similarity has been established, the author may either leave it or develop it; he may even take it up later on in the story.

The structure of the image. In *The Philosophy of Rhetoric*, Dr I. A. Richards has drawn attention to a curious and almost incredible anomaly. After all the endless discussions on the subject, there exists as yet no agreed terminology distinguishing between the two terms of a metaphor. To remedy this situation, Dr Richards suggests a distinction between *tenor* and *vehicle*. The tenor of a metaphor is the object or idea we are talking about; the vehicle is the term to which the tenor is likened. When we speak of the *teeth* of a comb, the tenor is the pointed projection whose shape reminds us of a tooth; the vehicle is the human tooth itself whose name is applied to the inanimate object. The common element, in this case the similarity in shape, is the *ground* of the metaphor.[1]

It is an essential feature of metaphor that there must be a certain distance between tenor and vehicle. Their similarity must be accompanied by a feeling of disparity; they must belong to different spheres of thought. If they are too close to one another, they cannot produce the perspective of 'double vision' peculiar to metaphor. A contemporary psychologist has coined the happy expression of a 'cocktail of spheres'[2] to bring out this feeling of disparity.

The distance between tenor and vehicle—the 'angle' of the metaphor, as Dr Sayce calls it[3]—produces an element of tension which is an important factor in the expressive force of the image. Modern writers are often tempted to heighten the tension by bringing remote objects or ideas into relation to each other. In this way, however, the impact of an image may

[1] *Op. cit.*, pp. 96ff. and 117.   [2] K. Bühler, quoted by Konrad, *op. cit.*, p. 99.
[3] *Op. cit.*, pp. 62f.

be strengthened at the expense of its appropriateness, and if the device is frequently repeated, it begins to pall. In Dr Richards' words, 'that tension is the spring of the bow, the source of the energy of the shot, but we ought not to mistake the strength of the bow for the excellence of the shooting; or the strain for the aim' (*ibid.*, p. 125).

The classification of imagery. Leaving aside some highly controversial attempts to establish a typology of images on psychological or aesthetic grounds,[1] certain simple criteria for classification can be derived from the linguistic background of imagery. Two of these have already been mentioned: the distinction between metaphorical and metonymic images, and that between implicit and explicit metaphors. The three elements of which every metaphor is built up—tenor, vehicle, and ground of the image—can each serve as a basis for classification. Among these, the grouping of metaphors according to the *vehicle*, i.e. according to the source of the image, is the most popular. It is fairly easy to tabulate imagery according to its provenance, and the temptation is great to draw psychological inferences, equating 'dominant metaphors' with the author's interests and experiences, and reconstructing his 'inner biography' in the light of his images. We have seen in the introduction (pp. 31ff.) the fallacies to which such a method may lead. Yet, within limits, the grouping of metaphors according to provenance can yield interesting results. Images may also be classified according to the *tenor*, the objects or ideas which are described in metaphorical terms. In this way one may hope to identify the main themes which invite images from other spheres; we shall see, for example, the multiplicity of metaphors through which Sartre tries to convey, and to make intelligible, the basic experiences of Existentialism.

The *interrelations of tenor and vehicle* provide a further criterion for classifying imagery. A rough scheme may be based on the interplay of concrete and abstract terms. Both tenor and vehicle may be either concrete or abstract, so that there are theoretically four possibilities: (1) from concrete to concrete; (2) from concrete to abstract; (3) from abstract to concrete; (4) from abstract to abstract. But if it is remembered that a certain quality of concreteness and sensuousness is a distinctive

---

[1] Cf. Wellek and Warren, *op. cit.*, pp. 205ff, and the works of G. Bachelard.

feature of the image, the fourth possibility will automatically lapse; one abstract idea can certainly be likened to another, but it is hard to see how an image could result from such a combination. Of the other three types, the first two are bound to predominate since an abstract term is hardly suited to give a graphic description of a concrete experience. Yet, as we shall see, such combinations are sometimes deliberately contrived by the modern writer: their very rareness and artificiality may produce a surprise effect and a kind of 'inverted expressiveness'.

The interrelations of tenor and vehicle may also lead to more specific conclusions when a particular sphere is consistently described in terms of another, or when there is continual interchange between two spheres, as for instance between the spheres of religion and love in Donne's poetry.[1]

The *ground* of the metaphor is less suited to serve as a basis for classification. Broadly speaking, the similarity between tenor and vehicle may be either objective or emotive. When we speak of 'focusing our attention' on something, we do so because there is a definite analogy between focusing a lens and concentrating one's attention on a problem. Here the resemblance resides in the two processes themselves. Elsewhere it will reside, not in the two terms but in the similar impressions which they produce. If we talk of an 'icy silence', we mean that the unpleasant impression caused by extreme cold is not unlike that caused by a certain kind of silence. The similarity here is emotive, not objective. This distinction, which can be further refined,[2] may be useful in the interpretation of particular images, but it could hardly provide a framework for classification. The same may be said of attempts to classify metaphors according to their *function*, distinguishing e.g. between 'illustrative, decorative, evocative and emotive intention'.[3] The intention behind an image is often very difficult to determine, and one must also allow for the presence of two or

---

[1] Wellek and Warren, *op. cit.*, pp. 213f.

[2] In his *La Science du mot. Traité de sémantique* (Louvain (1927)), A. Carnoy distinguishes between four types of metaphor: perceptual, synaesthetic, affective and pragmatic (ch. xx).

[3] Cf. F. W. Leakey's interesting article, 'Intention in Metaphor', *Essays in Criticism*, vol. iv, ch. 2 (1954), pp. 191–8. See also I. A. Richards' distinction between 'functional' and 'ornamental' metaphors in *Speculative Instruments* (London, 1955), p. 46.

more intentions in the same image. Nevertheless, all these criteria will have their usefulness in the analysis of specific cases.

In a short but provocative essay on the image in French literature,[1] Professor Bruneau has outlined a typology of contemporary imagery. In his view, the modern image dates from Baudelaire's theory of correspondences, and since then it has evolved on two main lines. Some poets, whom Bruneau describes as 'les chimistes', have developed it into a refined and recondite intellectual medium, a kind of super-language. Mallarmé and Valéry are the purest representatives of this tendency. A second type, 'les inspirés', are given to an entirely different kind of imagery: irrational, visionary, even primitive in some respects. Poets like Rimbaud, Apollinaire and Paul Eluard clearly belong to this group. Professor Bruneau also distinguishes between four main themes of modern imagery: sensations, impressions, feelings, and purely intellectual experiences, the last of these being more germane to the Valéry type. These categories are rather vague and over-simplified, but they undoubtedly correspond to certain broad tendencies in modern poetry; they also have some relevance to the novel which, in the matter of imagery, has moved much closer to poetry since the end of the last century.

As usual, one has to study a complete novel in order to determine the part which imagery plays, and the diversity of forms which it may assume, in the structure of a work of art. The material will be drawn from three novels very different in subject-matter and in style: one of Giono's early regional stories; a novel about post-war Paris by a young writer, Hervé Bazin; and the third part of Sartre's existentialist trilogy, which deals with the French collapse of 1940. Although imagery forms the most personal layer of a writer's style, a comparison of these three novels should give us some idea of the functions and potentialities of the image in contemporary fiction.

1. JEAN GIONO

Regain

The very title of this novel is metaphorical. Though the English translation is entitled 'Harvest', *regain* really means

[1] Ch. Bruneau, 'L'image dans notre langue littéraire', *Mélanges Dauzat*, pp. 55–67.

'aftermath, second growth', and, figuratively, 'renewal'. Both senses are relevant to the theme of the novel. It tells of the renewal of a man's life when he finds a woman who brings meaning and purpose into his lonely existence. But the change in his life also means the rebirth of the deserted little Provençal village where he lives, and of the untilled land around it. The story is simple, straightforward, with few incidents and characters; yet it derives deeper significance from the intensity of the emotions portrayed and from the originality of the author's vision and expression.

Even the most casual observer will be struck by the richness of imagery in the novel. 'What he has perceived is almost instantaneously rendered through images,' writes Professor Henry Peyre. 'Giono is one of the most prolific creators of images in modern literature. . . . He fixes the essence of reality through them and ennobles it at the same time; he simplifies, and yet he transfigures.'[1] This general impression is borne out and even strengthened by a detailed study of the imagery.[2]

The density of the metaphorical element in *Regain* is very great; at first sight, it might even appear excessive. The novel contains over 350 images, an average of nearly one and a half per page—and the pages are very small. In fact, it is hard to open the book anywhere without coming across an image or, more often than not, a whole series of images. One may legitimately wonder how a short novel, dealing with a narrow subject, can bear the strain of such a heavy load of imagery, and whether the exasperated reader will not exclaim, with the visitor from Sirius in Voltaire's *Micromégas*: 'Encore une fois, la nature est comme la nature. Pourquoi lui chercher des comparaisons?' That the reader does not do so is due partly to the quality of the images, the freshness of vision from which they spring, and partly to the important role which they have in the structure and impact of the story.

An interesting feature of imagery in *Regain* is the frequency of *comparisons*. This is not surprising in a writer like Giono, close to nature, nurtured on Greek classics, and hostile to urban

---

[1] H. Peyre, *The Contemporary French Novel*, New York (1945), p. 143.

[2] On Giono's imagery, see R. de Villeneuve, *Jean Giono, ce solitaire*, Paris (1955), ch. xii, and J. Pugnet, *Jean Giono*, Paris-Bruxelles (1955), pp. 58–65. Cf. also H. Harvitt, *The French Review* (1934), pp. 284ff., and H. Chonez, *Giono par lui-même*, Paris (1956), pp. 80ff.

civilization. His comparisons fit into the simple and epic tone of his style; some of them have a distinctly Homeric ring. They are mostly introduced by *comme*: 'Son corps est en travail *comme* du vin nouveau' (p. 82); 'un visage maigre et rouillé *comme* un vieux fer de hache' (p. 40); 'une terre malade de lèpre *comme* une vieille chienne qui perd ses poils' (p. 13); 'ce sentier qui est déroulé dans les collines *comme* la longe d'un fouet' (p. 115). But the pattern can be varied in a number of ways: 'les deux filles sont rouges, *à croire* qu'elles ont des tomates mûres sous leurs cheveux' (p. 186); 'Des corbeaux s'appellent; on les cherche, on ne les voit pas. *On dirait* que c'est la grande faïence bleue du ciel qui craque' (pp. 288–9); '*Il semble* qu'on a étiré le ruisseau, *il semble* qu'il y en a un, là-haut sur le plateau qui tire sur la queue du ruisseau et un autre, en bas dans les plaines qui tire sur la tête *comme* quand on veut écorcher une couleuvre' (p. 116). The explicit image verges on the implicit when a parallel is drawn without any actual comparison: 'tout saoulé de bonne soupe en dedans et tout saoulé de bonnes images en dehors' (p. 225); 'Et voilà le soleil qui a sauté les collines et qui monte. Et voilà Arsule qui a sauté le ruisseau et qui monte' (p. 176).

There are also various degrees in the *development* of the image. In many cases, the author adds a figurative touch and does not elaborate it any further. Some of his images are terse to the point of becoming somewhat cryptic: 'Et comme vent, celui qui s'est annoncé la nuit passée: ce vent-chèvre, le printemps' (p. 62).[1] But Giono is equally fond of complex images. Once his interest has been stirred by an analogy, he likes to develop the picture by adding one or more further details. Having likened, for example, an inner urge to 'une eau qui effondre tout', he goes on: 'Son coeur est une motte de terre qui fond' (p. 98). When the main character, Panturle, first appears in the story, his huge bulk standing erect among the plants, the author is suddenly reminded of a tree, and this leads on to a fresh image: 'Sa chemise pend en lambeaux comme une écorce' (p. 24). Elsewhere, the image is even further expanded:

L'ombre marche sur la terre comme une bête; l'herbe s'aplatit, les

[1] This is a case of what Bruneau has called a 'maximum metaphor': the bald juxtaposition of two nouns, which Hugo first introduced into French literature. Cf. Bruneau, *op. cit.*, vol. XII, pp. 239f., and vol. XIII, ch. 1, pp. 37f.

sablonnières fument. L'ombre marche sur des pattes souples comme une bête. La voilà: froide et lourde sur les épaules (pp. 75–6).

Il est las comme si on avait fait des trous à ses bras, des trous à ses jambes et qu'on ait laissé couler sa force. Oui, et qu'on ait mis à la place de cette force du lait avec des fleurs de sariette. Du lait. Il sent que ça coule le long de son corps, et ça le chatouille, et ça le fait rire (p. 58).

The structure of these passages, the repetition of certain words (*ombre, marche, bête; trous, coule, force, lait*), the throwing in of subjective elements like *oui* and *la voilà*, enable the reader to follow the images as they gradually unfold themselves in the author's mind.

It also happens that Giono takes up and develops an image later on in the story. The initial simile: 'Aubignane est collé contre le tranchant du plateau comme un petit nid de guêpes', evokes a little later the secondary image: 'il y a une maison qui s'est comme décollée, qui a coulé de haut en bas' (p. 23). The poetic comparison: 'le clocher bleu qui monte au-dessus des bois comme une fleur' (p. 10) is expanded three pages further on into 'la tige bleue du clocher de Vachères' (p. 13).

Images may also be generated by chain-reaction, with one metaphor setting off another until the initial impetus is spent. The elemental force of the wind—one of the main themes of Giono's imagery—is conveyed by such a series of interrelated images:

. . . le beau vent, large d'épaules qui bouscule tout le pays . . . le vent s'appuie sur lui de tout son poids, par larges coups, longs et lourds . . . le vent le presse comme une éponge . . . le vent toque du doigt contre lui comme contre un baril, pour voir s'il reste encore du jus (pp. 100–1).

Here we also see another basic tendency of Giono's imagery: his fondness for personification. Natural phenomena are often personified and organized into a kind of semi-pagan mythology.[1] The night is endowed with feet, hands and shoulders (pp. 32, 48–9, 86). The wind is pictured as a horse: 'il galopait bride abattue à travers tout le plateau, il avait un long gémissement pour boire tout le ciel' (p. 89). The morning sun stalks along the fields, 'enfoncé dans les herbes jusqu'aux genoux'

[1] Cf. Ch. Dietschy, 'Natur und Mensch in Gionos Sprache', *Festschrift für Tappolet*, pp. 71–7.

(p. 92). The soil fights a losing battle against the ploughshare: 'Elle a gémi; elle a cédé. L'acier a déchiré un bon morceau qui versait noir et gras. Et, d'un coup, la terre s'est reprise; elle s'est débattue, elle a comme essayé de mordre, de se défendre' (p. 175). Some of these personifications have a strange, almost hallucinatory intensity: 'Le printemps est cramponné sur ses épaules comme un gros chat' (p. 115).

Giono's imagination has no markedly synaesthetic bias, but the different senses are often intermingled in his metaphors. Light is transcribed in terms of touch: 'La grande lune entre dans ses yeux sensibles comme un couteau' (p. 122). The same simile serves to evoke a sudden noise: 'le bruit les a tranchés comme un couteau' (p. 201), while the impact of a shout on the ear is likened to that of a stone (p. 58). Some synaesthetic analogies are further developed: 'du bruit et des cris à vous rendre sourds comme si on avait de l'eau dans les oreilles . . . Il en coule (du café) un ruisseau de fumée et de cris' (p. 187). The most intricate series of transpositions occurs at the very end of the novel:

Il a des chansons qui sont là, entassées dans sa gorge à presser ses dents. Et il serre les lèvres. C'est une joie dont il veut mâcher toute l'odeur et saliver longtemps le jus comme un mouton qui mange la saladelle du soir sur les collines. Il va, comme ça, jusqu'au moment où le beau silence s'est épaissi en lui et autour de lui comme un pré (p. 239).

Here we have a real 'cocktail of spheres', with all five senses thrown into the mixture. But the various transpositions are uncoordinated and produce a somewhat strained and incongruous effect.

The tenor of an author's metaphors is not entirely at his discretion; it is to some extent imposed by his subject-matter. Within these limitations, however, there remains a wide margin of choice as to the *themes* which he wishes to interpret in metaphorical terms. In a novel like *Regain*, these themes will of necessity be drawn from a limited field, yet certain preferences and centres of attraction are clearly discernible.

Much of the imagery develops around the *forces of nature*. The wind in particular inspires an almost inexhaustible wealth of metaphors, only a few of which can be given here. Most of them are personifications: 'le vent le ceinture d'un bras tiède et l'emmène avec lui' (p. 102); 'cette grande main du vent plaquée à nue sur sa chair' (p. 84); 'le vent éparpille de la rosée comme un poulain qui se vautre' (p. 92). Such a profusion of analogies almost inevitably leads to mixed metaphors; it would not be easy, for instance, to reconcile the images packed into the following passage:

> . . . le vent . . . venait bien en face et il leur a plaqué sa grande main tiède sur la bouche. . . . Alors, le vent s'est mis à leur gratter les yeux avec ses ongles. . . . Le vent entre dans son corsage comme chez lui. Il lui coule entre les seins . . . il la rafraîchit comme un bain. . . . Elle le sent sur elle, frais, oui, mais tiède aussi et comme plein de fleurs, et tout en chatouilles, comme si on la fouettait avec des poignées de foin (p. 81).

The movement is too swift, and the images are too vivid, for any sense of incongruity to arise, but the transformation of the wind from a solid into a fluid disrupts the unity of the picture.

Other natural phenomena are presented in the same way. The brook has a moustache of weed (p. 229), the hill a hairy shoulder (p. 36) into which the sky drives an iron wedge (p. 116). A break in the winter weather is like the mellowing of fruit: 'l'hiver s'amollit comme un fruit malade. Jusqu'à présent il était dur et vert et bien acide, et puis, d'un coup, le voilà tendre' (p. 54). Plants are pictured in animal terms: leeks look like white fish (p. 223), and the bone of bare branches pierces through the skin of yellow leaves (p. 168). Light is materialized in transpositions reminiscent of Proust: 'un jour . . . épais comme de la paille d'étable' (p. 39); 'la lumière de la bougie est là comme un fruit roux sur la paille' (p. 85). Elsewhere, light and darkness are transmuted into fluids: 'le matin coulait comme un ruisseau d'or' (p. 227); 'la nuit, épaisse comme une soupe de pois' (p. 57).

Animals play a significant part in Giono's landscapes; their habits are carefully observed and depicted with a multiplicity of metaphorical terms. As if to emphasize the inner unity of nature, animals are often likened to plants. A young fox is like a white walnut (p. 110), while a lean and bony dog reminds one of a vine-stock (p. 104). Hunted animals tremble like flowers in the wind (p. 105); crows circle in the air 'comme des débris de bois autour d'une barque' (pp. 219–20); a swarm of bees is like 'une poignée de balles de blé que le vent porte' (p. 104). Inanimate objects also furnish some analogies: birds drop like a handful of stones (p. 92), and the bushes seem to play ball with them (p. 26).

The same metaphorical vision, obliterating the borderlines between the various realms of nature, pervades the portrayal of *human beings*. More often than not they are compared to animals. They are 'blêmes comme des oiseaux nus' (p. 94) or 'tout gonflée de joie comme un pigeon' (p. 200); they stretch themselves like cats (p. 147), and are glued to sweet-shops like flies to a jar of honey (p. 187). While these animal images are mostly comical or unflattering, those drawn from plants are more pleasant in tone: 'ces filles des champs qui sont comme des fleurs simples, avec du bleuet dans l'oeil' (p. 11); 'souple et qui se plie comme une gerbe' (p. 197). Other images are taken from inanimate objects: Arsule, the young woman who relieves Panturle's loneliness, beams with joy like the flame of a candle (p. 197) and is sunburnt like a brick (p. 193); the body of an old woman is yellow like an old candle (p.26).

Giono has a healthy interest in the human body and its sensations. The flow of blood and, more generally, the sense of physical well-being circulating in a young and robust body are conveyed by a number of graphic images: 'la force coule comme de l'huile jusqu'au bout de ses doigts' (p. 50); 'cette force folle que le printemps a mise au creux de ses reins et qui bout, là, comme une eau toujours sur le feu' (pp. 105–6); 'tous les réseaux de son sang se sont mis à chanter comme la résille des ruisseaux et des rivières de la terre' (p. 133). Equally expressive are the metaphors describing parts of the body. The skin on Panturle's hand is rough like the bark of a tree (p. 131). When he goes fox-hunting, his muscles are taut 'comme les longues cordes qui tiennent les seaux au fond des puits' (p. 119). The chest is pictured as a basket holding the heart like a fruit (p. 133). Occasionally, such images may have a humorous turn: 'sa tête se balançait en arrière comme une courge au bout de sa tige' (p. 226).

Giono's characters are firmly rooted in the physical world, and even their mental states are closely linked to their bodily experiences. Metaphors from concrete to abstract are therefore rare;

images like 'des coeurs simples comme des coquelicots' (p. 134) or 'il se sent amer et tout fleuri comme l'aubépine' (p. 108) are not at all typical.

If the author's hands are to some extent tied in choosing the tenor of his metaphors, they are entirely free in the choice of their *vehicle*. He can draw his terms of comparison from any source he likes. The only limitations are those imposed by the general tone of the narrative: in a novel like *Regain*, philosophical or scientific images would be obviously out of place. Otherwise he may range freely over the most varied spheres of experience, including those totally unrelated to his subject-matter.

A glance at the sources of Giono's imagery shows that he has scarcely availed himself of this freedom. Most of his images are drawn from a limited field; the same field, in fact, which forms the background of the story: plants, animals, the tools and activities of the farmyard. Naturally, there are exceptions; a number of metaphors are taken for example from the sphere of shipping: 'L'escadre des nuages a largué les amarres . . . on a vu bouillonner le ciel libre sous la poupe du dernier nuage' (p. 233). But such images are neither characteristic nor particularly expressive. The bulk of Giono's metaphors move, so to speak, in a closed circle: within the fauna, flora and rustic life of his own native country, the Basses-Alpes. In this world, limited and yet self-contained, there is between some spheres a give-and-take of images: as we have seen, plants are compared to animals and animals to plants. Elsewhere, there is mainly one-way traffic: human beings are described in animal terms, but not *vice versa*. But whether there is reciprocity or not, the author seems to be perfectly at ease within his self-imposed limitations and rarely ventures beyond them.

There is thus a fundamental contrast between the exuberant richness of Giono's imagery and the narrowness of its range. To account for this paradox, it might be tempting to assume that the images merely reflect the author's own interests and experiences, that he draws his analogies from those spheres which absorb his attention and are ever present to his mind. This is no doubt true, but it is not the whole truth. There were deeper reasons, intimately connected with the structure of the novel and with its basic inspiration, which determined the field of Giono's metaphors.

Firstly, by restricting the range of his imagery, Giono has safeguarded the stylistic homogeneity of the novel. In a story which introduces diverse characters or which passes through a variety of physical and social environments, the need for homogeneity does not arise. But in a book confined to the intensive study of one particular milieu and social type, homogeneity in style is essential if the language of the novel is to be in harmony with the rest of its structure: plot, characters, ideas.

Secondly, Giono's metaphors have an air of authenticity which they would lack if they were drawn from a wider field. He is thoroughly familiar with every detail of the objects which supply his images. He has watched and noted the flights of birds, the shape of plants, all the various activities on the land and on the farm, and he transcribes them with precision and self-assurance, with the differentiated vocabulary of country folk. And even where he does not do so, where he merely throws out a brief analogy, we know that he speaks from first-hand knowledge and experience. Who but a man steeped in country life would have thought of an image like 'une balayure de ciel . . . accrochée au clocher d'Aubignane comme du linge autour d'une pierre dans un ruisseau' (p. 233)? This note of authenticity would have been weakened if he had borrowed images from spheres with which he was less familiar.

But one must probe even deeper, down to the very roots of Giono's philosophy of life, to understand the full implications of his imagery. Profoundly suspicious of modern civilization, Giono preaches a return to nature very different from Rousseau's: not a sentimental and bucolic escapism, but a positive creed, an intimate communion and fusion between man and nature, sentient as well as insentient. 'All the errors of man', he proclaims, 'spring from his imagining that he is treading a dead earth, while his footsteps are imprinted in a flesh of good will'.[1] The peculiar structure of his imagery is the stylistic counterpart of this pantheistic communion with nature; the dense and homogeneous network of metaphors overlies and

---

[1] Quoted by Peyre, *op. cit.*, p. 147. Cf. also Dietschy, *loc. cit.*, p. 71, and esp. Ch. Michelfelder, *Jean Giono et les religions de la terre*, Paris (1938).

supersedes all borderlines and interknits the spheres which are normally kept distinct.

Giono's imagery is thus perfectly attuned to the aesthetic and ideological structure of the novel. But this attitude has its dangers: homogeneity may degenerate into monotony, and the disparity between tenor and vehicle, the 'angle' of the metaphor, may not be wide enough to produce an expressive image. The examples already given will have shown that, whatever the weaknesses of Giono's technique, he has successfully overcome these two dangers. There certainly is no monotony in the images of *Regain*. Working in depth rather than in breadth, the author's inventiveness in finding new and unsuspected analogies is quite inexhaustible. Even when the same metaphor is used twice, it may bring out different affinities between the two terms. We have seen (p. 219) how a meandering brook is likened to a snake. Here the resemblance is purely visual; but when, later on, the brook is again compared to a snake, the similarity will be acoustic: 'en sifflotant comme une couleuvre apprivoisée' (p. 201). Elsewhere, it is the wind, coiled and quivering against the skin, which is pictured as a snake (p. 110). The field of Giono's imagery may be narrow, but his knowledge of it is so detailed, and his imagination so fertile in positing analogies, that the number of combinations is virtually unlimited.

The danger inherent in the proximity of the spheres is also successfully averted. The examples already quoted will have given an idea of the expressiveness of Giono's images. One or two further illustrations will show that, though the angle of the metaphors is not very wide, the analogies are so unexpected, and the vision behind them is so fresh and unique, that the total effect is arresting even if not always convincing. They derive their impact, not from the distance which they span, but from the discovery of latent affinities between objects close and yet unconnected. Baudelaire has likened nature to a 'forest of symbols'; here we have the impression of walking in a strange world of hidden analogies, suddenly revealed and brought to life by the writer's imagination.

We have already seen how human beings and plants are often compared to animals. The same method is frequently applied to inanimate objects and natural phenomena. The sun,

drinking like a donkey, empties the basin in three gulps (p. 38);
the rain 'colle son ventre de limace contre les vitres' (p.
212); a new ploughshare has a smooth skin, without a wrinkle,
and 'le flanc creux des bêtes qui courent à travers la colline'
(p. 163); the plough is resting on the ground like a grass-
hopper (p. 173). In some cases there is no personification, but
this does not reduce the expressiveness of the image: 'Il y avait
un jour gris, doux comme un pelage de chat' (p. 222).

Plant images have a strong pictorial effect; most of them
are purely visual, based on some similarity in shape or in
colour. The night sky is pictured in terms of plants: the stars
look like grain in the field (p. 51), while the moon, naked and
lonely in the night, reminds the author of an almond (p. 88).
Some images are more differentiated: when Panturle grasps a
knife, 'la lame est dessous comme une feuille d'iris mouillé'
(p. 204). Not all plant metaphors have such a pleasant and
poetic quality: a pool of blood, for example, is likened to a
peony (p. 98), and the great silence of the night 'cracks like a
water-melon' (p. 82). Occasionally, plant analogies are applied
to mental processes: 'elle parle une parole douce venue de son
coeur doux comme une figue' (p. 44).

Images drawn from domestic and farming activities have a
homely air which is especially marked when they are used to
describe the forces of nature. It is as if these imposing and
terrifying phenomena where deliberately brought down to the
familiar level of daily routine. The sky is 'tout gelé comme un
linge étendu' (p. 29) or 'ouvert comme une porte de four'
(p. 95). Night has 'des bras tout humides comme une la-
veuse' (p. 202), or again it looks like 'du fer à la meule, avec
toutes ses étoiles en bouquet' (p. 57), while the wind planes the
fields with a huge trying-plane (p. 13).

It is thus clear that the expressiveness of Giono's images was
not affected by the narrowness of their range. There were,
however, other risks inherent in his technique: he had to pay a
price for the richness and intensity of his imagery.

At the time when he wrote *Regain* and his other prewar
novels, Giono was possessed by what Mallarmé called 'le
démon de l'analogie'.[1] He was himself clearly aware of this

[1] Cf. also Gide, *Journal*, p. 822.

bent of his imagination. In one of his early works he described himself as an 'accoucheur d'images'.[1] 'Le poète', he declared, 'est comme le teinturier: d'un blanc il fait le rouge.'[2] He visualized poetry as dynamite which blows up rocks, and spoke to his biographer of the 'chemical' process by which he scrutinized and tested a word before putting it to paper.[3] It is also significant that, following the great spiritual crisis which he experienced during the war, his manner changed completely: in his postwar novels there is little trace of the exuberant imagery of the earlier volumes.[4]

The most obvious risk invited by the superabundance of imagery in the early novels is that they may reach saturation point beyond which the reader's responses are dulled and his attention overtired. The constant flow of new and often bewildering analogies undoubtedly places a certain strain on the reader. Yet the conspicuous success of *Regain* and other novels of the period shows that the risk was worth taking. The pyschological explanation is quite simple: the freshness and expressiveness of the imagery, the simplicity and universality of its appeal provided a sufficient stimulus to overcome the strain.

There is also a danger that the excessive wealth of imagery will smother the story and divert attention from it, so that the novel disintegrates into a series of disjointed images. Clearly, this situation does not arise in *Regain*. The plot itself is so tenuous that, divorced from the imagery, the book would be quite inconceivable. Besides, the images are functional, not parasitic; they are part of the very fabric of the work. We have seen their role in the total effect of the novel, its aesthetic structure and its 'philosophical' implications. The forces of nature and their impact on man are just as important to Giono as man himself; and these forces are portrayed and brought to life through a multiplicity of metaphors which illuminate their various aspects. To take the most striking case of all, the wind

[1] Quoted by Dietschy, *loc. cit.*, p. 72.

[2] Quoted by Michelfelder, *op. cit.*, p. 118; cf. Peyre, *op. cit.*, p. 145.

[3] 'Avant d'écrire un mot, je le goûte comme un cuisinier goûte le produit qu'il va mettre dans sa sauce; je l'examine aux lumières comme un décorateur examine un vase chinois qu'il veut mettre en valeur; je le pèse comme un chimiste qui verse dans une éprouvette un corps qui peut faire tout sauter; et je n'emploie que des mots dont je sais la saveur intime et la puissance d'évocation et de retentissement' (quoted by Michelfelder, *op. cit.*, pp. 45f.).

[4] Cf. Peyre, *op. cit.*, p. 152.

is part of the basic inspiration of the story and one of its protagonists; the original title of *Regain*, under which parts of it
appeared in magazines, was *Vents de printemps*.[1] But the wind
could not play this role without the innumerable personifications and other metaphors through which every aspect of it is
identified and made sensible in the novel.

One minor point where Giono's technique is open to criticism
is the style of his dialogues. His imagination is so fertile in the
creation of metaphors that they sometimes overflow into reproduced speech. His characters will then talk, not like Provençal
peasants, but like the author himself.[2] It could be argued that
figurative turns of phrase are common enough in peasant
speech, but some of the expressions used bear the unmistakable
mark of Giono's own style. His characters seem to be just as
interested in words as their creator: 'L'homme est là à réflé-
chir, à faire sonner les mots en lui-même. Et ils ont bon son'
(p. 214). Some of the characteristic patterns of Giono's imagery
recur in the speech of Arsule: 'on a vu un grand morceau d'arbre
qui tombait . . . comme un paquet de linge . . . Vous filiez tout
raide sous l'eau comme un gros poisson' (pp. 124–5); 'Oh! ça
(viz. le soc) c'est beau; on dirait un devant de barque' (p. 166).
Even some metaphors from concrete to abstract find their way
into dialogue, where they will clash with the popular syntax:

> Tu sais, les domestiques, ça ramasse comme ça dix mots, une fois
> l'un, une fois l'autre, dans les choses qu'ils entendent et ça leur fait
> dix pierres à te jeter à la figure, après (p. 150).

So far we have been concerned with the difficulties arising
from the density and distribution of Giono's imagery. But the
nature of the images themselves raises a set of further problems.

Most readers will agree that Giono's images sometimes have
a repellent effect. This is not necessarily a criticism, and the
author himself, with his robust interest in the physical side of
life, would probably dismiss such objections as squeamish.
Animal imagery, which is always apt to acquire pejorative overtones,[3] supplies several unattractive parallels: 'il a sauté sur

---

[1] See Michelfelder, *op. cit.*, pp. 67f.

[2] On Giono's technique of regionalism see A. Roche, 'Les provençalismes et
la question du régionalisme dans l'oeuvre de Jean Giono', *Publications of the Modern
Language Association of America*, vol. LXIII (1948), pp. 1322–42, esp. p. 1341.

[3] Cf. Rees, *loc. cit.*, pp. 132f.

son matelas comme un poisson' (p. 107); 'tout saoul de cet orgue qui grogne comme dix pourceaux' (p. 197). Others arise in the description of animals, especially in the fox-hunting episode:

> Ça, lourd et juteux comme un fruit mûr et qu'il écrase, ça sent l'amer, ça sent l'aubépine. C'est le foie (p. 110).
> . . . un beau ventre large et velouté comme la nuit et qui était plein et lourd (p. 107).

In these passages there is a definite 'de-aesthetizing' process: the animal organs are, by a shock-effect worthy of Rimbaud,[1] compared to objects surrounded by a traditional halo of poetry: the liver to the hawthorn, the stomach to the night.

A more serious objection may be directed against the ground of some of Giono's metaphors: the alleged similarity between tenor and vehicle, or the manner in which the similarity is conveyed. Among the images quoted in this chapter, there were, besides many striking and illuminating ones, others which failed to carry conviction. It would be easy to multiply the number of such examples. In some cases, expressiveness is achieved through doubtful analogies: 'Il vient buter de la bouche contre une masse d'air dur comme de la pierre' (p. 120); 'On entendait l'eau qui descendait son gosier par blocs épais et ça s'entassait sous sa peau avec du vent' (p. 104). Elsewhere, the image is somewhat strained: 'des quartiers perdus où le ciel était collé si fort contre la terre qu'il fallait forcer de la tête pour passer entre les deux' (p. 94). Some metaphors have a precious air: 'ce poignet d'homme qui l'attache à l'homme, ce poignet qui est un pont par lequel le charroi du désir de l'homme passe dans elle' (pp. 132-3). The hallucinatory effect does not quite come off in 'il voit les longs doigts blancs du ruisseau qui se ferment sur lui' (p. 119); in 'son visage plein d'un contentement large comme le ciel' (p. 237), the parallel between concrete and abstract, which is never Giono's forte, remains unconvincing.

It was also inevitable that such an extravagant wealth of imagery should produce some mixed or incongruous metaphors. We have seen some examples of this tendency, and there are many more, though in the rapid succession of images they may pass unnoticed. The incongruity is especially marked when the

---

[1] On Rimbaud's 'anti-aesthetic' vocabulary and imagery, see F. H. Scarfe, 'A Stylistic Interpretation of Rimbaud', *Archivum Linguisticum*, vol. III (1951).

images themselves are open to doubt, when, for example, we find the night compared, in two consecutive sentences, to pea-soup and to the iron of a grinding-wheel (p. 57). Here we reach the limits of the technique: the demand on our capacity for visualization is so heavy, and the transition so abrupt, that the author's virtuosity defeats its own ends.

But even if Giono has the vices of his qualities, he is certainly one of the foremost creators of images in modern prose. Many of his metaphors have a gripping and almost haunting quality; but what is even more important is the fertility of his mind in discovering analogies. In view of the limited resources on which he draws, the sheer vitality of his imagination is all the more remarkable. No less significant is the complete integration of the imagery into the work of art: it is one of the chief means by which he expresses his vision, communicates his philosophy and achieves his aesthetic purpose.

After the spectacular success of his early novels, there has been of late a certain recession in Giono's influence.[1] Partial eclipses of this kind are common occurrences in literature; Anatole France is passing just now through such a phase. In Giono's case, however, the reaction has set in rather early, and it is also worth noting that D. H. Lawrence, to whom he is often compared, has not been affected by the same fate. The recession may be due to a variety of reasons. His attitude during the war and the completely new manner he has adopted in his postwar writings may have played a certain part; it is also conceivable that the present generation is less responsive to his art and ideas than was the public of the thirties to whose mood they were so strangely attuned. The waning of Giono's popularity may only be temporary; in fact, there are already signs of a come-back. It is too early to speculate on his final position in the history of the French novel, but one thing seems already certain: his place as a maker of images is assured.

---

[1] Cf. Pugnet, *op. cit.*, pp. 125ff. See, however, an interesting article by W. M. Frohock, 'Camus: Image, Influence and Sensibility', *Yale French Studies*, vol. II, 2 (1949), pp. 91–9, where the influence of Giono's imagery on Camus is traced in detail.

2. HERVÉ BAZIN

Lève-toi et marche

From the wind-swept plains of Provence and the vigorous out-door life of their inhabitants, we now move to the totally different atmosphere of a Paris sick-room. The contrast could hardly be greater, and it is further emphasized by a difference between generations. Hervé Bazin, who is still in his thirties, is twenty-two years younger than Giono, and *Lève-toi et marche* appeared in 1952, exactly twenty-two years after *Regain*.

Lève-toi et marche is the story of an invalid girl, dictated in the first person singular. There is an epilogue by a neighbour, a retired schoolmaster, which covers the final stages of her illness. The narrator, Constance, is a young woman of unusual intelligence and an original cast of mind, whose family was killed in a bombardment while she herself survived in a semi-paralysed condition. As the disease advances, her mind and outlook inevitably become affected and to some extent warped, but her vitality remains unimpaired: she is determined to go on living in a vicarious form, by shaping and influencing the lives of her friends. Her style, like her personality, is a curious compound of self-irony, a certain quizzical shrewdness, and irrepressible intellectual vitality.

Imagery in *Lève-toi et marche* is far less prominent than in *Regain*, but it is present on quite a substantial scale. Roughly, there is an average of one image per page; the pages, however, are much larger than in Giono's novel. But these figures are meaningless unless related to the quality of the images themselves, and here there is a sharp contrast: while most of Giono's metaphors are fresh and expressive, many of Bazin's are conventional. But there is a large residue which shows remarkable talent and originality of vision and plays an important part in the structure of the novel.

We can find a first clue to the function of Bazin's imagery in a conversation between Constance and her parson friend Pascal. Speaking of the tasks of a minister, Constance remarks:

S'il existe plusieurs cuisines, il n'y a jamais qu'un feu. Pour moi, Pascal, c'est ce feu qui compte. J'aime qu'il soit vif et . . .
—Et vous aimez les paraboles! me décocha Pascal.

Première touche: à son avantage. Je me gourmandais: 'Un peu de simplicité, ma fille!' (p. 117)

As Constance admits, the parson has laid his finger on a fundamental habit of hers. She likes to talk in parables, and once her imagination has been kindled by an analogy, she is inclined to dwell on it and develop it further. This habit is not confined to conversation; her thoughts and reminiscences, as she dictates them to her friends, are often expressed in the same form. Here, for example, is the way she conceives of her influence on other people:

Quand on jette un caillou dans la mare, on n'a pas le droit d'être étonné par les ronds qui s'élargissent, s'élargissent, à la surface de l'eau. Ni d'être agacé parce qu'elle est bénite (p. 129).

There are sound psychological reasons why Constance should be so fond of metaphorical language. It is not simply that she is a highly imaginative person whose mind naturally works that way. Metaphor is admirably suited to the type of mental activity induced by her illness. It is an oblique mode of expression and provides an effective vehicle for her humour and self-irony, for the serene wisdom and the moods of bitterness which alternate in the life an invalid. But metaphor is also a form of wit, of intellectual brilliance, and as her body is gradually invaded by the disease, the process is compensated by a hypertrophy of the intellect and of the linguistic resources through which it expresses itself. Language is the only means through which she can still act on others and dominate her own distress.

This also explains Constance's passionate interest in words for their own sake. Some of her boldest images arise around this theme:

Entre lui et moi, comme entre les noirs et les blancs, il y a un Sahara. Rassemblons une petite caravane de mots (p. 161).
. . . un mot terne, qui n'ose pas sortir et qui se recroqueville dans ma bouche comme le lapin dans son trou (pp. 160–1).
Comment résister au désir de lui écraser une belle formule sur le nez? Une formule tarte à la crème. Avec l'intonation, comme du sucre dessus (p. 127).

The last example shows that Constance is sensitive to phonetic nuances. Her remarks on the subject are amusing, though rather sophisticated. This is how she describes a sneeze:

A midi moins le quart, j'éternuai. Le plus discrètement possible: une simple lettre russe, un 'tché' dévié par le nez et presque étouffé dans le mouchoir (pp. 27–8);

or an unfinished sentence, with a doubtful *toutefois* suspended in mid-air:

Le 'toutefois' se prolongea en point d'orgue, pendant lequel la tuyauterie du service d'eau se mit à exécuter quelques traits de fantaisie (p. 39).

Constance is a shrewd observer of the speech-habits of other people. The parson's voice is characterized through a metonymic image:

. . . la voix du pasteur, une voix de fausset qui n'a pas d'onction et qui monte en chaire dès le premier mot, sans aucune nécessité (p. 46).

She is particularly scornful of technical jargon:

Dégringole un mot scientifique, inaudible. . . . D'autres mots techniques restent accrochès à sa barbe (p. 138).
. . . me cribler de ces mots techniques qu'évitent les véritables professionnels, mais sur lesquels se jettent les débutants pour créer autour d'eux un halo verbal (p. 144).

One of the main tasks to which Constance puts her verbal resources is a ruthlessly ironical portrayal of the *decay of her own body*. The story is punctuated with metaphors on this theme, which mark the successive phases of the inescapable process. The stage is set right at the beginning when she tries, with disastrous results, to prove to herself that she can still swim:

Ça, c'est moi. La belle loque! La belle fille à la poitrine rare, aux hanches plates, aux jambes de carton-pâte! Regardez-moi ces orteils, qui remuaient, qui grouillaient avec vivacité et qui ont l'air aujourd'hui d'une rangée de petits cailloux (p. 16).

She watches the gradual paralysis of her limbs with an anxiety only half-concealed by ironical similes: 'mes jambes se tassaient sous moi comme des pattes de pantin, bourrées de crin' (p. 85); 'mes mains, pleines de doigts paresseux, de doigts qui se dépliaient comme les tentacules de certaines étoiles de mer' (p.

154). She follows the gradual metamorphosis of her body into an inert object: 'De plus en plus je me transformais en soliveau' (p. 171); 'réduite à vivre comme un pieu '(p. 206). Eventually, the respiratory organs are attacked: 'l'air devient de plus en plus irrespirable et comme mélangé d'ouate au fond de mes poumons' (p. 227). On the last page of her narrative, the final stage is portrayed in a series of images reminiscent of Villon:

Ce visage que je n'ose plus regarder et qui se creuse partout, ces cheveux devenus plus ternes que le foin délavé, cette poitrine qui grince comme un vieux soufflet, . . . cette main qui a encore perdu un doigt et n'est plus qu'un affreux moignon (p. 247).

The account is completed in the epilogue written by her neighbour, Roquault, in slightly different but no less metaphorical language:

Sa poitrine se soulevait par ressauts, avec un bruit d'anche brisée, de soufflet crevé, restait un moment bloquée, puis redescendait, s'effondrait, côte par côte, secouée comme une nef qui perdrait ses arcs-boutants (p. 275).

These 'clinical' metaphors have a twofold function, aesthetic as well as psychological. They make the description of symptoms, which is an important element in the novel, somewhat less repellent; the very expressiveness of the images mitigates the unpleasantness of the subject. But they also help Constance to step back from and rise above her illness and view it with an air of ironical detachment. Naturally, she is merely acting a part, but this play-acting is an essential factor in her defence mechanism against the disease.

Preoccupation with her own body has in no ways lessened Constance's interest in other people. She describes their physical appearance with a few bold strokes; her portraits are often unsympathetic to the point of caricature. Given her metaphorical way of speaking, these sketches are mostly enlivened by figurative touches. The human eye has a particular fascination for her and suggests a number of curious analogies: 'Ses yeux jaunes m'observaient, cuits, inexpressifs: deux oeufs de moineau sur le plat' (p. 89); 'il me regarda d'un seul oeil, foré comme un trou de ver dans la pomme ronde et rubiconde de la tête' (p. 68). The pupil is pictured in the same way:

'des prunelles trop bleues, insolites, tombées sur le papier comme des boules de lessive dans une béchamelle' (p. 26); 'aux prunelles noires, menues comme des boutons de bottine et serrées dans l'étroite boutonnière rouge des paupières' (p. 41). Occasionally, the image has a more pleasant tone: 'Un regard monta vers moi, frais comme un crocus' (p. 76). In the epilogue, there are more images on this theme, including a deliberate echo of an earlier metaphor: 'un oeil fermé, l'autre ouvert, forant son trou de ver dans la pomme' (p. 275), which shows that Roquault too had been struck by the expressive force of that analogy.

Other parts of the body are portrayed in the same way, more often than not with an uncharitable bias. The similarity between the human face and an apple is extended to the lips: 'Un sourire, en coup de couteau, fend la pomme en deux' (p. 69). A spotty complexion looks as if it were riddled with pellets (p. 138); Constance's own hair, during her ill-starred swimming experiment, feels like sea-weed (p. 18). Some of these images are comical and even vulgar: 'ce menton de chair jaune, long, pointu, hérissé de gros points noirs et qui ressemble à un croupion de poulet' (p. 23). This refers to the devoted but unattractive young man who is in love with Constance. A certain bluffness and even coarseness in language, including the use of slang, is another piece in Constance's defences against her illness: to the end she fights against self-pity and sentimentality.

Several of the examples already quoted were *animal images* applied to human beings. This type is very common in *Lève-toi et marche*, as it was in *Regain*, but there are two essential differences. Firstly, most of Giono's metaphors were based on some physical similarity, whereas here the analogy can be either physical or moral. Secondly, the overtones of animal imagery are different. In *Regain*, as we have seen, some of these images had a pejorative note, but a great many others were free from any such stigma, as was only natural in a writer with Giono's views and sympathies. Constance has no idealistic notions about animals, and her metaphors from this source are almost invariably comical, sarcastic or grotesque. An image like the following, which evokes a semi-hallucinatory state of mind, is very exceptional: 'J'étais comme portée, emmenée je ne sais où, sur les ailes de cent mille oiseaux chanteurs' (p. 174). Most animal images serve mainly as an outlet for Constance's bizarre sense of humour, her irony and the air of toughness which she likes to affect. They are essentially caricatures, amusing or sinister as the case may be:

. . . il secoue la tête, ce hibou, comme s'il déchirait des entrailles de taupe (p. 167).

. . . sa mine d'oiseau qui rentre la tête dans le jabot (p. 84).

. . . la maladie démultiplie mes mouvements et leur impose cette langoureuse allure de poisson qui se meut dans un bocal (pp. 168–9).

. . . puis nous repartîmes, lents et gracieux comme des canards (p. 57).

In the last sentence, which refers to Constance and one of her protégés, a bandy-legged child, the irony is underlined by the pretentious Past Definite *repartîmes* and by the contrast between *gracieux* and *canards*.

Applied to the moral sphere, animal images may retain some visual element: 'il fait son beau entre Nouy et Thiroine comme un roquet entre deux dogues' (p. 68). Elsewhere, the moral analogy predominates and the image owes its expressiveness mainly to its comic quality: 'il joue en ce moment le rôle de la poule qui a couvé un canard' (p. 19); 'Tu as faim, petite phoque? Voilà . . . Je te jette mon poisson' (p. 109).

Traditional images are sometimes revitalized by adding a new touch to them or by placing them in an unusual context. The cat-and-mouse game is turned inside out: 'Ma chatte, je me fais souris pour soulager tes griffes' (p. 200). The chance homonymy between *caillette* 'frivolous person, flirt' and *caillette* 'petrel' is reinforced by an ornithological analogue: 'la téléphoniste, cette caillette à bec pourpre'[1]—a pun developed into an image. The very conventional simile of the spider lying in wait for the fly is modernized by being applied to the telephone which is one of Constance's main contacts with the outside world: 'le siècle a inventé la présence à distance, les P.T.T. vous louent une toile d'araignée toute faite, toute tendue, pour attraper vos mouches' (p. 92).

[1] *Caillette* 'frivolous person' comes from the name of a sixteenth-century court jester; originally, it was masculine, but it became feminine through being associated with its homonym *caillette* 'petrel', a diminutive of *caille* 'quail' (Dauzat and Bloch-Wartburg).

Occasionally, parallels are drawn between human beings and the inanimate world, mostly with a comic or ironical intention. There are some amusing plant images: 'Mathilde, cette châtaigne hérissée' (p. 145); 'du petit rire qui vous secoue, toute jaune, comme le vent de mars fatigue la jonquille' (p. 87). Milandre, her persistent admirer, once again becomes the butt of Constance's sarcasm: he is like a dandelion, 'il repousse entre les pavés, il dresse à l'improviste sa tête ronde dont les cheveux s'effilochent au vent' (p. 12). Inanimate objects provide similar analogues. The same Milandre is uncharitably likened to a beggar's wooden bowl: 'tendu comme une sébile vers la moindre obole d'attention' (p. 143); the swaying head of a girl is compared to a censer (p. 108).

As the narrator is forced to spend most of her time indoors, there are comparatively few descriptions of natural phenomena. Giving way for once to a poetic mood, she pictures the white sky as a chrysanthemum: 'Un ciel blanchâtre, où frisaient de lents tourbillons gris, renversait sur la banlieue son immense chrysanthème' (p. 49). The river Marne is described in metaphorical terms: 'un fleuve de coton descendait vers Paris, coulant au-dessus d'un fleuve de mercure' (p. 29); 'Je connais sa Marne d'hiver qui ressemble à une immense flaque de colle de pâte, sa Marne de printemps qui fait soupe de pois cassés' (p. 91). There are a few synaesthetic images, clever rather than convincing: 'celle-ci me débitait depuis un quart d'heure les consolations d'usage, d'une voix de source, tiédasse, imbuvable' (p. 34); 'un long silence s'établit, dense comme l'ombre qui envahissait peu à peu la cellule' (pp. 265–6).

One of the predominant forms of imagery in *Lève-toi et marche* are transfers *from concrete to abstract*. In *Regain* there was, as we have seen, little need for such metaphors; here, however, intellectual and moral analysis is one of Constance's main preoccupations, and it can be most effectively expressed in figurative language. There is a certain danger in this tendency: the edges of reasoning may be blurred by over-indulgence in images, and the metaphors themselves are apt to appear cold and *recherché*, without any graphic quality. On the other hand, the angle of such images is necessarily rather wide, the parallels drawn are often quite unexpected, and this surprise effect compensates to some extent for the absence of sensuous and pictorial values.

This element of surprise is particularly marked in a group of metaphors equating abstract phenomena with impressions of taste. In one case Constance herself admits that the parallel is far-fetched: 'du pére Roquault dont l'esprit me rappelait, je ne sais pourquoi, ces demi-noix qui ont la forme d'une petite cervelle et que certains confiseurs déposent à la surface d'une écorce d'orange amère' (pp. 179–80). Other images are less recondite: 'comprendre ses intentions, secrètes comme des amandes et, comme elles, amères' (p. 11); 'Je préfère ce qui résiste sous la dent à ce qui fond sur la langue' (p. 164); 'en conservant dans la bouche ce goût de lait vinaigré, d'affectueux mépris qui a toujours gâté mon intimité avec Luc' (p. 27).

When the analogue is visual, it is sometimes developed into a little drama: 'glisser mes petits avis dans la cervelle des gens comme des sous dans une tirelire défoncée' (p. 209); 'Son regard se disperse en petits coups d'oeil, plantant partout les épingles de sa curiosité' (p. 106). Some of these metaphors are drawn from military operations: 'C'est un homme (viz. the doctor). . . qui prodigue ses soins comme un poseur de mines essaie de retarder l'avance ennemie' (p. 219); 'Et de voir arriver la contre-attaque, toute fumante, fonçant sur vos intentions, ces marches lointaines où l'on a dépêché de vague éclaireurs' (p. 87). Trying to remember how to swim, Constance compares herself to the war blind: 'Comme un aveugle de guerre cherche à voir en se référant à ses souvenirs, je fais de la nage cérébrale' (p. 18).

The form of these intellectual images is very varied. Some are explicit and symmetrically constructed:

Tout en poussant l'aiguille, avec une adresse si touchante que le fil s'emmêla vingt fois, je poussais mes réflexions, elles aussi fréquemment embrouillées—en logique comme en couture, j'aime les grandes aiguillées qu'on tire de long (p. 78).

Elsewhere, the abstract element is delayed till the end of the sentence where it forms an unexpected climax:

. . . comme je l'avais fait dans la Marne, je piquai une tête dans l'éloquence (p. 37).

Je ne suis plus un gamin tourmenté par ces boutons qui s'épanouissent si facilement en fleurs de rhétorique (p. 86, extract from a letter).

A cliché may be enlivened by giving it a new twist:

Tout enfant, j'avais déjà horreur des phrases, des projets, des bonnes intentions (dont l'enfer est pavé, assure le proverbe, tandis que le ciel doit être couvert de mauvaises actions, de "tuile récupérée", comme disent les gens du bâtiment) (p. 207).

As in the case of *caillette*, the metaphor may be combined with a pun. Having received a letter from her parson friend, Constance reflects:

Cependant, ma joie reste prudente. Sceptique. Si j'ose dire: pasteurisée (p. 183),

a play on *pasteur* 'minister' and *pasteurized* milk.

The appearance of a second narrator at the end of the novel gave the author an opportunity for contrast effects in linguistic portrayal. But the two parts of the book are not in any way balanced, as they are, for example, in André Maurois' *Climats* or even in Gide's *École des femmes*; the final section is too short, and too much in the nature of an epilogue, for the narrator's personality to come to the fore. In fact, Roquault keeps himself deliberately in the background and we only see him from one particular angle: that of his relationship with Constance. Nevertheless, there are several skilful touches of portrayal through language, and subtle but significant differences between his and Constance's way of writing. Both of them are fond of metaphorical expressions, but the tone of their imagery is not the same.

One difference, which is partly due to the subject-matter, is the streak of sentimentality evident in some of Roquault's images. This comes as a slight surprise to the reader whom Constance had led to picture Roquault as a gruff and embittered old failure. The two facets of his personality are not entirely reconciled, though it is suggested that his friendship with Constance may have mellowed his character:

. . . ce vieux pion, caressé par elle à rebrousse-poil, en gardera jusqu'à la fin le cuir attendri (p. 252).

Moi qui vous parle, ratatiné dans mes habitudes—à mon âge on n'en change plus,—ratatiné dans ma peau comme un abricot sec, je ne me sens plus si creux, je me sens comme un noyau (p. 255).

In his summing up of Constance's character he uses the kind of imagery to be expected from a retired schoolmaster:

Un électricien dirait qu'elle avait trouvé le moyen de vivre à très haute intensité une vie sans potentiel (p. 253).
Constance n'était pas dure; elle était sèche. Sèche comme la noix de coco capable de vous assommer quand elle vous tombe dessus et qui pourtant est pleine de lait (*ibid.*).

It falls to Roquault to record the final phases of Constance's illness. His clinical imagery is clear and precise:

Les yeux bleus devinrent durs, secs comme du vitriol (p. 267).
. . . les battements insolites de cette paupière rêche où le kyste tremblait comme une baie rouge au coin d'une feuille de houx (p. 270).
Un fil de souffle s'étirait, s'enrayait, repartait, s'étirait encore à travers la filière bouchée de la gorge (*ibid.*).

The accuracy of these descriptions differs markedly from the more impressionistic images by which Constance had conveyed her earlier symptoms.

Looking back on the imagery in *Lève-toi et marche,* one is impressed by the author's verve and adroitness rather than by the quality of his imagination. Many of the analogies are clever; hardly any are memorable. His handling of metaphor is more imaginative than that of many other writers, but he is not a great creator of images comparable in any way to Giono. Nor would the medium in which he works lend itself to such treatment.

In one respect, however, the use of imagery in the novel is highly significant. It is very closely integrated into the structure of the book. Constance's addiction to metaphor, and the specific forms which her images tend to assume, reach down to the very roots of her personality; they are an essential part of her defences against disease and death. It would hardly be an exaggeration to say that, without the imagery, the book would be inconceivable in its present form.

Writing of this novel, Professor Henri Peyre has paid tribute to 'the intelligence, the gift of vivid characterization, and the stylistic verve of the author', but felt that 'the total impact of the book is uncertain'[1]. This is no doubt true, but the uncer-

---

[1] *Op. cit.,* p. 307.

tainty is to some extent unavoidable: it resides in Constance herself. Her attitude to her illness, to her friends, to herself, is fundamentally ambivalent, and this is also reflected in her style. Taken at face value, many of her images are harsh and even cruel. Set against the wider background of her general attitude, they reveal themselves largely as a pose and a necessary outlet. Her actions are not always matched by her words; she gets rid of her spite and bitterness, and has her fun, through the barbed witticisms of her language, and her conduct is dictated by quite different motives. We have seen the merciless irony with which she ridicules her assiduous admirer; yet this does not prevent her from tolerating his presence, showing some interest in his work, and intimating, just before she dies, that his love did not remain unrequited.

In the terms of Professor Bruneau's typology, Giono is a classic example of an 'inspired' maker of images, whereas Hervé Bazin belongs to the 'chimistes', the intellectual type. We shall now turn to a different variety of this second species: a writer whose imagery is harnessed to the expression of a philosophical doctrine.

3. JEAN-PAUL SARTRE

La Mort dans l'âme

The first three volumes of Sartre's tetralogy, Les Chemins de la liberté, are strangely heterogeneous in literary form. L'Age de raison is constructed on more or less orthodox lines. In Le Sursis, there is a complete change in narrative technique: outdoing Jules Romains and emulating Dos Passos, Sartre tries to bring out the simultaneity of events occurring in different places. The impact of the Munich crisis on a number of human lives is conveyed by switching over from one scene to another in the middle of a paragraph or even of a sentence. The effect is bewildering, and the dazed reader is left to wonder, in the words of a critic, 'whether Sartre, like Picasso, . . . has not starved his genius to feed his talent and his greed for experimenting'.[1] In La Mort dans l'âme, he reverts at first to a more traditional manner: he is still trying to present simultaneous happenings, but on fewer

---

[1] Peyre, op. cit., p. 231.

planes and with less abrupt transitions, and attention is mainly focused on the experiences of one character, Mathieu Delarue, during the final stages of the French collapse in 1940. In the second part of the novel, we are plunged into another experiment: a hundred pages without a paragraph, relating the first days in captivity of the Communist journalist Brunet. The device is largely typographical and not entirely new; nevertheless, it affects the rhythm of the narrative and imparts to it a feverish, irrepressible momentum. The concluding volume of the series, *La dernière chance*, will deal with French resistance during the German occupation.

In the great controversy raging around Sartre and his followers, so many fundamental problems—ontological, ethical, political, aesthetic—have been raised that his handling of language has received little attention. Yet existentialism is a literary as well as a philosophical movement, which requires, and has evolved, a language of its own. Tributes have been paid, even by hostile critics, to the quality of Sartre's style, and more particularly of his imagery,[1] but it is only by investigating these images in the context of an entire novel that one begins to appreciate their richness, their structural role and their intrinsic interest. Indeed it is somewhat surprising to find that, in the first part of *La Mort dans l'âme*, there are approximately 250 images, rather more than one per page. It must also be remembered that the novel is full of long dialogues, most of them in argot, which contain very few images, so that the density of imagery in the narrative and descriptive passages is considerable.[2] There are undoubtedly a number of conventional similes and metaphors, but many others are original, carefully worked out, and marked with an unmistakably Sartrean stamp.

Sartre's novels, like his plays, are literary works in their own right; they can be fully understood by readers unacquainted with existentialism. At the same time, they are permeated

---

[1] Cf. e.g. R. Picard, 'L'art de J.-P. Sartre et les "Hommes de mauvaise volonté"' *La France Libre*, 15 February 1946, pp. 289–96, esp. pp. 291f.; R.-M.Albérès, *Jean-Paul Sartre*, Paris-Bruxelles (1953), pp. 126f.; R. Champigny, 'L'expression élémentaire dans *L'Etre et le néant*', *Publications of the Modern Language Association of America*, vol. LXVIII (1953), pp. 56–64, where the part played by the four 'elements' in the imagery of Sartre's philosophical work is discussed in the light of the theories of G. Bachelard.

[2] I cannot therefore agree with M. Peyre when he declares (*op. cit.*, p. 233) that in Sartre, 'metaphors are scarce'.

with his philosophy, and designed to illustrate existentialist problems and experiences in the context of concrete human situations. The imagery, too, will have a twofold function, literary and philosophical, and the two are inextricably interwoven and stimulate each other.[1]

In the existentialist metaphysic, the material world is conceived of as something inert, dense, opaque, existing 'en soi', as distinct from man who is endowed with consciousness and therefore exists 'pour soi'. In Sartre's philosophical treatise, *L'Etre et le néant*, the inanimate world is characterized by epithets peculiar to solid matter: *compact, massif, dense, opaque, empâté* etc.[2] The experience of existence as such, which is as fundamental to existentialism as the *Cogito* is to Cartesianism, was forcefully evoked in Sartre's first novel, *La Nausée*. This experience does not enter directly into the imagery of *La Mort dans l'âme*, but the tendency to solidify the phenomena of nature, and even to materialize those which have no material substance at all, is evident in a series of curious images. The news of the Armistice—which later on turns out to have been premature—reaches Mathieu and his platoon in the languid atmosphere of a summer day:

. . . un éclair d'acier, puis le silence; la molle viande bleue de cette journée avait reçu l'éternité comme un coup de faux (p. 67).

Here the day is visualized as a fleshy substance whose tissue is lacerated by the news. Elsewhere, the night is made palpable:

La nuit était douce et sauvage, la chair tant de fois déchirée de la nuit s'était cicatrisée. Une nuit pleine et vierge, belle nuit sans hommes, belle sanguine sans pépins (p. 140).
. . . il flottait dans cette grosse nuit brute qu'elle caressait du bout des doigts (p. 155).

Mathieu's friend Daniel, waiting in the empty streets of Paris for the arrival of the first German troops, subjects the

---

[1] It is outside the scope of this book, and the competence of its author, to give even a brief account of the existentialist doctrine. A good introduction will be found in P. Foulquié, *L'Existentialisme*, Paris, 1946 ('Que sais-je?' series). Cf. also Peyre, *op. cit.*, pp. 216–39, where further references are given.

[2] Cf. Champigny, *loc. cit.*, pp. 57f.

atmosphere of that Sunday afternoon to a kind of chemical analysis:

Un dimanche tout fait, quelconque, à peine un peu plus raide qu'à l'ordinaire, un peu plus chimique, trop silencieux, déjà plein de croupissures secrètes[1] (p. 79).

Air and water are also solidified: 'un air chaud et lourd comme de la bouillie' (p. 192); 'l'eau était froide et nue comme une peau' (p. 42).

Under the gaze of some strange soldiers, Mathieu himself experiences a kind of metamorphosis, as if he were merging into the inert world around him—the 'pour soi' turned into 'en soi':

Sous ces yeux d'un autre âge, Mathieu se sentit fondre en herbe, il était une prairie regardée par les bêtes (p. 136).

When Mathieu and his companions try, by an act of gratuitous heroism, to hold up the German advance, he has a sudden and overpowering experience of his own solidity and that of the world around him:

. . . la route s'arrêta de couler, la route s'immobilisa, Mathieu sauta sur ses pieds, épaula, ses yeux durcirent: *debout et dense dans un monde de solides*, il tenait un ennemi au bout du canon de son fusil et lui visait tranquillement les reins (p. 186).

The strong alliterative effect—six 'd' sounds in close succession—helps to underline the sense of firmness, poise and solidity.

The examples already quoted reveal another distinctive trait of Sartre's imagery, and of his style in general. Everything is presented as seen and felt by the characters themselves, in a kind of perpetual and loosely constructed free indirect speech.[2] It is one of the basic tenets of the existentialist doctrine that the world, inert and 'absurd' in itself, only acquires meaning and existence proper when perceived by human consciousness; the 'en soi' is brought to life by the 'pour soi'. It follows that the world is not rigidly uniform: each individual will perceive and interpret it in his own particular way.[3] The linguistic corollary of this relativist position is an extreme form of the free indirect technique: objects and events are presented not as they

---

[1] *Croupissure*, which I cannot find in the dictionaries, may be a Sartrean neologism; for similar examples see Picard, *loc. cit.*, p. 292.

[2] Cf. above, p. 174.   [3] C. Foulquié, *op. cit.*, pp. 73ff.

are, but 'phenomenologically', as experienced by a particular mind.[1] This has important consequences for Sartre's images: it gives them wide scope, great freedom, and a strongly subjective, at times almost visionary quality.

The raw material of physical experience can be treated by the mind in a number of different ways. We have seen how water, air, and even light and darkness can be solidified. But the process can also be reversed, by turning solids into liquids:

> Elle regarda avec regret l'herbe noire et douce, elle se baissa et la tâta comme de l'eau (p. 157).

> Mathieu regardait la route: elle s'échappait de la nuit, à deux cents mètres, coulait en blancheur incertaine jusqu'à ses pieds et s'en allait baigner derrière lui les maisons aux volets clos. . . . Elle avait retrouvé la sauvagerie des fleuves antiques; demain elle portera jusque dans le village des navires chargés d'assassins (p. 145).

In the last example, the visual image is developed into an intellectual symbol. The night itself, which has the power to make solids appear as fluids, is pictured as 'black water':

> . . . des soldats en tirailleurs . . sortaient un à un de l'eau noire de la nuit (p. 145).

Twilight, too, can suggest strange analogies by dissolving the contours of objects:

> C'était l'heure où les objets débordent leurs contours et fusent dans la brume cotonneuse du soir; les fenêtres glissaient dans la pénombre d'un long mouvement immobile, la chambre, c'était une péniche, elle errait; la bouteille de whisky, c'était un dieu aztèque; Philippe, c'était cette longue plante grise qui n'intimidait pas; l'amour, c'était beaucoup plus que l'amour, et l'amitié, ce n'était pas tout à fait l'amitié (p. 140).

Once again, a series of visual images is given an intellectual twist at the end.

When we look at the world around us from an unusual angle, the result may be a similar 'recomposition de la réalité'. Lean-

---

[1] 'Ce qui serait chez un autre écrivain narration objective reste chez lui tout *imprégné du goût particulier de la conscience humaine qui le vit.* Nous n'assistons pas seulement aux petits événements que vit Mathieu, nous y assistons avec le même goût dans l'arrière-bouche qu'a Mathieu, avec le même relent qui est au fond de son esprit. . . . Les scènes de la rue que voit Mathieu, nous les voyons comme lui à travers le même état viscéral et coenesthésique qui est le sien' (Albérès, *op. cit.*, p. 124).

ing against the parapet of his observation tower, Mathieu feels as if 'la terre haussait . . . son visage renversé, le ciel chaviré coulait à travers lui avec toutes ses étoiles' (p. 175). This is a faint echo of an earlier dream of his which is related in almost surrealist language:

Une boule rouge se mit à tourner, des visages de femmes se penchèrent au balcon et se mirent à tourner aussi. Mathieu rêvait qu'il était le ciel; il se penchait au balcon et regardait la terre. La terre était verte avec un ventre blanc, elle faisait des bonds de puce (p. 93).

Images induced by abnormal experiences may have the obsessive quality of a nightmare. Walking in the empty streets of Paris, which remind him of ruins and of a frozen star, Daniel suddenly notices the swastika on the Hôtel Crillon:

Oh! le pavillon en viande saignante sur la soie des mers et des fleurs arctiques.

Au milieu du chiffon de sang le rond, blanc comme celui des lanternes magiques sur les draps de mon enfance; au milieu du rond, le noeud de serpents noirs, Sigle du Mal, mon Sigle. Une goutte rouge se forme à chaque seconde dans les plis de l'étendard, se détache, tombe sur le macadam: la Vertu saigne (p. 116).

Then an aeroplane appears in the sky:

Il accueillit avec soulagement la déchirure sonore du ciel: l'avion brillait au soleil, c'était la relève, la ville morte avait un autre témoin, elle levait vers d'autres yeux ses mille têtes mortes . . . S'ils lâchaient leurs bombes! Ce serait une résurrection, la ville retentirait de bruits de forge comme lorsqu'elle était en travail, de belles fleurs parasitaires s'accrocheraient aux façades.

But there are no bombs, and the town relapses into 'planetary silence'.

The subjectivism inherent in the existentialist doctrine, and the visionary streak running through much of Sartre's imagery, almost inevitably lead to a *synaesthetic* mode of expression. In *L'Etre et le néant* he had dogmatically stated: 'Si je mange un gâteau rose, le goût en est rose.'[1] He frequently introduces analogies from other senses. The effect is sometimes so intense that it verges on hallucination. When the painter Gomez

---

[1] Quoted by Champigny, *loc. cit.*, p. 62; cf. Picard, *loc. cit.*, p. 292.

whose artistic work had been interrupted by the Spanish Civil War, visits for the first time an art gallery in New York, the impact of the colours on his mind is pictured in a series of violent synaesthetic images:

> . . . c'était comme si on l'avait opéré de la cataracte: toutes les couleurs s'étaient allumées en même temps et lui faisaient fête . . . les couleurs battaient à grands coups dans les choses, comme des pouls affolés; c'étaient des élancements, des vibrations qui s'enflaient jusqu'à l'explosion . . . les couleurs l'assaillaient par côté, elles lui éclataient dans les yeux comme des ampoules de sang et de fiel (pp. 25–6).

Other sensations are also transcribed in synaesthetic terms. Silence is assimilated to touch and to smell: 'Il sentait dans son dos la pression magnétique du silence' (p. 79); 'Il ouvrit la fenêtre, se pencha au-dessus du vide, et respira l'odeur de violette du silence' (p. 140). The human voice, detached from its owner, sucks his blood like a parasite:

> . . . sa voix se tirait de lui toute seule, elle vivait de lui comme un énorme parasite qui lui eût pompé les tripes et le sang pour les changer en chansons (p. 106).

One sense may be transmuted into another:

> Il plongea la tête dans l'abreuvoir, le petit chant élémentaire devint cette fraîcheur muette et lustrée dans ses oreilles, dans ses narines, ce bouquet de roses mouillées, de fleurs d'eau dans son coeur (p. 42).

Even smells can be visualized:

> . . . après les oiseaux, les herbes et les prés s'éveillaient; elles jetaient leurs odeurs comme ils avaient jeté leurs cris: 'C'est vrai, pensa Mathieu, il y a aussi les odeurs.' Des odeurs vertes et gaies, encore pointues, encore acides: elles deviendraient de plus en plus sucrées, de plus en plus opulentes et féminines, à mesure que le ciel bleuirait (p. 45).[1]

In Sartre's philosophy, the *human body* occupies an ambiguous position. It is part of the 'en soi', the inert material world; yet at the same time it forms the 'permanent structure' of our being and is essential to the existence of consciousness.

---

[1] Cf. in the second part of the novel: 'le jeune goût jaune de bois tendre' (p. 233); 'la paille lui saute au visage, il respire son odeur jaune' (p. 251).

The affinity of the body to inanimate nature underlies some images which picture it in vegetal and even in mineral terms:

Pinette était transparent au soleil, la vie montait, descendait, tournoyait si vite dans l'arbre bleu de ses veines (p. 75).

Quand il me touchait, je devenais de velours. A présent, mon corps est de terre sèche; sous ses doigts je me lézarde et m'effrite (p. 175).

Other images describe the curious sensation one has when some part or function of the body seems to detach itself from the rest and acquire a separate existence. We have seen how the human voice can be visualized as a gigantic parasite. Breath can give a similar impression:

Sur sa gauche, un souffle râpeux. Elle l'entendait depuis cinq minutes sans y prendre garde. Il se glissa en elle, s'installa dans ses bronches, devint *son* souffle (p. 23).

Metaphors assimilating parts of the body to inanimate objects are by no means unusual, but in Sartre they have a peculiar quality. Some of the analogies are purely visual: 'il avait un visage las et flou; un brouillard au-dessus de son col déboutonné' (p. 99); 'elle sentit, sous le regard, son nez s'allumer comme un phare' (p. 156). Others present the body in mechanical terms:

Le type se détendit comme un ressort (p. 187).

. . . son biceps saillit, comme gonflé par une pompe (p. 130).

. . . sa paupière gauche s'était mise à battre dans son visage cendreux comme un volet par un jour de vent (p. 68).

Crowds, too, are likened to inanimate objects. The analogy, not very novel in itself, between a crowd and the billowy sea, is developed into an ample image:

. . . la foule roula sur lui sa marée, les vagues portaient à leur crête des gerbes d'yeux brillants et morts, le trottoir tremblait, les couleurs surchauffées l'éclaboussaient, la foule fumait comme un drap humide au soleil . . . l'écume blanche de leurs regards le frôlait au passage (p. 31).

More concisely, the crowds of refugees moving slowly on the roads of France are likened to black pitch: 'la poix noire des piétons recouvrit la route' (p. 17).

Animal imagery is very prominent in *La Mort dans l'âme*. It is perhaps more than an accident that the book both begins and ends with such an image. The opening sentences compare the New York heat-wave to a huge octopus:

Une pieuvre? Il prit son couteau, ouvrit les yeux, c'était un rêve. Non. La pieuvre était là, elle le pompait de ses ventouses: la chaleur.

This image has an obsessive quality; it reappears later in exactly the same form: 'Dehors, la pieuvre, mille ventouses le pompèrent' (p. 30).

The second part of the book ends with an animal image which is also a symbol: 'demain viendront les oiseaux noirs'. As we have seen in an earlier chapter (p. 187), this is one of the very few examples of inversion in the novel: the *crescendo* word-order leads up to the sinister climax of the image, and the whole book ends on the word *noirs*.

As usual, most animal images have a pejorative connotation. They are mainly applied to human beings, reducing them to animal level or underlining some unpleasant trait in their physique:

. . . la bête immonde qui proliférait dans la nuit de sa chair (p. 176).

. . . Au-dessus du bandeau, Mathieu voyait ses yeux fixes et ronds de vieille poule (p. 114).

. . . il aperçut un crapaud qui rampait vers la bataille. Pendant un moment, Mathieu regarda cet animal plat avec indifférence, puis le crapaud devint un homme (pp. 185–6).

Occasionally, there is a more pleasant image:

. . . elle avait l'air noble, ombrageux et triste, comme un cheval (p. 132).

Daniel se sentait aussi insolite qu'un chamois fixant sur des alpinistes son lent regard vierge (p. 80).

Inanimate objects, too, are compared to animals. Houses are shut like oysters (p. 83); the empty Boulevard Saint-Michel reminds Daniel of a dead whale:

Le boulevard Saint-Michel, hier longue coulée d'or vers le sud, c'était cette baleine crevée, le ventre en l'air. Daniel fit sonner ses pas sur ce gros ventre creux et ballonné (p. 81).

This is one of the many repellent images which Daniel's fevered imagination conjures up during his walk in the deserted streets.

Daniel also has a vision of an air raid, and his bitterness against his smug fellow-citizens vents itself in a grotesque animal metaphor:

Ils courent, les témoins, les juges, les hommes de bien, ils courent sous le soleil et l'azur pond des avions sur leurs têtes (*ibid.*).

At about the same time, Mathieu and his platoon experience a real alert:

... les mouettes avides et indolentes tournèrent un peu au-dessus du village, cherchant leur pâture, puis s'en allèrent en traînant après elles leur casserole qui rebondissait de toit en toit (p. 83).

Elsewhere, planes are likened to tadpoles swimming in the water of the sky (p. 24).

Even abstract phenomena can be assimilated to animals:

... nous sommes le rêve d'une vermine, nos pensées s'épaississent, deviennent de moins en moins humaines; des pensées velues, pattues courent partout, sautent d'une tête à l'autre: la vermine va se réveiller (p. 89).

This last image is one of a large and interesting group drawn from the world of *insects*.[1] The heaviest concentration of such metaphors occurs in the account of the great exodus from Paris, seen through the eyes of Sarah Gomez and her little boy, who are among the refugees. The roads are blocked with cars:

... les longues fourmis sombres tenaient toute la route. ... Les insectes rampaient devant eux, énormes, lents, mystérieux . . . les autos grinçaient comme des homards, chantaient comme des grillons. Les hommes ont été changés en insectes. Elle avait peur (pp. 20–1).

Les autos passaient devant elle et elle se sentait *vue* par des yeux cachés, par d'étranges yeux de mouches, de fourmis (p. 21).

La route et les carapaces qui se traînaient dessus (*ibid.*).

Gradually, the insect image widens in range, until it includes the whole crowd moving down the road:

... nous sommes pris dans la foule et la foule marche et nous marchons; nous ne sommes plus que des pattes de cette interminable vermine (p. 24).

Insect images recur at various points in the novel, with the persistence of an obsession:

[1] Cf. above, pp. 33f.; on insect images in Malraux, see Rees, *loc. cit.*, p. 135.

... cette larve grise qui remuait doucement à ras du sol et poussait vers eux ses têtes multiples (p. 85).

Tout son corps *faisait le mort*, comme les insectes qu'un danger menace (p. 117).

Des retardataires couraient en tous sens, des fourmis affolées (p. 170).

The insect motif leads on to the even more hideous image of the insecticide:

Ils se taisaient: elles n'avaient qu'à se taire, les abjectes vermines qui souillaient cette belle journée de juin. Patience! L'exterminateur viendra, on passera toutes les rues au Flytox (p. 84).

Such images play a crucial part in that mood of nausea which, according to the existentialists, is an essential stage in man's spiritual development.

Metaphors from *concrete to abstract* are one of the predominant forms of Sartre's imagery. Some of the existentialist problems and experiences, studied 'en situation', could hardly be made sensible without concrete analogies. But two other tendencies are equally noticeable: strong shock-effects are derived from unexpected associations, and many of the images have a pejorative tone, they become an outlet for the mood of bitterness and pessimism with which the characters are filled.

Both tendencies are at work in a number of cynical images applied to certain moral values—goodness, charity, fraternity:

La bonté monta dans ses seins comme du lait. . . . Sa bonté inemployée la gonflait comme un gaz (p. 23).

Il décida, et, à l'instant, son coeur scrupuleux et pitoyable dégringola de branche en branche; plus de coeur: fini (p. 174).

. . . il lui restait de la veille, au fond de la bouche, un goût refroidi de fraternité (p. 99).

It also happens that a poetic image is evoked and then cancelled out as a mirage:

. . . bien sûr l'innocence rayonnait dans le soleil matinal, on pouvait la toucher sur les feuilles d'herbe. Mais elle mentait: le vrai, c'était cette faute insaisissable et commune, *notre* faute (p. 50).

Pejorative imagery can also work more directly by stressing

the ugly aspects of a vice. Thus hatred is pictured as a squirting fluid: 'la haine allait gicler jusqu'au ciel' (p. 185).

Similar effects may be obtained from metonymic images: 'Ils passèrent entre deux haies d'hostilité molle' (p. 146); 'il dressait sa tête au-dessus de cette docilité touffue' (p. 138). By using the abstract nouns *hostilité* and *docilité* instead of *gens hostiles* and *femme docile*, the author achieves greater concision and at the same time isolates the quality and erects it into a substance—a device familiar to us from our study of the Goncourts. There are also more complex patterns: 'son éternité de statue se cassa, vola en éclats de rire' (p. 69).

Abstract processes and experiences are transcribed in terms of physical sensations—touch, heat or sound:

Dans un rêve pâteux, il entendit des cris (p. 185).

Il avança ses longues mains comme pour tâter précautionneusement la nouvelle (p. 67).

. . . cette gloire qui passait de la terre à son corps comme une chaleur animale (p. 138).

Une seconde des souvenirs bruissèrent comme un feuillage sous le vent (p. 174).

. . . j'agitais le grelot des mes problèmes (p. 69).

The spectacle of the French collapse suggests a number of curious analogies. France is like an immense mechanism thrown out of gear:

A présent, la France s'est couchée à la renverse et nous la voyons, nous voyons une grande machine détraquée et nous pensons: c'était ça (p. 46).

During his nightmare walk in Paris, Daniel suddenly has the feeling that the city is not really empty—it is hollow:

Paris n'était pas vide à proprement parler: il se peuplait de petites déroutes-minutes qui jaillissaient dans tous les sens et se résorbaient aussitôt sous cette lumière d'éternité. 'La ville est creuse', pensa Daniel (p. 80).

Transmuted by moonlight, Paris strikes him as 'de la pierre confite dans les sucres de l'histoire' (p. 155).

The intimate connection between Sartre's philosophy and his imagery is seen most clearly in the metaphors which arise around some of the great themes of existentialism.

The pivot of that doctrine is the concept of *choice*. Man has freedom of action, but he must choose all the time; even abstention is a form of choice. Through his successive choices he will inevitably commit himself, and this *engagement* will limit his future freedom. At the same time, there are no absolute norms dictating his choice; as far as man is concerned, 'existence precedes essence', there is no *a priori* ideal which could guide our decisions.

The human predicament in general, and the acute form which it assumed in the summer of 1940, are presented in a number of images. Making a choice and committing oneself is like venturing into a forest:

S'enfoncer dans un acte inconnu comme dans une forêt. Un acte. Un acte qui engage et qu'on ne comprend jamais tout à fait (p. 77).

In a defeated France, freedom of action will be curtailed and stultified:

Il se tut. Il pensa brusquement: il faudra vivre. Vivre, cueillir au jour le jour les fruits moisis de la défaite, monnayer en déroutes de détail ce choix total qu'il refusait aujourd'hui (p. 50).

Hence a mood of despair which is crystallized in an almost mythical image:

. . . *tragiques*: même pas, *historiques*: même pas, nous sommes des cabotins, nous ne valons pas une larme; *prédestinés*: même pas, le monde est un hasard. Ils riaient, ils se cognaient aux murs de l'Absurde et du Destin qui se les renvoyaient (p. 69–70).

Faced with these hazards, man is filled with a feeling of *anguish*. This is one of the main themes of existentialism and was already foreshadowed by its precursors, Pascal and Kierkegaard. In Sartre's novel, a number of images are introduced to evoke anguish and describe its workings. Most of them bring out the physical symptoms accompanying it. The image may be brief, confined to one aspect only: 'il sentait l'angoisse monter en lui comme une marée . . . l'angoisse recula' (p. 125); 'l'angoisse le fendit en deux' (p. 144). Elsewhere, the process is studied in greater detail:

Et de nouveau, l'angoisse. Elle commença prudemment, comme une caresse et puis elle s'installa, modeste et familière, au creux de son estomac. Ce n'était rien: tout juste du vide. Du vide en lui et autour de lui. Il se promenait dans un gaz raréfié (p. 89).

Collective anguish is also described through its physical symptoms:

... ils se regardaient et ils se faisaient peur .. personne n'en parlait, mais il cognait à grands coups dans les poitrines, on le sentait dans les bras, dans les cuisses, douloureux comme une courbature, c'était une toupie qui tournait dans les coeurs (p. 83).

Yet *solidarity* with other people is the best defence against anguish. Throughout the novel, Mathieu is desperately fighting for such a sense of solidarity:

Par moment il n'était qu'un vide anxieux et à d'autres moments il devenait tout le monde, son angoisse se calmait, les pensées de tout le monde sourdaient en lourdes gouttes dans sa tête et roulaient hors de sa bouche (p. 84).

In the same way, the individual becomes physically part of the crowd during the great exodus from Paris:

... au bout d'un moment, cette marche collective la pénétra, remonta de ses cuisses à son ventre, se mit à battre en elle comme un gros coeur forcé. Le coeur de *tous* (p. 22).

Anguish is felt so poignantly that it can even be personified:

L'angoisse tournait en rond au milieu des verdures et des légumes joufflus comme sur le visage de Charlot; elle n'arrivait à se poser nulle part (p. 43).

There is also another form of anguish. In moments of heightened sensitivity, the absurdity of the world and of man's situation in it are so acutely borne in on us that we are seized with a kind of panic, a metaphysical horror:

Sous ses mains, sous ses fesses, Mathieu sentait la vie enchevêtrée de l'herbe, des insectes et de la terre, une grande chevelure rêche et mouillée, pleine de poux; c'était l'angoisse nue sous ses paumes. Coincés! Des millions d'hommes coincés entre les Vosges et le Rhin par l'impossibilité d'être hommes: cette forêt plate allait leur survivre, comme si l'on ne pouvait demeurer dans le monde, à moins d'être paysage ou prairie ou n'importe quelle impersonnelle ubiquité (p. 131).

And the internal monologue continues by a curiously twisted image comparing a concrete experience to an abstract one: 'Sous les mains, l'herbe était tentante comme un suicide.' Eventually, there is a complete fusion of concrete and abstract, human and non-human, as though the boundary between the two worlds had been obliterated:

> . . . l'herbe et la nuit qu'elle écrasait contre le sol et les pensées captives qui couraient ventre à terre dans cette nuit et ce faucheux qui se balançait près de son soulier, qui se fendit brusquement de toutes ses pattes immenses et disparut.

Another existentialist theme, the experience of *time*,[1] underlies some of Sartre's most remarkable images. Their starting-point is a metaphor as old as philosophy itself: the idea of the 'flow of time', the Heraclitean πάντα ῥεῖ.[2] This motif is seized upon, expanded and developed by Sartre. In the torpor of the summer heat, time flows slowly and languidly: 'Le temps coulait doucement, tisane attiédie par le soleil' (p. 70). It may even seem completely at a standstill, though a sudden movement will rouse it: 'Le temps ne coulait même plus: il tremblotait, affalé sur cette plaine rousse. Un mouvement trop brusque et Mathieu le sentirait de nouveau dans ses os, comme l'élancement d'un vieux rhumatisme' (p. 135). In a bold image, the stopping of time is compared to the clotting of blood:

> . . . leur départ fit une rapide lézarde dans la fraîcheur du soir; un peu de temps coula par cette déchirure. . . . Et puis la saignée s'arrêta, le temps se cailla de nouveau (p. 137).

The existentialist conception of time is dominated by the *future*. This is hardly surprising in a philosophy which lays so much stress on free will and on choice. To the existentialist, the future is a *project* in the ordinary and the etymological sense of the term: it is a plan and also an act of projection.[3] As in his time images, Sartre has the gift of materializing these highly abstract experiences with uncanny precision. Terrified by the

---

[1] On Sartre's conception of time, see R. Campbell, *Jean-Paul Sartre ou une littérature philosophique*, Paris (1945), ch. III.

[2] Cf. Poulet, *op. cit.*, p. 10. The formula itself may, however, be apocryphal; see B. Russell, *History of Western Philosophy*, 3rd impr., London (1948), p. 64.

[3] 'Tâchez de saisir votre conscience et sondez-la, vous verrez qu'elle est creuse, vous n'y trouverez que de l'avenir. Je ne parle même pas de vos projets, de vos attentes: mais ce geste même que vous attrapez au passage n'a de sens pour vous que si vous en projetez l'achèvement hors de lui, hors de vous dans le pas-encore' (from an article by Sartre on 'La temporalité chez Faulkner', quoted by Campbell, *op. cit.*, pp. 51f.).

bleak prospect ahead of him, Mathieu tries to stop time. For a little while he succeeds:

Moi, je suis *là*. Le Temps s'effondra, avec son grand avenir-épouvantail. Il ne resta qu'une vacillante petite durée locale. Il n'y avait plus ni Paix ni Guerre, ni France ni Allemagne: tout juste cette lueur pâle sous une porte qui allait peut-être s'ouvrir. S'ouvrira-t-elle? Rien d'autre ne comptait (p. 94).

This is the existentialist version of Faust's attempt to stop time, though for very different reasons. But the illusion cannot last long: 'A l'instant, le Temps lui fut restitué, la petite perle d'avenir se dilua dans un avenir immense et sinistre.'

There is one aspect of Sartre's imagery which has to be emphasized if one is to see it in its proper perspective. The distribution of the images is perfectly normal: hardly any occur in dialogue, and those which do are mostly uninteresting.[1] What is, however, unusual is the gulf which exists in this novel between the style of the dialogues and that of the narrative.[2] It is hardly an exaggeration to say that the dialogues in *La Mort dans l'âme* could not reproduce actual speech more faithfully, and more unselectively, if they had been transcribed from a tape-recorder. Most of the characters, the educated as well as the illiterate, are given to a slangy and vulgar way of speech and seem to delight in obscenity. Determined to give an accurate picture of their language, Sartre makes no concessions to good taste or to variety: the same coarse expletives are constantly repeated, with a monotony which deprives them of much of their shock-effect. This tendency is common enough in contemporary French fiction, but it has seldom been carried to such lengths. All this concentrated vulgarity and obscenity provides a strange background for the efflorescence of intricate and highly intellectual images, especially as the transition from one style to another is often quite abrupt.

This clash between two styles is perhaps a special aspect of a

[1] Occasionally, there is an interesting image in dialogue; when, for example, Daniel conceives his plan of 'corrupting' Philippe, he tells him: 'Tu seras guéri quand tu m'auras rejeté comme une vieille épluchure' (p. 130).
[2] Cf. Picard, *loc. cit.*, pp. 292f.; N. Cormeau, *Littérature existentialiste. Le roman et le théâtre de Jean-Paul Sartre*, Liège (1950), pp. 38f.; Peyre, *op. cit.*, p.p 233f.

wider contrast. In a penetrating article, Raymond Picard has argued that Sartre's technique has many affinities with Symbolism: transpositions, evocation of intimate, vague and semi-visionary experiences, skilful handling of the suggestive and musical values of words.[1] At the same time, his theme is in many ways naturalistic, and the rich resources of his style are brought into play to describe feelings of nausea and other repulsive phenomena. M. Picard writes:

> Ce qu'il y a d'étrange chez J.-P. Sartre, c'est qu'il a mis en oeuvre un art qui rappelle le *Symbolisme*, dans un dessein apparemment *naturaliste*. Avant lui, on pensait que Rimbaud excluait Jules Renard et Verlaine Zola; après lui on peut en douter.[2]

These words were written three years before *La Mort dans l'âme* appeared, but they are fully applicable to that novel, except perhaps that the feeling of revulsion and nausea is more motivated in the historical context of the French collapse. To these objections Sartre would no doubt retort that nausea is an essential stage in the development of the mind, and that existentialism, with its insistence on free will and responsibility, is ultimately a virile and humane philosophy;[3] yet it cannot be denied that *La Mort dans l'âme* and the novels preceding it have only shown one side of the doctrine.

These criticisms concern the wider context of Sartre's imagery; others may be directed against the nature of the images themselves. That many of them are repellent and 'anti-aesthetic' is, as we have seen elsewhere, no valid criticism. The modern image is meant to be expressive rather than attractive, and neither the theme nor the mood of the book were such as to invite pleasant associations. Besides, the unpleasantness of the images is redeemed by their novelty and forcefulness, and, on the whole, the flashes of imaginative vision provide a welcome relief from the sullen vulgarity of the dialogues and of some of the narrative passages.

Many of Sartre's images may also appear strained and bizarre. One critic has spoken of a 'déferlement d'images incontrôlées'.[4]

[1] Cf. for example the onomatopoeic structure of one of the sentences quoted above: 'les pensées de *tout* le monde *sour*daient en *lour*des *gout*tes dans sa tête et *rou*laient hors de sa *bouche*'; see also above, p. 245.

[2] *Loc. cit.*, p. 293.

[3] Cf. Sartre's essay, *L'Existentialisme est un humanisme*, Paris (1946).

[4] Cormeau, *op. cit.*, p. 45.

In actual fact, they are seldom incomprehensible, and even the more baffling ones can be interpreted in the light of Sartre's philosophy. But the untutored reader who approaches the novel without previous knowledge of existentialism may well be bewildered by images like the clotting of time, scars on the torn flesh of the night, or the soft blue flesh of a summer day. Such metaphors will only be appreciated by those attuned to the author's idiosyncratic mode of expression. At the same time it must be remembered that most of the images occur in internal monologues, in Sartre's particular brand of free indirect style. He is trying to record the associations arising spontaneously in the minds of his characters; the thoughts are theirs, not his own. It is not suggested that the free indirect method affords an easy alibi for every kind of licence, but it is certainly relevant to the interpretation of Sartre's imagery.

This imagery does not, however, need any alibi. Whatever weaknesses it may have are outweighed by its richness, energy and intellectual brilliance. Sartre is not an inspired creator of images like Giono, walking in the world with almost childlike wonderment, discovering unexpected affinities everywhere, and building up a mythology of his own. Sartre's imagery is that of a 'chimiste', a thinker whose vision has been sensitized by his thought. As a philosophical doctrine, existentialism may be open to many doubts, but it unquestionably endowed Sartre with a new view of life, an original way of looking at the world, and these are fully reflected in his imagery. Indeed, the image is one of the most effective means through which this vision is communicated in a concrete and artistic form. We have here the fullest possible integration of a linguistic element into the inner structure of a work of art.

With imagery we have arrived at the deepest layer of the stylistic system. In these essays, we have worked our way gradually downwards from the surface. We began with some features of vocabulary: the use of foreign words, archaic and dialect terms and argot as elements of local colour. Then, probing deeper down and following at the same time the evolution of French prose itself, we examined the stylistic implications of certain tendencies in syntax: free indirect speech, nominal and impressionist sentence-structure, new patterns of word-order. Finally, we reached the deepest stratum, that of imagery, which is most intimately related to the writer's temperament and experience, and most directly involved in promoting his artistic aims.

Having considered twenty-four modern novels from a variety of angles, we shall now have to face the crucial question: *What is the importance of style in fiction?* Are we to believe, with Mr. Martin Turnell, that 'the study of the French novel is primarily a study of the alterations which have taken place in the French language and of the novelists' use of their resources'![1] Or are we to heed Professor Peyre's warning that style is not all-important in this *genre* and most not be over-stressed?[2] If one is thinking in terms of value-judgements, then it cannot be denied that some outstanding novelists are indifferent stylists. Balzac's style had many flaws; Zola wrote, as André Gide once put it, with a badly sharpened pencil;[3] and other examples come readily to one's mind.

If, however, one looks at style from a functional point of view, the answer to the question will be very different. As we have seen, certain linguistic features may play a significant, sometimes even a vital part in the structure of a novel. The method of analysis practised in *Madame Bovary* and the *Education sentimentale* would have been inconceivable without the resources of free indirect style. The impressionist technique of the Goncourts received a powerful reinforcement from their nominal syntax. Some of Proust's principal themes were clothed in synaesthetic metaphors; Giono's pantheism and Sartre's existentialist vision are indissolubly bound up with their imagery. Even such a seemingly trivial device as inversion can, in the hands of a Proust and a Giraudoux, become an effective instrument of portrayal and a source of pathos and irony.

To study the integration of a stylistic device into the structure of a novel, one must examine it at the level of the *entire work of art.* Such an approach opens up new perspectives which cannot

[1] *Op. cit.*, p. 7.

[2] *Op. cit.*, p. 5. Cf. also J.-J. Marchand's statement in the volume *Problèmes du roman* (ed. J. Prévost, Paris, no date, p. 174): 'Le bon prosateur cache toujours l'aspect verbal de son art. . . . Il y a là une loi générale de toute prose, *le style ne doit pas y être apparent*, ce qui ne veut pas dire qu'il doit être plat, car la platitude frappe l'esprit: on doit exactement pouvoir "oublier le discours"'.

[3] *Journal*, p. 1207. Cf. also R. Barthes, *Le Degré zéro de l'écriture*, Paris (1953), esp. pp. 108 ff.

be discerned in any other way. It throws light in particular on three sets of problems: (1) the density and distribution of the device throughout the novel; (2) the various forms of the device, their relative importance, their implications and overtones; (3) most significant of all, the uses to which the device is put, and its role in the general economy of the work.

This does not mean that there is only one level at which stylistic studies can be profitably pursued. On the contrary, stylistics can operate at a number of different levels, ranging from the analysis of short texts to that of the language of an author, a movement, a period or a *genre*. But the particular perspective aimed at in this book will only open up at the level of a complete work; beyond that we need not go, short of that we dare not stop. At the same time, such studies may form part of a wider inquiry: one can compare the use of the same device in different novels, as I did for example in tracing the development of inversion since the beginning of the nineteenth century.

The method I have followed has its limitations and its pitfalls. The choice of suitable material presents some difficulties. How is one to know beforehand which novel will repay investigation? Unless the ground has been previously covered, the choice will be largely impressionistic, starting from casual observations and proceeding by trial and error. As we already know, such difficulties are unavoidable in any study of style which aims at something more than an inventory or a frequency count.

Rather more serious is the risk that, by tearing passages out of their context, one may miss important connections and come to view the material in an artificial vacuum. But it is hard to see how any inquiry transcending the limits of short extracts can avoid this danger. This is the price one has to pay for keeping one's eyes fixed on the work of art as a whole. The risk can be reduced if the student pays attention to the context of his examples and notes any features of it which may be relevant to their interpretation.

Another risk inherent in the method is less obvious and more difficult to guard against. By confining one's attention to a single element of style, one may arrive at a result perfectly correct in every detail and yet somehow out of focus, giving an erroneous impression. One is reminded of Valéry's dictum: 'Tout point de vue est faux.'[1] To give a concrete example, anyone who has not read *La Mort dans l'âme* might, in the light of the imagery discussed in this chapter, come to an entirely wrong conclusion about the style of that novel; this might conceivably prompt him to read the book, and he would then be amazed and appalled by page after page of monotonous vulgarity. The student of style should therefore be careful to correct any false impressions and point out any discrepancies between his material and the general tone of the work.

Stylistic studies of this type are astride the borderline between linguistics and literature. Future progress in this field is bound to be beneficial for both of the neighbouring disciplines. It will enrich literary criticism with a technique which seeks to combine precision with sensitivity. It will have a humanizing effect on linguistics at a time when influential schools of thought threaten to rob it of its humanistic content. It will also help to heal the fatal split between philology and literature which has arisen in the modern humanities. Stylistics will demolish the old and deeply-rooted conception which regards language as something purely external, a mere 'dress of thought', as Dr Johnson called it. Here as on many other points, Flaubert anticipated our modern ideas when he proclaimed:

Ces gaillards-là s'en tiennent à la vieille comparaison: la forme est un manteau. Mais non! la forme est la chair même de la pensée, comme la pensée est l'âme de la vie.

[1] *Variété*, Paris (1924), p. 23.

BIBLIOGRAPHY

1. LIST OF NOVELS DISCUSSED

(*The numbers in brackets refer to the chapters in which the novels are examined.*)

H. DE BALZAC, *Splendeurs et misères des courtisanes*, M. Lévy (I, IV).

H. BAZIN, *Lève-toi et marche*, Grasset (VI).

F.-R. DE CHATEAUBRIAND, *Les Martyrs*, Garnier (IV).

G. FLAUBERT, *Novembre*, Conard (II).
    La première éducation sentimentale, Conard (II).
    Madame Bovary, Conard (II).
    Salammbô, Conard (II).
    L'Éducation sentimentale, Pléiade (IV).

A. GIDE, *Les Faux-Monnayeurs*, N.R.F. (IV).

J. GIONO, *Regain*, Grasset (VI).

J. GIRAUDOUX, *Suzanne et le Pacifique*, Grasset (IV).

E. AND J. DE GONCOURT, *Renée Mauperin*, Charpentier (III).
    Manette Salomon, Charpentier (III, IV).

V. HUGO, *Notre-Dame de Paris*, Nelson (I, IV).

F. MAURIAC, *Thérèse Desqueyroux*, Grasset (IV).

P. MÉRIMÉE, *Carmen*, Calmann-Lévy (I).

M. PROUST, *Du Côté de chez Swann*, N.R.F. (IV, V).
    A l'ombre des jeunes filles en fleurs, N.R.F. (V).
    Le Côté de Guermantes I, N.R.F. (V).

J. ROMAINS, *Les Amours enfantines*, Flammarion (IV).

G. SAND, *La Mare au diable*, M. Lévy (I).

J.-P. SARTRE, *La Mort dans l'âme*, N.R.F. (IV, VI).

STENDHAL, *La Chartreuse de Parme*, Pléiade (I, IV).

A. DE VIGNY, *Stello*, Conard (I).

2. SOME GENERAL WORKS ON STYLE

A. Alonso, 'The stylistic interpretation of literary texts', *Modern Language Notes*, vol. LVII (1942), pp. 489–96.

D. Alonso, *Poesía española; ensayo de métodos y límites estilísticos* (1950).

E. Auerbach, *Mimesis. Dargestellte Wirklichkeit in der abendländischen Literatur* (1946) (English translation: *Mimesis: The Representation of Reality in Western Literature*).

Ch. Bally, *Traité de stylistique française*, 3rd ed. (1951).

——. *Le Langage et la vie*, 3rd ed. revised (1952).

Ch. Bruneau, 'La stylistique', *Romance Philology*, vol. V (1951), pp. 1–14.

M. Cressot, *Le Style et ses techniques* (1947).

G. Devoto, 'Introduction à la stylistique', *Mélanges Marouzeau* (1948), pp. 125–39.

——. *Studi di stilistica* (1950).

S. Dresden, 'Stylistique et science de la littérature', *Neophilologus*, vol. XXXVI (1952), pp. 193–205.

W. J. Entwistle, *Aspects of Language* (1953).

H. J. G. Godin, *Les Ressources stylistiques du français contemporain* (1948).

R. de Gourmont, *Le Problème du style* (1902).

M. Grammont, *Essai de psychologie linguistique. Style et poésie* (1950).

P. Guiraud, 'Stylistiques', *Neophilologus*, vol. XXXVIII (1954), pp. 1–11.

——. *La Stylistique* (1954).

H. Hatzfeld, 'Stylistic criticism and art-minded philology', *Yale French Studies*, vol. II (1949), pp. 1–9.

——. *Literature through Art. A New Approach to French Literature* (1952).

——. *A Critical Bibliography of the New Stylistics Applied to the Romance Literatures, 1900–1952* (1953).

El Impresionismo en el Lenguaje, 1936 (articles by Ch. Bally, E. Richter, A. Alonso and R. Lida).

Introducción a la Estilística Romance, 2nd ed., 1942 (articles by K. Vossler, L. Spitzer, H. Hatzfeld; translation and notes by A. Alonso and R. Lida).

W. Kayser, *Das sprachliche Kunstwerk* (1948).

BIBLIOGRAPHY

G. Lanson, *L'Art de la prose* (1908).

H. Lausberg, *Elemente der literarischen Rhetorik* (1949).

Literature and Science, 1955 (articles by H. Hatzfeld and P. Guberina).

A. Malblanc, *Pour une stylistique comparée du français et de l'allemand* (1944).

J. Marouzeau, 'Quelques aspects de la question du style', *Conférences de l'Institut de Linguistique de l'Université de Paris*, vol. vii (1939), pp. 29–42.

——. 'Comment aborder l'étude du style', *Le Français Moderne*, vol. xi (1943), pp. 1–6.

——. 'Extraits d'articles de J. Marouzeau sur la stylistique', *Mémorial des études latines* (1943), pp. 104–16.

——. *Traité de stylistique latine*, 2nd ed. (1946).

——. *Précis de stylistique française*, 3rd ed. (1950).

E. P. Morris, 'A science of style', *Transactions and Proceedings of the American Philological Association*, vol. xlvi (1915), pp. 103–18.

J. Middleton Murry, *The Problem of Style* (1922).

W. Raleigh, *Style*, 2nd ed. (1897).

D. W. Rannie, *The Elements of Style. An Introduction to Literary Criticism* (1915).

I. A. Richards, *Practical Criticism* (1935).

——. *The Philosophy of Rhetoric* (1936).

——. *Principles of Literary Criticism*, 2nd ed. (1938).

E. Richter, 'Sprachpsychologie und Stilistik', *Archiv für das Studium der neueren Sprachen und Literaturen*, vol. clvi (1929), pp. 203–14.

R. A. Sayce, *Style in French Prose. A Method of Analysis* (1953).

H. Seidler, *Allgemeine Stilistik* (1953).

H. Spencer, 'The Philosophy of Style', *Essays, Scientific, Political, and Speculative* (1858), pp. 228–61.

L. Spitzer, *Aufsätze zur romanischen Syntax und Stilistik* (1918).

——. *Stilstudien* (1928).

——. *Romanische Stil- und Literaturstudien* (1931).

——. *Linguistics and Literary History. Essays in Stylistics* (1948).

——. *A Method of Interpreting Literature* (1949).

——. 'Les théories de la stylistique', *Le Français Moderne*, vol. xx (1952), pp. 165–8.

H. Steinthal, 'Zur Stilistik', *Zeitschrift für Völkerpsychologie und Sprachwissenschaft*, vol. iv (1866), pp. 465–80.

C. F. P. Stutterheim, 'Modern stylistics', *Lingua*, vol. i (1947–8), pp. 410–26; vol. iii (1952–3), pp. 52–68.

BIBLIOGRAPHY

S. ULLMANN, 'Psychologie et stylistique', *Journal de Psychologie*, vol. XLVI (1953), pp. 133–56.

J. A. VERSCHOOR, 'Parole, langue et les deux stylistiques. Questions de terminologie', *Neophilologus*, vol. XXXIX (1955), pp. 184–91.

R. WELLEK-A. WARREN, *Theory of Literature* (1949).

E. WINKLER, *Grundlegung der Stilistik* (1929).

INDEX

(Clarendon type denotes main references. Purely bibliographical references in the footnotes have not been included.)

267

INDEX